the Developing Child

Creative Play for the Developing Child

EARLY LIFEHOOD EDUCATION THROUGH PLAY

Clare Cherry

Director, Congregation Emanu El Experimental Nursery School and Kindergarten San Bernardino, California

Photographs by Sam Cherry

David S. Lake Publishers Belmont, California

Dedication

In memory of Betzena Weinrob, whose early lifehood is reflected in the eyes of the children.

Library of Congress Catalog Card Number: 75-16950.

Printed in the United States of America.

Contents

Preface

The purpose of this book is to illuminate the value of play in relation to child development during the first few years of life. It stresses the importance of play-learning attitudes and environments as opposed to the more formalized work-teaching concept of traditional educational systems. These attitudes are based on trusting, friendly, and helpful relationships in which honesty, freedom, and mutual respect for others are nourished. Play as an approach to learning is not a new idea. Too often, though, what the child is able to learn naturally through play has been confused with what adults feel they must teach the child through formal lessons.

Long-term goals for the children involved in the creative play program are secondary. Primary goals are for moment-to-moment, hour-to-hour, and day-to-day achievements, rather than remote objectives based on what they might be expected to know the following year when they are twelve months older. Step-by-step growth enhances the quality of life and encourages each individual to realize his or her potential.

In developing the creative play program, I have taken an overview of that research with which I am acquainted, and have added to it my own theories which have developed over the years as a result of many kinds of experience. The result is an eclectic curriculum that is wholly compatible with our present-day system of early lifehood education. It is usable, flexible, and adaptable. It leans heavily on the importance of movement in relation to what children learn, overall development rather than one single aspect of growth, the totality of an experience rather than isolated parts of it, and creative environments in which both children and adults are encouraged to explore, imagine, invent, innovate, express feelings, display emotions, and —above all—enjoy life. My approach is phenomenological. It emphasizes the inner-world of the individual. The experience comes first, with its accompanying sensations and reactions. Self-evaluation and struggle for understanding come next. Evaluation with and clarification by the help of others follow.

In this book we will review many of the phenomena that influence the play environment, discuss the overall goals of creative play, and present an overview of many of the kinds of play activities enjoyed by young children. It is of course not practical to describe all of the play activities that children experience or all possible types of materials and equipment. Illustrating many of the activities are candid photographs taken over a one-year period of many of the children with whom I play. The conversational excerpts that accompany the photographs are genuine. They were made by children between two and six years of age while they were at play, but many are by children other than those in the photographs. A brief history of children's play and a play-learning theory-reference guide is included in the appendix.

While writing this book, I was completing my twenty-first and twenty-second years as Director of the experimental nursery school sponsored as a community service by Congregation Emanu El of San Bernardino, California. I appreciate the support given me by the Congregation in the development of our creative play program and open classroom model. I could not have accomplished the program, however, without the close interaction I had with the children who were involved. Their openness, naturalness, love, honesty, trust, and playfulness were my constant guides. I am also indebted to their parents for permitting the use of their children's photographs in this book and for patiently waiting on many occasions while we completed photographic sequences.

I wish to express my deepest appreciation to my co-workers at the school, including Alyce Smothers for assisting in the research with two-year-olds, Helen Sunny Wallick for assistance in recording conversations and play sequences, Lois Ledbetter for evaluating my observations and conclusions, Diana Wearne for taking care of so many details that I was freed to spend time on the needs of the book, Marjory Brown, Barbara Stangle, and Robin Valles for their assistance in the development of the central room arrangement plan, and Peter Horton and Evelyn Paytas for their ongoing cooperation.

My appreciation also extends to the participating parents and student teachers, whose assistance allowed the professional staff to constantly revise their own plans to meet my needs. I also wish to thank the members of the Child Development class of Arrowview Junior High School of San Bernardino for their long hours of service, which gave us an opportunity to see creative play at work between children and adults. For their participation in and assistance with many aspects of my research, I wish to thank the students of my classes at the College of the Desert in Palm Desert, California, the University of Redlands, California, and California State College, San Bernardino Extension, and Doctor Nikolai Khokhlov for his valued guidance.

I am especially grateful to Mary Manz Simon for first suggesting this book, to Barbara Harkness for her continual encouragement and suggestions, and to my many other friends and colleagues whose interest, correspondence, manuscripts and research papers, and discussions concerning the premises of this book were a constant source of inspiration. I also want to thank my mother for her many contributions of time and assistance, Linda Weitzman and Robin Valles for their help in indexing, and my husband, without whose patience, creative ideas, practical assistance, and understanding, this book would not have become a reality.

Clare Cherry

Developing a Philosophy
of Play

PART ONE

⅂ The Importance of Playing

When Debra comes to nursery school each day, she is ready to play. When Jimmy arrives, he says, "I'm gonna play with my friends." Another time he says, "Play with the dumper." I asked Katie's mother what she expected Katie to do at school one day. Her reply, somewhat resignedly, was, "Well, I expect she'll just play." When Joey and Jennifer arrive too early, I say to them, "Your teacher isn't here yet. You may go to Miss Alyce's room and play until she comes." When their teacher arrives, she says, "I'm going to put out the red clay to play with today." When Betsy is ready to go home, I ask, "What are you going to do after you have your lunch?" "Play-ay-ay-ay!" she says, drawing the word out with relish as though she hadn't played for weeks. When any parent who has ever had a child in nursery school or a kindergarten that is not trying to emulate first grade asks "What did you do today?" he or she hears on many occasions, "Oh, nothing—just played," even though the child knows full well that the mother's face will reveal tremendous feelings of disappointment. On the other hand, as Eric was leaving school one day, one of the teachers asked him, "Eric, did you do anything special today?" His eyes lit up with enthusiasm as he said, "Yeah! I played!"

One day, I asked a group of eighty-five experienced nursery-school and kindergarten educators at a university seminar, "What in your collective opinion is the reason children want to come to your schools?" "To play!" they shouted in unison, as though the answer had been rehearsed. This answer was given in spite of the fact that over half of those educators worked in situations where play was downgraded because the emphasis was on teaching language and concepts, with tightly structured formats to follow.

The common denominator in these incidents is the free and natural use of the word *play*. That is how it should be. No matter what the program, no matter how the adults may try to turn it into something else, the primary occupation of most children before cultural inhibitions and formal schooling take over is *play*. Play is their way of coping with life. Play is early lifehood education at its best.

Theories about the influence of play on the development and education of children are based on observations of children at play naturally. They are observed through various stages of growth. Then, in most formal situations, complex programs and models are devised to insure that the children are *taught* these things at the appropriate ages, instead of concentrating on giving them the kind of environment and offering the guidance in which they will learn what they are ready to learn anyway.

By the time children reach four years of age, they have learned many things without formalized teaching programs. Somehow, by that age, normal children everywhere learn to walk, run, jump, climb, tumble, hide, tease, say "no," and maybe "please." They learn about hot and cold, and the way things taste, and to push, pull, stack, and knock things down. They know what bugs are, as well as airplanes and trees. They can tell the difference between one chocolate cookie and three, whether they can verbalize that difference or not. They can classify people as to whether they are family, friends, or strangers, even though they may not necessarily be able to use the word "stranger." They can tell you which is their neighbor's apartment or house and which is the family's, that they like the smell of some things and dislike others, that they can reach certain things and that other things are too high—or too hard, or too far, or too tight. Much of their knowledge depends on their cultural background, but it is extensive in any case when compared to what little knowledge they have at birth.

Yet, about the time that children are showing evidence of the vast amount of learning they have acquired along the way, we start inhibiting the process of learning by denaturalizing it in the name of education. We look at a child and say, "You've played around long enough. Now it's time to learn something." To do this we must assume that we know what all children are thinking and what they are interested in and what they will react to at any given moment. The result is overprogrammed curriculae, rote teaching, line standing, patterns, testing and retesting, no-talking rules, competitiveness, comparisons, and other well-known classroom techniques. Too often these unrealistic goals overwhelm the individual and sacrifice his worth as a human being to the all-powerful objective.

Children learn through the processing of sensory information. They hear, feel, see, smell, and taste. The sensory input usually comes from some kind of movement, or it results in producing a movement, voluntary or involuntary. When the brain receives sensory information, some kind of muscular activity takes place at almost the same instant it is processing that information. The sensory information is relayed to the brain and then back to those parts of the body that will respond. When this response takes place, perception occurs.

A simple example might be given of Kevin, who is playing with blocks. He puts one block on top of another and then adds a third one. He's done that before and it is easy. Now he adds a fourth. He has made a small tower. Then he puts a fifth block on, but it doesn't set exactly the way he meant for it to and one end is sticking over the edge of the tower. He sees the tower wobble back and forth for an instant and then it collapses. After three or four such experiences, Kevin will probably have formed the perception that when the tower he is building starts to wobble, that means it is going to fall in another instant. This perception will be further strengthened when he begins to anticipate the collapse and, as he observes the wobbling, he experiences a sinking feeling inside of himself, in anticipation of his disappointment. Or perhaps his muscles tighten in anger at his failure. Meanwhile, the foundation has been laid for the formation of concepts regarding balance, stacking, gravity, wobbling, apprehension, and so on.

Play is a natural function, and the learning it leads to is achieved by the well-accepted process of "doing," by a sequence of exploration, testing, and repetition. Books may provide us with facts and patterns. Lectures may give us clues. But actual learning comes through doing. Through doing we learn to drive automobiles, to cook and sew, to write and paint pictures, to repair machinery, roller skate, play tennis, and do all the other activities that make up our daily lives.

The creative play philosophy is based on the premise that the more our emotions are involved, the more sensory information we receive, the more easily learning takes place. This is why play is important. The natural world of our less sophisticated past provided opportunities for "learning by doing" either through the freedom and the space for play, or though the need, for economic, cultural, and societal reasons, to participate in community responsibilities at a very young age, and to assume family responsibilities even younger.

Friedrich Wilhelm Froebel (1782–1852), along with the American philosophers William James (1842–1910) and John Dewey (1859–1952), and many others, promoted the principles of learning by doing, learning through play, and the right of a child to a joyful childhood. The idea of relating education with happiness and joy has met considerable opposition in our society. Many people still retain a strict, almost punitive, attitude toward schooling.

It is important that we discontinue viewing the child as some unique creature that will one day be a human adult. Rather, we should take joy in being able to participate in the lifehood of a person who is undergoing a process of growth and development that will continue, to some degree, through his entire life.

There is presently a great deal of research on play in relation to learning. From it has grown a number of new theories, each vying for acceptance and adding to the confusion of those who may be looking for one pat answer, when, in fact, there is none. One of the problems in using theory to arrive at an understanding of play is the difference between the perceptions of adults and children. Being adults, we can consider play with adult perceptions. We know that because of their immaturity, children have views that differ from ours. We can understand and accept that their perceptions are different, but in no way can we perceive as they do. Even if we record their responses to one stimulus a thousand times, we still have to interpret them from an adult's point of view. So we cannot be certain of knowing the children's real world or of understanding what drives them to play. The closest we can come is to relive periods of our own early lifehood that come to mind and try to recapture some of the emotions, thoughts, and feelings of the time.

2 Attitudes and Points of View

The field of nursery education has grown rapidly during the twentieth century, especially since the 1950's. Considerable experimentation and research has led to the development of many different kinds of programs.

There are many excellent programs worthy of serving as models for others. They start with the traditional with its typical schedule: Arrival, free play, circle (or rug) time, toilet, juice, rest, music, story, outdoor play, dismissal—either in that order or some other order. Some programs are extremely innovative with schedules indicating arrival and going home times with learning experiences in between.

Some schools emphasize language development, some cognition, some emotional health, some highly structured learning tasks. Others stress reading and writing and still others concentrate on the learning of concepts. In some schools children are expected to pursue their exploration of didactic materials without talking, in others there is a noisy, ongoing verbal interchange.

In all of these programs, staffing ranges from the highly paid professional to paraprofessionals, volunteers, parents, and trainees. Whatever the program, its success and its value to little children is not totally dependent on the format of the curriculum or the specific nature of the school. The adults and their attitudes toward the children make a program either meaningful or meaningless. It is the relationships between the adults and the children that can make every moment count or make many moments wasteful.

The creative play program depends on trusting, friendly, and helpful relationships. These relationships are two-way experiences in human interaction. As much consideration is given to the needs of the adults as to those of the children. Attitudes are based on such concepts as "I'm your friend and I want you to be my friend; I trust you and I want you to trust me; I'll help you and I want you to help me."

Essential to such attitudes is honesty. With honesty, there can be freedom, which is essential to creative play. Freedom does not mean license to do *anything*. It means that children are given play environments in which options are available. They can make choices as to what they want to do, how long they want to do it, whether they want to do it slow or fast, whether they want to do it alone or with another person or with several others. As long as they are considerate to people and things, they do not always have to conform. They are encouraged to be innovative, inventive, and creative.

Freedom means that you respect the children's point of view. Because of age differences and other individual differences, there is no way for you to perceive things the same way they do. But by showing children the respect that every human has a right to, you invite respect in return. They cannot understand why your point of view is different from theirs. But you can help them to know that you have the same right to your point of view that they have to theirs. Through this type of mutuality, friendships grow and learning flourishes.

POINTS OF VIEW

Each person involved in the play activities of children has an individual point of view and individual goals in mind. For example, when you arrange a "crawl-through" place, a child might consider it to be a "climb-over" space. When you provide a setting for a quiet, restful respite from gross motor activities, a child might view it as the ideal place for turning somersaults. Or when you provide a cardboard tube and materials with which to decorate it for an art project, a child might decide the undecorated tube is just what he needs to use as a telescope or a horn for his own make-believe. I once painted some patterns in the tricycle yard that I thought the children would enjoy following. Their point of view has remained constant for several years: those painted lines are the places to stay away from.

Listed below are some of the areas that help to form the differing viewpoints of the adults and children involved in a mutual program:

For Yourself   Meeting the overall goals of learning through play.
Meeting the needs of a developing child.
Providing for the health and safety of the child.
Staying within the limits of your budget.
Creating an atmosphere of trust, friendliness, and help-
fulness.
Growing professionally.

7

Providing yourself with an income.
Having the freedom to express your own feelings.
Having the freedom to express yourself creatively.

For the Child Being able to respond to the impulse to move.
Being able to touch what is visible to the eye and within reach.
Being trusted.
Being given opportunities to be in control.
Having options.
Having friends.
Feeling safe, protected, and secure.
Being able to manipulate and change some things.
Being respected as an individual.
Having play experiences that are relevant to his age and needs.
Feeling welcome and loved.
Having fun.

For the Parents Feeling welcome.
Being made comfortable.
Knowing that their child is being cared for.
Knowing that the school program is as advertised.
Learning about child growth and development.
Meeting with other parents with common concerns.
Not being made to feel troublesome when asking for help.
Not being made to feel guilty when problems concerning the child or family relationships arise.
Knowing that confidences will not be betrayed.
Being free to pursue own activities while child is in school.
Being needed to assist for special events, emergencies, and, if available, participation programs.
Feeling free to observe.

For the Visitor Feeling welcome and comfortable.
Being able to touch what is visible to the eye and within reach.
Being able to observe at an individual pace.
Being able to sit down if desired.
Being able to converse with others and to ask questions.
Being able to stay as long or as short a time as wished.

For the Custodian Being able to move things easily.
Being able to touch what is on top of areas to be cleaned.
Being able to feel welcome and comfortable.
Not having to cope with flimsiness.
Not having to cope with sloppiness.

For Aides Feeling welcome and comfortable.
Being trusted to help meet the needs of a developing child.
Growing professionally.
Earning an income.
Having the freedom to express personal feelings.
Having the freedom for creative expression.
Not having to do all the menial tasks.
Being respected as a professional or paraprofessional.

For Student Teachers Feeling welcome and comfortable.
Being trusted with responsibility.
Growing for professional competence and certification.
Having the freedom to express personal feelings.
Having the freedom for creative expression.
Not having to do all the menial tasks.
Being respected as a professional-in-training.
Preparing for a means of future income.
Being free to pursue directed assignments expected of the supervising institution, if not your own.

For the Office Staff Feeling welcome and comfortable.
Being trusted with responsibility.
Having the freedom to express personal feelings.
Having the freedom to plan own work sequences.
Not having to do menial tasks for teachers in the classrooms.
Having privacy for personal belongings.
Being considered an equal with the teaching staff.

For the Community Being confident that the program is as advertised.
Being able to rely on the school to meet the needs of the community in providing an early lifehood education facility, without prejudice.
Being able to call on the school for advice.
Being able to visit and observe.
Being made to feel welcome.

Viewpoints and goals vary according to the individual's role in the school environment. It further varies according to individual personalities, cultural and economic backgrounds, education, and similar factors.

Because of these variations, a strong element of trust is necessary. By the time most young children are ready to enter nursery school, they have already learned not to trust most adults. Trust is a two-way street. I want to let children know that I trust them and that they can trust me. We need to be honest with them and patient. We have to show them that we trust other adults and that other adults trust us. Through mutual cooperation, it is possible to establish an atmosphere of mutual trust within the school community.

Relevance is another necessity in the creative play program. Experiences in which the children participate, materials they are given to use, and ideas you share with them should be relevant to their interests, needs, abilities, and understandings. Naturally, if you have meetings with parents, parent-education programs, open houses, or other school or public relations events, you are going to base those events on subjects that are relevant to the adults who will be involved, subjects in which they will be interested. But the same people who apply this principle to adult relationships often neglect to consider it with children. For example, many nursery school teachers tell the story of Thanksgiving pilgrims for two or three weeks during November. One day I spoke with Anna (4½) at a school I was visiting. She said, "I have a pilgrim, too." With that, she put her hand in the pocket of her jacket and took out a miniature rubber penguin she had brought from home. As a result, I interviewed forty children between 3 and 5 years of age at three other schools I visited that week in different cities. I found that three out of four of the children in these widely separated locations thought, when the teacher spoke of pilgrims, that they were talking about an Arctic bird.

Another example of relevance occurred to me when I spoke to a group of young mothers and asked if any of them had ever left an iron plugged in. "Iron?" I had forgotten about the permanent pressed materials and how they have changed the ironing problems since my own children were young. And so I took a second look around the school. I found that approximately half of the children (from middle-class homes) knew what an iron was for, but had absolutely no familiarity with it nor any desire to use it in their housekeeping activities.

Most people want to be able to express their feelings. Establishing an environment where this can be done without self-consciousness helps everyone involved to be more aware of both their own feelings and those of others. Only through such awareness can children learn from our example to make use of their emotions in appropriate ways, but keeping them under control while doing so rather than allowing them to control their actions.

Being in control is one of the important aspects of play. Through play children have opportunities to control situations, environments, and other persons. They also have control over whether or not they even want to participate and the extent of that participation. Their control, however, is subject to the control exercised by other children in the play group as they compete with each other in their struggles for dominance. By helping children recognize the many times when they are in control of a particular situation, they can be helped to learn to overcome the frustration they feel when they are not in control.

Movement is emphasized over and over again as an essential aspect of the creative play program. Environments should be planned to provide for maximum movement. Equipment and activities should be considered for their value in relation to movement experiences. Children should be challenged to move in as many ways as possible. This freedom to move enhances the total learning value of the program.

Communication, both verbal and nonverbal, is the ongoing tie between all persons involved in creative play. Through communication, all of the foregoing factors can be achieved. Nonverbal communication accounts for a very large number of the messages that people send to each other. Verbal communication is pertinent to the development of skills for future reading experiences. Before children can read, they need to understand words. In order to master the uses and meanings of words, children must be able to talk. Therefore, the encouragement to use and enjoy language underlies the creative play program.

Joy is one more important factor essential to creative play experiences. Without joy, all of the other elements are meaningless. However, if all the other elements exist, joy should be the natural outcome. When there is mutual trust, friendliness, and helpfulness, with accompanying freedom, relevance, and awareness, both children and adults will have *good* experiences. If a child or an adult has five minutes of good experiences, and then the next five minutes are also good, and so are the next five, the next, and the next, and if this can be continued for an entire school period, the total experience will have been satisfying. Satisfying experiences are joyful experiences. All we have to do is let them be so.

GUIDELINES FOR ADULTS

In the creative play program, it is assumed that a caring and understanding adult is involved at all times in whatever activity the children are participating in. The role of the adult is not that of an instructor or entertainer, but rather of a friend whose presence will insure the quality and appropriateness

11

of the experiences in which the children engage. There are three primary types of involvement. They may be going on separately or they may overlap one another.

1. *Participant*. The adult actually participates with the children in the activity, such as creative movement, a make-believe teaparty, or perhaps in developing a garden.

2. *Facilitator*. The adult gives necessary guidance and assistance as needed, but does not participate.

3. *Observer*. The adult can see the children and be seen by them, giving them the security of knowing that they will have help if they lose control of the materials they are using or of their emotions.

Whatever the type or degree of involvement, there are several guidelines for effective teaching:

1. Express yourself naturally.

2. Listen to what the children are saying, both verbally and through body language, and respond as needed. Appropriate responses include direct verbal interaction, communication by touching or some other form of nonverbal expression, providing new materials or other stimulation to enlarge a learning situation, and storing away of information to help meet their changing needs during the course of an activity or at some future time.

3. Be aware at all times of what type of learning is most likely to occur as a result of the play that is going on at any given time, making sure to consider the development and abilities of each individual partici-pant.

4. Know and understand the needs, interests, abilities, and handicaps of each child in order to arrange the play areas in a way that is most beneficial to each individual.

5. Be aware of which of the following categories the play activities fall into:

    a. Adult-anticipated but child-initiated.
    Although you have arranged the equipment, toys, and other materials in the play areas, the child is free to choose where he wants to play, how he wants to pursue that play, and how long he wants to do so. The role of the adult here is to help the child learn to make choices, and to show that you can really be trusted to allow him to abide by that choice. If help is needed with materials or skills, it should be given. Suggestions for expanding the activity or comments that will enhance the awareness or understanding of

accompanying stimuli should also be given if they are needed. If health and safety are not threatened and if the child is being considerate, his own ideas and pursuits should be encouraged.

b. Adult-anticipated and adult-initiated.
This is play where a single process is followed, as in cooking. It is appropriate only if it is set up in such a way that the child can handle the process by himself, with the adult acting as facilitator.

c. Nonanticipated, child-initiated.
Sometimes the child will initiate play that is independent of any prestructuring or environmental preparation. As long as the behavior is not undesirable, he should be allowed the freedom to pursue such play.

6. Speak quietly to children who are displaying undesirable behavior or are ignoring known rules. Make every effort to avoid embarrassing the child in front of his peers. Removing him temporarily from the situation or group stimulation may help the child to reorganize his feelings and regain control of his actions and emotions. Such removal should be considered a way of helping the child, rather than as punishment. Punitive attitudes teach children to be punitive. Helpfulness teaches children to be helpful. Since it takes two people to make an argument, refusing to argue with a child will help to reestablish an atmosphere of mutual cooperation.

7. Allow children of comparable size and ability who are quarreling to work out their own problems insofar as they do not disturb others. If they begin to lose control of the situation, suggest that they discuss it with each other, either where they are or in some other place. They will learn to appreciate this confidence you show in them.

8. Maintain positive attitudes.

9. Play.

GUIDELINES FOR CHILDREN

In implementing the creative play program, it is important to present the children with appropriate guidelines, too. The following list is simple and practical, and within the understanding of young children:

Be *yourself.* "Yourself" is the best kind of person to be.

Stay within the boundaries of the play areas.

Observe the health and safety rules.

13

Be polite and helpful to others.

Ask for help when you have a problem you can't handle or when something you want to do is too hard.

Help keep the play areas clean.

If you need something that you don't see, ask for it.

Express your feelings when you need to.

OVERALL GOALS OF
THE CREATIVE PLAY PROGRAM

In addition to the attitudes and points of view I have listed, the overall goals of the creative play program need to be considered. Activities are based on the natural growth and development of children. We provide an environment rich in materials, choices, space, time, and guidance, one that is geared towards meeting the varying needs of individuals as they occur from moment to moment, hour to hour, and day to day.

Learning occurs as the result of step-by-step achievements, based on individual abilities, natural potential, and experiences. Many different types of learning may be occurring simultaneously in an individual, each representing a different stage of growth for that particular child. A sequential order to development governs the growth of all human beings, although the time that any given aspect of development occurs varies in individuals. Some learning problems occur when that sequence is disrupted or a particular stage of development is skipped due to some inner deficiency or outer interference. There are certain sensitive periods at which optimum learning of a particular kind will occur for a particular child if the opportunities to do so are present. In the creative play environment, the opportunities for many kinds of appropriate learning are present at all times. Children are limited in what they learn from these opportunities only by what they are ready to learn at any given time. They are, by the same token, not expected to learn anything they are not ready to learn in their natural course of growth.

Creative play emphasizes activities that involve *tasting, seeing, smelling, hearing,* and *touching,* coupled with *movement* experiences of all kinds. As children develop their *sensory motor abilities* they also begin to grow in *perceptual skills.* They learn to make simple *classifications* according to *use, shape, color, texture, materials, graspability, fragility,* and other ways in which they can compare *likenesses* and *differences.* This also involves the ability to *compare* things according to various means of measurement such as *size, weight, distance,* and *time.* Children are simultaneously learning to separate primary stimuli from background stimuli (*figure-ground perceptions*). These stimuli may be things that are heard, smelled, seen, felt, touched, or tasted.

As children become more skilled at integrating these various learnings, they also become more skilled at recognizing their *position in space*, their *relationship to* the *space* around them, and the relationship between three-dimensional and two-dimensional space. They develop a sense of *laterality* (two-sidedness), and *dominance* (one side is the dominant side) and *kinesthesia* (knowing the location of a part of the body in relation to space and other external stimuli). They refine other skills such as *large* and *small muscle control, eye-hand coordination*, and the increasing ability to change the *focus* of the eyes from near to far or far to near. They also learn to visually follow through a sighting pattern as from left-to-right, or down-to-up, or round-and-round (*scanning*). They become skilled at *sequencing* objects according to size and *categorizing* them in many other ways.

Because they have many opportunities to use language in many different ways, they become skilled at verbally *recalling* past events, *sequencing* two or three events according to time, and *projecting* two or three future events sequentially. They acquire experience in *reporting, questioning, evaluating, conversing*, and *expressing thoughts, feelings*, and *ideas*. They are constantly practicing *problem-solving* and *decision-making* skills at increasingly complex levels.

Underlying all of these developing abilities and the accompanying accumulation of knowledge is the encouragement of wholesome *social relationships* with peers. The development of *ego-strength* and a sense of *self-worth* which evolves are crucial to all of the other goals of the program. Regardless of other abilities or lack of them, these attributes will ensure a joyful early lifehood for every child.

Creating the
Play Environment

PART TWO

3 Physical Influences

CREATING THE PLAY ENVIRONMENT

Facilities used by children can be divided into three categories:

1. Those areas used for storage of personal belongings and for materials and equipment.
2. Those areas used for routine physical care: eating, resting, napping, washing, toileting, and isolation for sick children.
3. Those areas used for play and other learning experiences which are indulged in by the children but which you may choose not to call play.

These last areas are the ones that we will be concerned with in these pages, although in many instances, especially in homes, the areas of these various categories may overlap. These areas are variously described as work or play centers, according to what the adults concerned think should take place within them. In this book they are referred to as *play areas*. Play areas may be any of the following places:

Interest center	Concept display center	Water play area
Learning center	Table	Gardening area
Discovery center	Corner	Table toy center
Science center	Playground	Manipulative toy center
Art center	Patio	Reading center
Activity center	Lawn	Mathematics center

Open area	Backyard	Construction center
Rug area	Front yard	Carpentry center
Story area	Play yard	Group activity center
Block play center	Bike area	Work area
Housekeeping center	Bike path	Listening center
Dramatic play center	Digging area	Language center
Quiet center	Sand play area	
Alone place	Sandbox	

Whatever area is available for the play environment, regardless of its location, size, or condition, it will influence the way the children using that area will play. By giving careful consideration to the physical environment, you can use it to the fullest advantage. Of course, there are always many things over which you have no control. Still, you can use those things over which you do have some control to the greatest possible extent. The creative play program is *not* dependent on any particular sort of area or physical structure. It *is* dependent on the time, materials, freedom, and space available to the children.

The materials, though part of the interest-arousing aspect of the program, need not meet any particular standards other than that they are safe and that the children will respond to them.

ARRANGEMENTS

A basic principle for preparing areas where children will play is to think in terms of *maximum challenge to body and mind*. Although there should be many open spaces, there should also be many areas that will initiate complex movement patterns.

For ease of supervision in outdoor playgrounds, it is usually necessary to place equipment primarily around the perimeter so that children at play aren't hidden behind large objects. Also, since running is usually encouraged, this arrangement allows for open space where the children are able to do so. Still, these spaces should be so arranged that even though they are fairly open, they require the children to look and think about where they are going because some objects may be in the way. Enough items should be movable so that the pathways through the play areas can be changed from time to time to prevent children from running automatically to any one place, both indoors and out.

Indoors, the open areas should consist of many small places around the perimeter of the room rather than one large central "rug" area in the middle.

This arrangement will require the children to move around the furniture. It not only encourages movement but speech as well. Supplies should not be too close to the areas where they will be used, which will require the children to carry them from one place to another. Materials and furnishings should be moved to different places in the play areas from time to time. Some changes should be made every few days.

Not everything should ever be changed at the same time. But enough changes should be made so that children entering the play areas must look and think before they can decide where to go. Classrooms used by two-year-olds should never be changed very much. Two-year-olds like routine, sameness, and repetition. Three-year-olds like surprises. They like the challenge of new ideas and new things as long as not everything is different. Four- and five-year-olds respond well to innovative ideas, complex movement patterns, and new environments.

One way to encourage movement is to limit the number of chairs in any one area or classroom. It's not even necessary to have one chair for each child. Hopefully, you will seldom have them all sitting at any one time. And if you do, they can always use rugs, cushions, and other down-on-the-floor places to sit. Children will limit their movements in places where there are too many rules and restrictions concerning the furnishings. They will move hesitatingly in areas where there are many things they are not allowed to touch. They will move comfortably when they are trusted to be considerate of the things in the environment.

GROUND AND FLOOR SURFACES

Children spend so much of their time sitting on the floor or the ground primarily because they are close to those surfaces. Therefore, these surfaces form an important part of their play areas. Many schools cover the play areas with indoor-outdoor carpeting, which cuts down on noise and provides comfortable surfaces to sit and walk on, but it has the drawback of limiting the overall use of the surface. For instance, certain areas may be left uncarpeted to provide areas for painting, waterplay, and other messy activities. In such cases, these activities are then restricted to only those uncarpeted areas. On the other hand, the use of many different sizes, textures, and colors of area rugs makes it possible to create new arrangements and varied play areas at will. Whatever the floor surface, however, it is important to consider its upkeep, janitorial services and costs, as well as the comfort, health, and safety of the children who play on it. Both indoors and out, try to provide as much variety in play surfaces as your budget and facilities will allow.

Decomposed granite is preferable to sand or dirt for the main outdoor play area. It consists of about 70 percent silicate, packs down better than pure sand, but is not as solid as dirt. In windy weather it doesn't blow as much as sand. It drains well and doesn't get muddy like dirt. The disadvantage of decomposed granite is that it is more abrasive than sand, and it may have to be replenished about every three or four years. After two or three years it usually becomes well blended with the original dirt surface, and overflow sand from the sandpile has mixed in enough to make a clean, comfortable ground cover.

Dirt surfaces are inexpensive and can be formed and shaped to make terraces, hills, and slopes. Some schools plan the outdoor area with dirt as the foundation. Then the equipment area, where most of the climbing apparatus is located can be covered with several layers of decomposed granite which will gradually blend into the dirt. Large amounts of sand can be placed directly under the climbing apparatus. Sand is good to fall in and good to jump in. It also has the advantage of being easy to mix with water and can then be used for building play hills, tunnels, and other forms. Naturally, it is used for sandplay areas. The disadvantage of it as an overall ground cover is that it will cling to shoes and feet and get tracked into the building. Also, it will blow and shift in the wind and has to be replaced more frequently than the decomposed granite.

If possible, arrange to have one or two grassy areas to play on. Naturally they will need watering, mowing, and frequent reseeding. However, anything growing is good for the oxygen it produces and the relationship to nature it provides. Grass is good for physical play when its dry, but can be slippery when wet. It will also stain clothing when wet.

21

In addition to the sand, granite, dirt, and grassy areas, there should also be some hard surfaces on which to use wheel toys and to play certain kinds of running games. Asphalt is the least expensive but it has the disadvantage of heating up in the summer and developing cracks. These cracks can be repaired at nominal cost. In fact, it is simple to repair it yourself. Concrete is sometimes the only surface available for wheel toys. It can be dangerous if these places are used for running and other physical activities. Concrete is good to use for anchoring equipment under the ground, and for walkways, especially around areas that are likely to become muddy during wet weather.

To add beauty and variety you might consider paving part of the play area with bricks. These can be tapped right into sand and will hold each other in place. Keep them away from climbing equipment, however, because they can be dangerous to fall on.

At some schools, large outdoor concrete areas are covered with indoor-outdoor carpeting. This holds up very well and is quite serviceable. It is certainly an improvement over the bare concrete. However, it is not very resilient. It can be padded underneath, but that adds greatly to the expense. Also, it takes some getting used to because it doesn't look very natural outdoors. But when it is used in conjunction with some of the other types of surfaces, it can be quite useful.

Materials to use under swings and climbing apparatus include tanbark and mixtures of peat and cinders. The tanbark is expensive and will need to be replaced almost yearly. The peat and cinders mixture is not so expensive and gives a resilient surface. It too must be replaced yearly.

For further variety, wood can be used for walkways or small portions of the general play area. However, wood is very expensive so its use should probably be limited to building projects where no substitutes are satisfactory.

TEXTURES AND MATERIALS

Play areas must be considered in their totality, making it important to pay attention to the materials from which they are constructed. Walls, whether they are plastered, brick, wallpapered, or painted wood, provide the basic setting for the environment. Brick walls sometimes look dull and they are difficult to clean. So are rough plaster walls. Wallpaper, unless it is waterproof, may require too many restrictions in the use of messy materials. Painted wood and smooth plaster can always be repainted, so their use may allow the children just a little more freedom. Formica walls, or other washable, smooth plastic finishes, allow for much messiness such as may be involved in waterplay and similar activities. However, these materials are often sterile looking, they reflect too much light for comfort, provide poor acoustical effect, and are often cold to the touch.

The ideal play area, both indoors and out, is one that incorporates many different textures and types of materials, thus enabling the children to become accustomed to the different properties of these materials. A variety of materials provides an ongoing input of sensory information—and the more the senses are stimulated, the more learning occurs.

In considering building materials, think in terms of acoustics, color, floor and ground surfaces, lighting, and dimensions and proportions. Also think in terms of the structure's age.

It is fun to move into brand-new buildings, especially if you have had some say in their construction or their decor. They are usually very clean, sanitary, shiny, light and airy, and sterile. However, they are not necessarily advantageous in terms influencing children's play compared to the warmth of well-used wood, wear-polished floors, and well-worn pathways. Places that have been previously used may provide an important sense of involvement and "belonging." So much in our world of today is too shiny, too flimsy, or untouchable. Therefore, we often find comfort in things from the world of yesterday.

The use of older facilities may also present problems. Wood may be so weathered that it's splintery. Peeling paint is unsightly and it can be hazardous to health. Storage facilities may be limited. The rooms may be too small and the ceilings uncomfortably high (although children like high ceilings). Windows may be inadequate. Ventiliation may be bad. Termites may have invaded the underlying structure.

Ideally we should try to blend the old with the new. For instance, new facilities can be partially furnished with some old warm, wooden equipment. By the same token, old pieces can be brightened up by such touches as new plastic table tops or new handles or other trim. Whatever the plan, avoid having everything so new that the unrealness of it restricts the freedom to play. At the same time, you don't want everything to be so old that too much of your budget has to be diverted to constant repairs and replacements.

DIRECTIONAL FACTORS

The direction the play area faces can greatly influence the people who use it and the type of play they will engage in. We seldom have much control over directional factors unless we are building from scratch. But we can still consider them when we plan for the arrangement and uses of these areas.

Remember that southern exposures will have both morning and afternoon sun. If you are located where there are many warm summer months, southwestern exposures would be more satisfactory because they provide more shade. Outdoor play areas should be located in a way that will give the children both sunny and shady places to play throughout the year. If your play area is away from any large structure, solid fences and brick walls can provide some shade during part of the day. Overhead climbing platforms, playhouses, and storage sheds can be located so that they will provide shade.

An interior room that has an eastern exposure will always be bright and cheery in the mornings. Even in warm months it will be comfortable because the sun will quickly move overhead. However, during winter months such rooms may become gloomy as the day progresses. Colors, furnishings, and lighting can be arranged to counteract this effect so that the room appears to be restful rather than gloomy. Rooms with western exposures will work just the opposite. They will be darker and cooler in the mornings, which is good during hot weather. But on cold, wintry days, warm colors should be introduced to keep these rooms from becoming depressing. But again, the afternoon sun will brighten up the room considerably. These factors must be taken into consideration when you plan how you are going to use the areas available to you. For maximum comfort, you may need to use some rooms in the morning and others in the afternoon, reversing the procedure for winter and summer. Northern exposures will generally be on the cool side and somewhat dull during winter months. Southern exposures will be bright, cheery, and sunny in comparison.

The directions rooms face are not only important because of the effect of the sun. The view from play areas can be overstimulating, pleasant, depressing or perhaps it may have no effect at all. If the view is pleasant, such as one of open spaces or attractive buildings, the children are fortunate. But if the view is depressing or distracting, such as moving traffic or ugly buildings, you should do something to make it less so. Screening devices in the form of fences, shades, hedges, trees, and other decorations can be used. Such devices should not be so prominent that they are in themselves distracting, but they can help to provide pleasing views for all the persons using the areas.

Another directional factor that is often overlooked by most people, especially classroom teachers is that people of all ages, including children, frequently must face certain directions in order to feel comfortable. For example, some persons are more comfortable when they can see all of the other people in the area. Others like to be where they cannot see most of the other people. Some prefer the brighter area of a room or the shady area of an outdoor play spot. Some like to be at the rear of the particular area. Others like the front or the center. Some prefer to have other people on their left. Others prefer the opposite. Therefore, it is important to let children choose their own places for playing, sitting, listening, resting, and other activities whenever possible.

24

In the central room plan, a wide variety of open places on every side of the room allows for a considerable amount of choice of location. In group situations, the need sometimes arises to separate two or three children temporarily from one another. You can sometimes anticipate this need and suggest certain positioning arrangements that would keep these children apart. In doing so, give them some choices, especially as to which side of the group they prefer and the direction they wish to face. Comfortable positions encourage relaxation and cooperativeness. Sometimes changing a nonparticipant's directional position will encourage participation.

Changing what the child sees is also important. From time to time, find a different place for the children to sit while they listen to stories. Vary the areas where they rest, work puzzles, play house, and paint so that the child's view is not always the same when he or she repeats an activity. Changing arrangements with thought to changing the directional factors stimulates the imagination, prevents boredom, arouses curiosity, refreshes attitudes, and promotes participation. When new movement patterns are used, new learning occurs.

COLORS

The colors used in the school environment play an important part in creating the atmosphere. They should be taken into consideration in planning play areas. Many people have some favorite, comfortable color schemes from which they do not want to vary greatly. The same should hold true in the classroom. Although I encourage a flexible, changing environment, some things should be kept fairly constant, such as a harmonious, functional color scheme.

Colors have a direct effect on our moods, nerves, and emotions. Some color schemes are soothing and restful. Some encourage animation and gaiety. Some may be depressing. Much depends on proportions, lighting, room arrangements, and similar factors. My own experiments have demonstrated that children's moods and the way they play can be influenced by the predominance of certain colors in a room. The use of red lights and decorations to create an almost completely red environment was fun, playful, and exciting. The room aroused curiosity and stimulated the imagination. But neither children nor adults wanted to use the room for very long. After fifteen minutes, everyone began to be hyperactive, and after another fifteen minutes, everyone felt fatigued.

In another experiment we prepared a room in which the lighting, walls, tables, and countertops, and many of the accessories were all yellow. Even the wooden cabinets and other trim was blonde wood. The door was painted yellow. The floors were ivory, and reflected the yellow of the colored lights. In this room movements appeared to be either lethargic or automatic. Faces were expressionless. Both children and adults were bored and uncomfortable.

Blue was the next color chosen to experiment with. We trimmed an entire room with blue butcher paper and blue corrugated paper so that all walls and furnishings were blue. All accessories and toys brought into the room were blue. The lights, windows, and doors were covered with blue cellophane or blue crepe paper. This room was very lovely. There was a gentle hint of mystery. Movements within the room were extremely slow and graceful, almost delicate. But it was difficult to function normally because of the tremendous distortion of shadowed areas. No one stayed in the room for more than twenty or thirty minutes, and some of the children left after only ten minutes. Everyone who left the room went back to it several times. Everyone, including the children, appreciated its beauty, but the effect was too powerful to enable anyone to stay in it very long.

The most satisfying color used in this series of experiments was green. The all-green room we created had the most calming and most organizing influence on the children's play. There was a happy, relaxed feeling, and much tolerance of one another's actions. Children played in the room for one- and two-hour periods, and came back to it several times. Adults found it pleasant and said it had a "woodsy" or "nature" feeling. They also commented on the underlying sense of order and well-being.

Red, yellow, and orange are usually considered to be the "warm" colors. They can be used to make a room seem smaller, because they seem closer when you look at them than do other colors. To make rooms appear to be cooler or to give the illusion of more space than there actually is, concentrate on blues and greens.

By carefully balancing warm and cool colors, you can achieve a day-long, year-round color harmony that will be just as comfortable on hot days as in cold weather, and just as cheerful on gloomy days as in bright weather.

In planning color patterns, be sure to consider the room from every side. A room may seem well-balanced from the side or front, but the colors may be off balance when they are viewed from the back or from the opposite side. Also, when planning new facilities, it is a good idea to consider how the color patterns look at various times of day and in different types of lighting.

Once the basic color scheme has been established, you can add accents of intense color. These can be introduced in the toys, small containers for games and puzzles, and other small items. The basic color scheme can be varied throughout the year to keep in tune with seasonal activities and moods. For example, floral arrangements, paintings, and wall displays of warm browns, yellows, and muted greens would be very appropriate during the fall season. Pastels are more appropriate for spring. The use of complementary colors (any two colors directly opposite each other on the color wheel) will brighten up a dull wintry day; analogous colors (colors adjacent to each other on the color wheel) will be more restful for a hot, summery day.

In equipping the classroom, consider very carefully the colors of the things you decide to use. Brightly colored small toys are acceptable, but some of the brilliantly colored larger pieces of plastic play equipment are overstimulating, attention diverting, and fatiguing. They limit the imagination and their intensity soon becomes monotonous. I prefer more subtle tones that pick up changing shadows and reflect changing light patterns.

The color pattern in the room will also be influenced by the colors of clothing being worn by the children and adults in the school. Wearing clothes of colors that are at least somewhat in harmony with the room environment will help you impart feelings of security and comfort to children. Clothes that clash violently with the room colors are sometimes fun and exciting, but they may interfere with your ability to maintain a calm, relaxed atmosphere. Obviously we can't control the colors of the clothing people wear to school, but knowing the ways that children react to different colors we can be aware of the strength of their influence on the way children play. You can use this knowledge to motivate different types of activities from time to time.

LIGHTING

Light often creates cheerfulness. Yet, too much light can get on the nerves and become irritating. In planning the interior lighting for your playrooms, you can take another approach. Consider the lighting as part of the overall decor. At certain times you may want as much light as possible, especially in areas where children are cutting, writing, pasting, playing with intricate puzzles, or other close work. On the other hand, you may be able to provide adequate lighting for these activities with only half the usual amount. The best way to find out is to try using the lesser amount.

As the day progresses and the children start to slow down, the sudden addition of light by using all available light can give spirits a lift. After a while, however, this additional light may become overstimulating and tiring. When that happens, reduce the amount again. When play is very quiet or during periods of relaxation and rest, the area can be darkened even more. As the seasons change, your lighting scheme may need to be adjusted to accommodate to the changing path of the sun.

One important factor to consider at all times, whether indoors or out, is safety. Areas that cannot be lighted adequately for children to see what they are doing should be considered off limits to them. Either find some way to

27

light such areas or provide some kind of barrier that will prevent access to them. Do not consider them a part of the play area. Some such areas may be unsafe during a certain part of the year or day, but perfectly fine during times when the sunshine is more direct.

Some researchers are now of the opinion that fluorescent lighting can cause or at least accentuate hyperactivity. Many schools have this type of lighting, and there is little likelihood of having it changed. If this is your situation, you may remedy it to some extent by bringing portable light fixtures that use incandescent bulbs into the playrooms. Use them in place of the overhead lights during part of each day. These lamps can also give you the opportunity to experiment with colored lights.

In evaluating lighting needs, consider the brightness of the colors and materials in the play areas. Smooth, shiny materials reflect light, and thus may require the use of less artificial lighting than dull, rough, or otherwise nonreflective surfaces. By the same token, table surfaces that are too bright and shiny can be overstimulating and tiring to the eyes. Such surfaces are easier on the nervous system if they are not too glossy. Semiglossy enamels provide a hard and easy-to-keep-clean finish without being as overbearing as high-gloss paints. Some formica tops have somewhat subdued reflective powers, but their smoothness will still reflect good lighting patterns.

In addition to the energy level and safety factors, the aesthetic effect of the lighting should be considered. Good indoor lighting should be balanced throughout the play areas. If some areas are very bright, and others quite dark, a room might be off balance visually. If you use portable lighting, try to arrange it so that the lighter areas are well-balanced in relationship to those areas that may be more shadowy.

Windows, particularly those which cover an entire wall, may cause too much glare in the play areas. This might come from direct sunlight or from being surrounded by white or shiny materials. Glare should be subdued with curtains, partial draping, blinds or outdoor awnings.

SOUNDS AND ACOUSTICS

The sounds in the environment have a direct influence on the child's play. When play areas are noisy and acoustics are bad, voices become sharp and impatient. When play areas are quiet enough for the children to hear only themselves, they take more care in what they say and in how they use their voices.

Sometimes the acoustics are so poor that sounds echo back into the room. This situation can be easily remedied by putting rugs or carpets on the floors, drapes or other curtaining at the windows, and acoustical tile on the ceiling. An inexpensive remedy is to hang a parachute immediately below the ceiling. Another is to partially carpet one or more walls. The larger the area, the more important such measures become.

In some locations, you may be annoyed by noise from the machinery of neighboring factories or bypassing traffic. These sounds can be very hard on the nerves and cause both children and adults to become irritable and impatient. Outdoor noise can be muffled by plants, porous screens, and solid fencing. Closed windows can help to shut out annoying sounds when you are indoors.

Whatever your particular circumstances, evaluate your play areas frequently for their noise levels. If they are annoyingly high, use the calm and quietness of your own voice to influence the children to lower their voices. If the sounds are simply those of children talking, playing, laughing, arguing, singing, shouting, and being themselves, be pleased. These are normal, healthy sounds and should be encouraged.

In arranging indoor play areas, the central arrangement referred to earlier has the value of encouraging verbalization. When play areas and learning centers are pushed up against walls, children talk relatively little—people don't like to talk to walls. When the play areas are in the center of the room, creating open space all around the child, talking increases. It is easier to talk when you see other faces and other activities taking place near you.

The continuous sound of air-conditioning machinery in the background is another irritant of which some people are not aware. Try turning the machinery off to observe the difference. Everyone will speak more softly and move more gently. It will seem almost as though some great weight were lifted from you. Since you probably need the air conditioning, you can look for ways to lessen the noise. The problem can sometimes be solved by the use of acoustical materials in the equipment room.

ODORS

No matter how much you may have to say about planning the play environment there are sometimes scents and odors over which you have no control. They will have an effect on the way children play, and they should be taken into consideration when planning the use of the play areas. For example, in one school I know of there is the daily smell of fresh baked goods drifting into the play yard from a nearby bakery. This so stimulated the digestive juices of both children and adults that constant feelings of hunger occured. They finally revised their timing for use of the outdoor areas, avoiding those times when the smells of the baking are at their strongest. Plantings of shrubs, trees, vines can help to offset odors.

Strong scents and odors permeating the interior areas can be absorbed with deodorant bottles (the wick type) placed wherever they are needed. Be sure that they are well out of the children's reach. One way to keep them out of curious hands is to hang them from a hook near the ceiling with a cord looped around the neck of the container to hang it from. Oppressive odors beyond your control can be dealt with by complaining to your local Board of Health.

WEATHER

The weather will affect the uses of play areas. If you familiarize yourself with a few basic guidelines, you will be able to use the weather to your advantage.

For the most part, the school year begins in September. As the days of autumn progress, changes begin to take place. In some parts of the country, wind becomes an important factor. Windy days mean that outdoor play should take place in protected areas. Several days of windy weather can make normally relaxed adults become irritable. Children may experience some changes too, but to a lesser extent. However, they readily react to the tensions of the adults about them. If you sense weather-induced changes coming on, arrange your plans to provide for quiet, relaxing activities. Keep groups small. Introduce music more frequently. Talk about the wind. Provide opportunities for the children to relieve their tensions, by encouraging them to play with clay, carpentry tools, and the punching bag, and by encouraging them to participate in creative movement activities. Do scientific experiments involving air movement. Help the children accept the changes of nature as something beautiful—a key to exploration and learning.

On cold, wintry days the wind may present different problems. It may be easier to run and play outdoors, but again, protected areas should be provided for. Be sure the children are dressed adequately, but not overdressed. As they exercise their muscles, their body temperatures will rise. The resultant perspiration may cause their clothing to become wet if they are dressed too warmly. Two or three thin layers of clothing are easier to control than one heavy outer wrap.

When the season of rain and snow arrives, you will find yourself having to make greater use of your indoor play areas. If you have the space, move as much of your playground equipment as possible inside. Children like to use boxes, planks, climbing apparatus, wheel toys, and other materials for vigorous physical play no matter what the weather is like outdoors. To accommodate this equipment, you might have to move the usual furnishings to the far corner of a hallway or a storage room.

Children do not seem to respond to adverse weather as much as adults do. Consequently, they can often withstand extremes more easily than adults. However, they also learn to react emotionally to the ways they see adults respond to the weather.

When the days become longer, children become completely revitalized. The quiet child becomes rambunctious, busy, and social. The child who played alone the month before now wants to be with others. During the spring months, biological changes seem to take place, in all human beings encouraging people to make closer physical contact with one another. Anticipating this, you can provide opportunities for children to be close to each other without allowing their play to become too rough.

Recognizing that toys and things become less important than people at these times, the curriculum can provide greater stimulus for dramatic and social play experiences. Plan picnics, parties, and other social events. Set off new areas where small groups can play together. Make use of smaller rooms, if they are available. At the same time, provide for vigorous outdoor activity such as nature walks and gardening, in order to offset the fighting and unpleasantness that often results from innocent touching games.

In some sections of the country, high humidity is a common problem. Humid days bring on slower movements, laziness, less energy. At these times, it is important to recognize the child's right to do nothing.

At the other extreme, some areas experience exceptionally low humidity at times. Breathing hot, dry air dries out the mucous linings of the nose and throat, and causes excessive thirst. Except for waterplay, children should avoid vigorous outdoor activities when the temperature is high and the humidity low. Indoor heating and air-cooling systems can also cause the indoor humidity to fall to unpleasantly low levels.

Foggy days may be the most depressing kind of weather of all. Some people experience a feeling of helplessness when they are not able to see more than a short distance ahead of them. Children may become confused, and this confusion will be reflected in their play. If you live in an area that gets foggy, talk to the children about fog and help them to understand that it is a natural part of the environment.

VENTILATION, SMOG, FRESH AIR, AND TEMPERATURE

Ventilation and heating arrangements must be considered in preparing play areas. Poor ventilation can cause headaches, even in young children. It can cause irritation and fatigue, and bring on upper respiratory tract infections.

Many homes and buildings are equipped with air-conditioning systems. As the nature of the outside air deteriorates, air conditioning becomes increasingly important.

In industrialized and urbanized areas where smog is common we have to consider the quality of the air before we permit children to play outdoors. Playing in the smog is harmful to children at any time. Therefore, it is important to know when air pollution has reached an unacceptable level. At those times, any unnecessary physical movement of two-,three-, four- and five-year-olds out of doors should be avoided. If smog is prevalent in your area, you should provide for alternate indoor play areas.

Too much moisture in the air tends to make people lethargic. Too little moisture can be irritating to the mucous membranes. Like poor ventilation, it can bring on headaches, allergy problems, and upper respiratory infections. The use of humidifiers can help to offset this problem. Steam from boiling water can be of relief—but use this method only if you can boil the water without endangering the children.

In good weather, the windows should be opened to let fresh air into the rooms. If the windows cannot be opened, leave the doors open instead. Fresh air, if it is not smoggy, should be brought into the interior play areas as often as possible. In some locations, industrial smoke, rather than smog, may be a problem. Do not allow the children to play in an outdoor area if there is smoke in the air. Substitute indoor play instead.

Thermostats or thermometers should be available so that you can maintain suitable temperatures. You should have some type of supplementary heating system available in case the regular system fails. Portable electric heaters with thermostat controls can be used to heat up an area rapidly. However, they must be placed out of the children's reach. Of course, if they are placed too high up, much of their benefit will be lost because the heat will rise. But they can be placed on shelves slightly above the reach of children—preferably back from the edge of any shelf—and still be effective.

It is more difficult to provide supplementary cooling devices. However, if your air conditioner breaks down, take the children to shady and cooler areas and encourage them to play quietly to avoid overheating.

In considering the temperature of indoor play areas remember that children are closer to the floor than you are. Unless you, too, get close to the floor, you may not be able to assess the situation properly.

⑷ Human Influences

Everyone who becomes a part of the school community is automatically a part of the play environment and thus influences the type of play that occurs in that environment. In addition to the children, this includes the teaching staff, supportive staff, parents, volunteers, visitors, student teachers, and sometimes neighbors. Anyone seen or heard by the children while they are playing is involved in that play even though it may be only for a fleeting second or two. Any person entering the play area takes up some of the space, adds to the sounds, colors, scents, and other phenomena that are already affecting that space.

Open, nondiscriminating environments accept and respect each person as an individual. If you are aware that each person influences every other person and, that this influence works both ways, you will be in a position to modify the environment as required to accommodate these influences.

DENSITY

Another influence on children's play is the number of people in the play area in relation to its size and amount of open space available in it. In school settings, the amount of space per child is governed by legal regulations. However, the regulations don't take into consideration the number of adults in the area. In observing how any given number of children in an area play, we must consider any adults present as well.

In my state (California) the law requires nursery schools to provide 35 square feet of indoor space per child. This provision is quite valid when we consider what happens when less space is available. Even though these spatial provisions are adhered to, a flexible curriculum can allow for great variations. After closely observing an average of sixty children a day for a week, I concluded that when no more than fifteen or sixteen children (the legal number for that school) were in any particular room, the entire program functioned smoothly, although there were numerous cases of aggression and some isolated cases of nonsociability and hyperactivity. These incidents were accepted as normal for the group since similar behavior is traditionally observed in most schools. Two adults were present at all times.

When the number of children in the room was doubled, bringing the total to thirty or thirty-one, the number of incidents of aggression greatly increased. *Many* children became overstimulated and apparently did not know where to direct their energies. In the resultant confusion, many of them finally withdrew (under a table, to a corner of the room, to an "alone" box, or even—in the midst of a crowd—into a daydream). Few children sat on the floor, and only a few sat at tables. Two out of every three remained on their feet. There was little movement; but what movement there was seemed disoriented. When the furniture was rearranged so that it was clustered near the center of the room providing many open areas around the perimeter, children were able to space themselves more easily and aggression decreased.

Conversely, when half the usual number of children were in the room, almost all aggressive behavior ceased. These eight children showed a greater ability to work out their own disagreements, space was more readily shared, and even the quiet, withdrawn children seemed to join one or another activity in the room.

There was a tremendous change in behaviors of most of the children being observed when the number was further reduced to five or six. Those who were normally shy or withdrawn continued to be so for a time. But gradually, as they realized how much space was available to them without threat of interference, they ventured into more active use of the entire space. After five to six such experiences (varying with the individual), these children were generally better able to cope with their shyness in larger groups and they participated more readily in all activities.

Another observation made during periods when only a few children were using space that was generally used by a larger number was the breakdown of certain social inhibitions relative to conscience. Without the support of other children or adults some children find it difficult to control their impulse in situations where they find themselves with a great deal more territory to do with as they please. Some will direct this tendency to innovative and creative uses of familiar materials. Others will become careless and destructive.

Sometimes there may be so much furniture and play materials in a room that there is not enough space left for people to move freely. Continuously evaluate your playrooms and discard or store surplus items.

The amount of space required for outdoor play varies from 75 to 100 square feet per child. The size of the play area is not more important than the way it is arranged, how it can be supervised, and the variety of play opportunities available in it. "The range of no less than one-third to no more than one-half uncovered surface is appropriate to good organization. Larger numbers of children appear to need the extra space provided by having more empty surface."[1]

In addition, there should be a minimum of at least two places for each child to play even if every child is playing alone. Thus, if twenty-five children are playing at one time, there should be at least fifty different places for them to choose to play.[2]

For outdoor play, two adult supervisors should be on duty for the first fifteen children, three adults for fifteen to twenty-five children, four adults for twenty-five to thirty-five children, and five adults for thirty-five to forty. When more than forty preschool children play in an outdoor play area at the same time, they exert too much pressure on one another no matter how many adults are supervising. When that number is reached, divide the group and find another area for the other children—if possible.

PERSONAL SPACE

When a new individual enters a play area, there is immediately less space available to others. An intrusion may appear threatening to a child who is using the space, has used it, or plans to use it, but hasn't done so yet.

What constitutes "personal space" varies with the size and personality of the individual. Some people seem to shrink into the space they are occupying, scarcely noticed and without threatening anyone. Others make their presence known in various ways, pleasant or unpleasant, seemingly occupying much more space than their actual physical bodies take up. If the "aura" of such people is positive, everyone makes room for them, even if the area is already crowded. But when a child's "aura" has negative inferences, other children shy away from him, resent his presence, and feel that he is literally taking up more than his rightful share of the available space.

[1] Sybil Kritchevsky and Elizabeth Prescott, *Planning Environments for Young Children* (Washington, D.C.: National Association for the Education of Young Children, 1969) p. 17.
[2] Clare Cherry, Barbara Harkness, and Kay Kuzma, *Nursery School Management Guide* (Belmont, CA: Fearon Publishers, 1973) p. 59.

The desire to have a place that is one's own is a normal human trait. All of us need from time to time a place to be alone, a place where no one can intrude and where we can feel safe and protected from others. This desire manifests itself in children at an early age. They frequently set up private little enclosures, or mark off an imaginary line that shows the boundary of their own territory. As long as no one else encroaches on that space, all may be well. But if someone wants to enter it, share it, divide it, or possess it, then the child may feel threatened. These situations require the child to modify his actions, which may lead to quarreling, sharing, giving up, intervention by an adult who will bring about a compromise, or it may result in the complete loss of the threatened child's emotional control.

Adults who work with young children should recognize these natural desires to control a particular space and what goes on there. Try to set up suitable spatial arrangements to accommodate children's desires to control a particular "territory." When conflicts arise, nonjudgmental interaction with the children involved can help them reach a compromise. Try to help the children understand one another's feelings, but always be aware that this normal human trait will influence the play experiences.

AGE

Children of different ages play in different ways. Toddlers spend much of their time in solitary play (playing alone), onlooker play (watching others), and parallel play (playing alongside of others, perhaps doing the same thing, but not mutually involved with one another).

Many children lead isolated or inhibited lives before they start to nursery school. Adults interfere with the toddler's free explorations of the environment, sometimes for very legitimate reasons, such as health and safety. Too often, however, they interfere for reasons of personal convenience or from a misunderstanding of how children learn, which has the effect of stifling the child's normal curiosity. Children frequently learn to perform socially acceptable actions by means of instructions like these:

- Go away, be quiet, play by yourself. I have work to do.
- Stop being a baby and get up off that floor.
- Stop crying. Big boys don't cry.
- Don't interrupt. We are talking.
- Go play somewhere else. We have company.
- Say hello to the company. Answer questions. Don't bother anyone. Talk only when someone talks to you.
- Play by yourself. Don't bother your sister.

Children learn to look, but not to touch; answer questions, but not to volunteer information; play alone, but not with adults—especially not with visiting adults. Although people are by nature social beings, children learn at an early age to suppress their desires to be sociable.

When children start to nursery school, abrupt changes take place in their lives. Not only are they separated from the person with whom they have probably socialized the most, their mother, but they are suddenly expected to start socializing with others. Other children, whom the child may not have been allowed to play with before, because they were "too big" or "too dirty" or "too rough" or "didn't belong" or, because they weren't even around, suddenly become playmates. But by this age, children have already learned to keep their distance. They would like to play with others, but they have learned to be cautious in their social relationships. It takes time for children to figure out what to do in a totally new environment. What they do is participate in the artificially created phenomena that is so widely considered still to be *parallel play*.

Watch children who are engaged in what is said to be parallel play. Often they are really playing *with* each other. What adult observers sometimes fail to see is that these children *are* communicating with one another. They *are* interacting, primarily by means of body language. Since their natural inclinations have been suppressed, they use this means to begin the socialization process on new terms, slowly learning to identify with their peers, both as individuals and as members of a group. At the same time, they are learning to reaccept the interaction of other adults, provided they have been shown that they can be trusted.

When three- or four-year-olds first enter a school situation, they frequently do not talk to people they don't know. But they are easily involved in play activities that will lead to social interaction and cooperative play. They begin to enjoy dramatic play activities, and by time they are four, they participate in it during much of their play time. The child who doesn't can usually be motivated by increased interaction with playful, playing adults.

When older children play with younger children, they influence the play of the younger ones. Usually the younger children will feel more confident in whatever they are doing, seeming to absorb some of the confidence that older children exude when they are "helping" with younger ones. One or two younger children playing with several older children do not have as much influence on the play of the older children. The younger ones are often ignored, or they may be pulled into the play with little regard to the fact that they may not be able to perform at the same level as the older children. Three-and-a-half-year-olds are somewhat careless with two-year-olds. Fours are somewhat more aware of the fact that the smaller children should be treated more gently, but they cannot always be depended on to do so. Five-year-olds will

37

waver between being very considerate of younger children and ignoring them, depending on the type of play activity that is going on.

The ages of the supervising adults also affect the way children play, not only because of the way they act because of their respective ages, but also because of the way some children react to people of various ages. For example, children seem to have a different kind of rapport with young teenagers than they do with college students. They seem to have a greater affinity for one another, as though they recognize that much of their emotional needs are the same.

Personality, size, and other aspects of an individual also have an influence on the age factor. So though the ages of the persons involved are important to consider, the other factors must also be taken into account.

ORDINAL POSITION

Ordinal position in the family influences the way children play together. (This factor, of course, influences the adults in the environment, too). First children of a marriage are often accepted by their parents more readily than succeeding children. Parents often show greater concern for these children, and have higher expectations for them. Their parents often expect them to be the very best in everything. By the time the second and third children arrive, the parents have usually become somewhat more relaxed in their expectations and therefore put less pressure on the children to succeed. The pattern, however, has already been set with the firstborn. Research seems to indicate that firstborn children do, in fact, achieve greater success in school and employment than younger members of the family. Part of this may be caused by the learning opportunities that result from tutoring their siblings in a wide variety of skills. The other siblings apparently exert some influence too, because these firstborn are usually higher achievers than only children.

Second and third children, perhaps because they are not pushed for such high academic achievements as the first, often have more freedom for developing creative habits and individualism. When there are three children in the family the middle one may feel pushed out. Too old for the attention the baby gets and too young to do all the things the older one does, such children sometimes become withdrawn, morose, or rebellious.

The child's ordinal position may be further influenced by the fact that with each succeeding child, the family may feel increasing economic pressures. The mother is obviously not going to have as much time to play with later children as with the first or second. However, these children do have their older siblings to play with. Statistically, the higher achievers may be the oldest and, in large families, the next oldest children. But the children in large families, in spite of economic pressures, frequently have much better adjusted personalities than do those who are only children, or are one of a group of two or three siblings.

If you know the ordinal position of the children with whom you interact, you can use that knowledge for better understanding how each particular individual influences the play that is occurring.

SIZE

The sizes of the various children in the play areas will influence one another. Large children obviously take up more space than smaller children. Children who are large for their age may be clumsier than smaller children and may unwittingly get into other children's way. Children who are small for their average age are generally quicker moving than some of the larger children. Sometimes, however, smaller children may feel overwhelmed, and hesitate to move at all, though this is not so true of preschool children as it is with older ones. Children who are small for their age will more likely react according to their personalities than their sizes. They seldom realize that they are smaller, although very large children usually realize that they are larger than the others.

Unfortnately, we often expect too much of those who are large for their age, forgetting that even though they may be large in size they are still as immature emotionally and socially as children who are physically smaller.

Children's play will not only be influenced by the sizes of the players, but also by the sizes of the adults in the area. Very large or tall persons may seem threatening if space is limited. All adults should sit down among the children as often as possible to avoid towering over the play group.

NONVERBAL COMMUNICATION

Awareness of body language leads to empathic human interaction. The infant has this awareness. Infants are dependent on body language for communication. But as we grow older, we allow this ability to subside into our subconscious. As people who are concerned with children, we should try to reawaken our own awareness of this type of communication in ourselves and in the children and others with whom we spend our time. This language can be divided into three groups: silent, vocal but nonverbal, and nonsilent but nonvocal.

Silent

Facial Expressions Natural
Forced
Voluntary
Involuntary
Distorted

Mouth Position, shape, size
Movement of (including speed of movement)
Size of opening when in use
Position of tongue (between teeth, between lips, biting of,
movement of, speed of movement)
Color
Moisture

Eyes and Eyebrows Position, shape, and size
Movement
Frequency of movement
Focus
Color
Attention
Flicker of lids
Raising or lowering of brows
Lashes

Forehead Shape and size
Wrinkling
Tension
Perspiration

Jaw Tension
Position
Size
Prominance
Set

Head Tilt
Movement
Direction facing
Hair (styling, color, looseness or tightness, length, sheen)

Expression Accepting, nonaccepting
Threatening, nonthreatening
Positive feelings, negative feelings
Good mood, bad mood

Posture   Stance
Tension
Arch of back
Tilt of shoulders
Hunched shoulders
Erect or slack
Lopsidedness
Flexibility

Arms and Hands   Gestures
Palms (open, closed, loose, clenched)
Positions (extended, withdrawn, raised, lowered, fluid, rigid, folded)

Legs and Feet   Position
Movements
Gestures
Tension

Skin   Flushed, pale, pallid, moist, dry, perspiring, goose bumps, hair raised

Vocal, but nonverbal

Humming, tongue clicking, smacking lips, hissing, blowing, whistling, Tsk! Tsk!, Shhhh, clicking teeth, sucking cheeks inward, sighing, squeezing sounds in cheeks, squeezing sound through closed lips, snapping lips together to form *ppppp* sound.
Coughing and other throat noises
Sneezing, smacking lips, heavy breathing, rate of breathing, laughing, giggling, snickering.

Nonsilent but nonvocal

Hands   Clapping, swishing, opening and closing with force, snapping fingers, tapping fingers, scratching, tapping fingernails together, winging arms against sides, shuffling, clicking palms, chopping.

Feet   Stamping, shuffling, clicking heels, tapping shoes, tapping ball of foot, clicking ball of foot, swishing heels, swishing toes.

Touch

From the moment of birth, infants are handled and touched by other human beings. This touching becomes an important part of the infant's early

41

communication and interaction with others. "There, there" may be accompanied by soothing strokes on the shoulder or arm. "Mama loves you" may be accompanied by a gentle hug or squeeze. "Go to sleep now" may call for soft patting of the back. Petting, stroking, tickling, massaging, holding, stretching, swatting, spanking, slapping, and similar types of touching movements are very much a part of the normal infant and toddler's tactile experience. Much of children's earliest learning comes through their ability to touch, and to receive sensory impressions from this action. Through the sense of touch they find out about the world and the things in it. As a result of being touched they find out about themselves and their relationships to other persons.

There have been many reports of infants who have been deprived of touch during their early months of life. These infants are often dull and listless. As they grow older, and touch is still denied, they frequently develop learning difficulties and behavior problems. Some schizophrenic personalities have been found to be persons who were not given normal physical handling as infants.

Unfortunately, as children reach the age of two or thereabouts, our culture begins to impinge on their tactile freedom. They are told not to touch certain parts of their own bodies. They are told not to "communicate" with others by touching (hitting, pinching) them. The adults who loved them and touched them since birth suddenly do not "baby" them with tactile messages. Instead, they are *spoken to*. The older they get, the more verbalization replaces tactile communication.

In spite of efforts at suppression, and in spite of the lessening of the amount of touching from adults, children will and do touch one another. During certain periods of the year, especially during the early spring, children display an urgent need to touch one another even more so than usual. Teachers should be aware of the importance to children of this familiar, comfortable, unmistakable means of communication—touch.

Because of their inherent need for touching behavior, how they touch one another, how you touch them, and how you allow them to touch you, all are part of the important ways that persons in the environment influence the play of children in that environment.

When children arrive at school each day, I give them a "health check." My technique is to first hold the child gently by one arm as I draw him close to me. He tips his head back and opens his mouth so that I can check for redness or other unusual coloring in his throat. At the same time, I reach up with my left hand and feel his neck for swollen glands.

Once in a while I may say to a child, as I'm talking on the telephone or am otherwise busy, "Hey, you look o.k. Just go on to your room." When I do this, no one ever budges. They just stand there and wait. If I glance into their open mouth, they still don't move. Not until I touch their throats and arms. The touch, apparently, starts their day off human.

Clothing

The type, color, style, age, and material of the clothing each person—child or adult—wears is a form of nonverbal communication. Not only does the clothing we wear reflect something of our own cultures and personalities, but it tells others things about our economic circumstances, our attitudes, and the role we are playing at the time. Because our clothing does play a strong part in how we communicate to others, it follows that it influences the way children play.

People who are inappropriately dressed are generally uncomfortable —in a social sense as well as a physical sense—and they tend to make people they are with uncomfortable too.

Children who are sent to school in their best clothes are also uncomfortable, particularly when they have been cautioned by their mothers to be careful to keep their clothes clean. These children may feel inhibited in their movements. Their play will be affected, which in turn will affect the play of others.

Little girls sometimes become very jealous when another girl is allowed to wear jewelry to school. Otherwise well-behaved boys may suddenly become completely different personalities for a while when they arrive at school wearing a new cowboy outfit. They feel so superior and so sure that everyone believes they are a real cowboy that they may become very belligerant in playing the role.

VERBAL COMMUNICATION

Although nonverbal communication is exceedingly important, people are far more aware of verbal communication. The verbal language we use can be placed into several categories. These include, but are not limited to, the following:

Questions

Answers

Description of sensory impressions
  (visual, auditory, olfactory, gustatory, tactile, kinesthetic)

Description of sensory observations

Verbalization of emotions

Statements of contradiction

Repetition of someone else's statements

Random expressions of thought

Creative expressions (poetry, songs, prose)

News reporting

Story telling

Dramatization of real or imaginary events

Imitation

Recall of past events

Directions

Commands

Laughter

Threats

Hopes

Projection of future events

Stream-of-consciousness

Nonsense words

Children's play will be influenced by the categories of the words they hear. Some kinds of verbalizations will not interfere with the play that is going on; other kinds may have such a negative influence that they will cause play to stop instantly. Some verbalization may help to extend the play that is taking place. Some may motivate play that has not yet occurred. Actually, an even greater influence on the actions of others, and thus on the play of children, is the type of voice and method of presentation that is being used. Some of these variations by both children and adults that may affect how children play are:

Pitch   High, low, shrill

Clarity   Smooth, hoarse, musical, gruff

Intensity   Screaming, loud, very soft, whispered

Tempo   Extremely slow, drawling, fast, very rapid

Meaning   Understandable, not understandable

Attitude   Emotional, nonemotional, friendly, angry, boastful, superior, dictatorial, abrupt, hesitant, whimpering, whining, tender, casual, intense, secretive, etc.

Some teachers find it necessary to keep up steady streams of remarks, directions, and corrections, throughout the school day. Some children soon learn to stop hearing such persons almost completely, resulting in a total lack of communication. Be aware of how much and for what purposes you use language. Awareness will help it to be more meaningful, helpful, and positive as an influence on the children's play and other activities.

Be aware of how children who play together talk to one another. Some of these children get turned off by the others, too. You may need to help some children learn how to talk without whimpering or to be less boastful, or to speak more slowly, or to make some other type of modification that will help them in socializing with others.

RHYTHMS

The natural rhythms of our bodies are crucial to normal, healthful living. We all function under our individual physiological timing systems. By becoming aware of these, you can learn to recognize how they differ from one person to another. You can look for their effects on how an individual acts and how they influence the way in which people react to one another. You can consider their effect on how children play.

Cicardian rhythms are those body functions that operate on an approximately 24-hour cycle. They control such functions as blood pressure, pulse rate, body temperature, hemoglobin, blood sugar, respiration, and others. They influence our energy level, stress tolerance, hunger, need for sleep, etc. Although these functions are common to all, the particular 24-hour period or the precise length of the cycle, may vary greatly in the members of any group. Your schedule, based on your own rhythmic needs, may not exactly coincide with the rhythms of many of the children in a group. Some people start functioning at maximum capacity early in the day, others may not begin until midmorning, and still others are at their best in the afternoon or evening. Naturally, children who are playing together in a group may be operating on different rhythmic cycles. We also experience cycles based on hourly, monthly, or seasonal periods.

These natural rhythms differ also in their regularity. Some people are very regular in their timing and are able to regulate their lives accordingly. Others are irregular, or arhythmic, their changes in body functions unpredictable. These people, especially children, may be affected greatly by being forced into schedules that demand a regularity they are physiologically unable to meet.

Another influence of body rhythms is the personal pace of the individual. Some people are generally slow moving and have an overall slower metabolic and rhythmic functioning than others. Some may be exceptionally fast. When people with different tempos are interacting with one another, they continuously need to make adjustments to one another. The difficulty involved in making these accommodations may lead to various types of interaction that require different types of people to try to understand one another.

Children can sometimes be exasperating to one another, as well as to adults, especially when adults insist that the children adjust their rhythms to those of the adults, rather than vice versa. Children are always having to adjust their rhythms to adult demands. Interestingly, during their play, they readily adjust to one another's rhythms. They seem to sense the need to do so in order to facilitate harmonious relationships between one another and a continuation of the play activity.

SEX DIFFERENCES

No matter what the reasons behind the differences in the way boys and girls play, the differences are there. Girls giggle more, chatter more, react verbally with expressions of feelings. Boys move more vigorously, shout more, hit others more, and tend to be less verbal about their changing moods. I suggest the following experiment: Listen to and watch five girls playing together. Then listen to and watch five boys doing the same kinds of things. Then combine the two groups and observe the boys and girls playing together. You will notice differences in noise level, movement, spatial relationships and use of personal space, touching of one another, verbal disagreements, physical disagreements, and many other things. If you do this for several days in a number of different play situations, you will be able to develop some personal guidelines for arranging the environment, placing materials, and helping children become more fully involved in wholesome play with one another.

Girls appear to develop their fine motor abilities at an earlier age than boys, thus being able to spend more time than boys sitting and looking at books, scribbling, and working with the smaller muscles of their hands. They do this at a time when most boys generally want to exercise their gross motor skills as much as possible and, along with their vigorous movements, seem to be more physically aggressive. It is often easier for the mother to relate positively to the girl who enjoys sedentary activities once in a while than to the boy who wants to keep moving without stopping. What started out as biological and physiological differences at the time of birth is therefore reinforced by adults through their natural responses. When girls get to the age of four or thereabouts, they often go through a period of excessive motor activity, seeming to need to catch up with what they may have missed. At around the same age, boys begin to enjoy sedentary types of play more, although they may not stay at it for as long a period as do most girls.

In mixed groups at nursery school or kindergarten, boys and girls are influenced by each others' levels of activity—that is, the type of play engaged in by boys will influence the type of play engaged in by girls and vice versa.

We could get more deeply into the discussion initiated by some women's groups concerning the stereotyping of sex roles. That is not the goal of this book. It is important, however, that educators who spend much time with young children be alert to the ways in which the two sexes influence one another. Although both girls and boys should have the same opportunities and types of toys to play with, to equalize things so that they would all play and react alike would not have very positive results. In the creative play environment, both girls and boys play with dolls, high heels, beauty shops, trucks, carpentry tools, and electricity. At the same time, boys are helped to understand themselves as individuals and as boys, and girls as individuals and as girls.

ECONOMIC BACKGROUNDS

Children from different socioeconomic backgrounds have different needs and skills. These differences will influence their play with one another. It will influence how children react to and use the play environment. By the time severely economically deprived children reach nursery school, they have already incorporated into their personalities the attitudes of mistrust and skepticism they have observed in their parents and neighbors. They are often fearful and uncertain. Sometimes they seem to be already so beaten and defeated, you wonder if they'll ever be happy. These children don't expect much. They are used to seeing and wishing, but they know that they rarely get what they see and wish for. These children need much ego-building support. They need approval. They need opportunities to participate in colorful, stimulating environments that will help to counteract their home surroundings. Their language, like their environment, is often limited and boring. Children from more affluent homes may not be able to interact with them. Some adults, in fact, have difficulty interacting with such children with love and understanding.

Economically overprivileged children are frequently faced with as many disadvantages as the economically deprived, although they lack the accompanying despair. Some of them come to school with set patterns of arrogance and superiority. From their parents they have learned that one can give orders and expect them to be followed. Sometimes they are selfish and demanding, and have difficulty in relating to other children. They often try to "buy" relationships by "granting privileges" such as, "You can hold my doll," or, "Sit by me." These children are frequently very insecure. Because of the need to give and take within a group, they feel their position of superiority being threatened by both adults and by the other children. Although the very poor and the very well-to-do represent the extremes, other children, from whatever their home backgrounds, also bring with them complex behavior patterns that reflect their families' particular status in the community. Your role is to try to understand each child's individual needs and to help him fulfil them.

RACIAL AND CULTURAL BACKGROUNDS

Another area that influences the needs, skills, and interest of children is their family backgrounds. However, children with racial and cultural differences generally have less difficulty relating to one another during their play than do children from widely different economic backgrounds. Teachers who are aware of some of the unique outlooks of various cultures represented by their students can help children understand and accept each other's conventions and ways of doing things.

Most children seem to take great delight in knowing children who are somehow different from them. The adult, however, must always keep in mind the fact that the child has a different perception. For instance, here is a conversation overheard between two boys, age five:

lst boy: I'm a Christian. I know I am. Because I go to church. My mother said I'm a Christian.

2nd boy: I don't know how you can be a Christian and a boy, too.

Conversation overheard between two girls, age four:

lst girl: These will be the chopsticks.
2nd girl: Chopsticks! What are you going to chop? My nose?
lst girl: No, you have to eat with them.
2nd girl: You're silly. Nobody eats with sticks! Chop, chop, chop. I'll chop off my nose!

Conversation between three five-year-old boys, two of them Mexican-Americans and the third not.

lst boy: My uncle isn't going to work in the fields with my papa anymore.

2nd boy: My papa went to the field today.

1st boy: The immigration is looking for Uncle Lupe. He's going to stay with Cousin Martha. She hides him.

3rd boy: Well. Let's play.

It was obvious that the third boy, even though his father was a farm worker too, didn't understand the problem about "immigration"—a topic obviously familiar to the two Mexican-American boys.

Inviting parents of various racial and cultural backgrounds to bring samples of special foods and holiday objects can widen the understanding between the younger children and satisfy some of their curiosity. But this is a matter for enrichment. The children usually accept one another on the basis of their personalities and the kinds of attitudes they have during play times rather than on the basis of ethnic background.

PERSONALITY

Each individual's personality is evident at birth and, obviously, has its beginnings before birth. In addition to genetic influences, certain prenatal environmental influences may contribute to the fact that even identical twins may show widely different personalities as infants. Some of these influences may include the position of the fetus in the womb, the amount of movement of the fetus while in the various positions, the reaction to the mother's diet, and hundreds of other variables that occur before birth. In the case of twins, who experience genetic and environmental *sameness*, two distinctly different personalities emerge. These differences become more apparent as their world widens, their contacts with others increase, and they have more and more opportunities to make choices.

Imagine, then, the widely differing personalities that exist in any play group. Although the children will all be influenced by the common physical setting and their own personal attributes and those of others, their genetic inheritances and environmental backgrounds react on each individual in a unique way.

It is useful to be aware of these influences, but it is dangerous to try to generalize about them. Any possible kind of influence must be considered in coordination with *all* other influences.

Interaction between differing personalities sometimes leads to conflict and misunderstandings. But when children have the common interest of playing and learning together, such differences can serve to enhance the personality and potential of each one.

Implementing the
Creative Play Program

PART THREE

5 Movement Experiences: Gross Motor Activities

Movement experiences start even before birth. Because they are so important to the growth and development of children, they form the basis for the creative play program. Children's entire orientation to the world develops through movement. Through play, their understanding of the world is enhanced. Wholesome play involves movement of all kinds. It provokes the reception of accompanying sensory information, and brings about an awareness of feelings and thoughts. Every action of a child at play relates to learning, self-image, self-awareness, and self-esteem.

In planning for movement at school, the entire environment must be taken into consideration in order to provide the maximum challenge to body and mind. When the child's body and the mind work together as an integrated unit, he is able to maximize his learning potential.

The most effective type of learning involves movement. Books may provide facts and patterns. Lectures may offer clues. But actual learning comes through *doing*. Through doing, we learn to type, drive, cook, sew, write, repair machinery, rollerskate, play tennis, read, and perform all the other activities that make up our daily lives.

The experiences listed in this section on movement are those in which the motor experience is the primary goal. Chapter 5 will discuss activities that involve the large muscles and whole body of the child. These are gross motor experiences that should be made available to children throughout their playtimes. In designing and equipping play areas, the first thing to do is obtain materials and equipment for these physical activities.

Chapter 6 will consider activities that are primarily geared toward the development of the smaller muscles of the body, and the refinement of fine motor abilities involving manipulative skills and tactile awareness.

Chapter 7 deals with rest and relaxation, a completely different type of movement experience, yet one that is every bit as important as the others. Rest and relaxation skills are the ultimate refinement of general motor skills and sensory-motor awareness.

Many activities discussed as movement experiences could just as logically appear under other categories. For example, although sand, water, and mud play are included under the category of manipulative-tactile experiences they could just as well have been placed in Chapter 9 on the exploration of natural materials.

Actually, all play experiences involve some type of movement. No single experience is sufficient in itself. The entire program depends on interweaving one type of experience with another to achieve what Piaget calls "the equilibrium of self."

CLIMBING

If I had room for only one piece of play equipment, my unhesitating choice would be something to climb on. As soon as seven- or eight-month-old infants start to creep, they climb over any objects they can that get in their way. They are very adept at learning to manage differing heights. They have an innate sense of depth perception from about the age of nine months. Climbing strengthens muscles, develops postural control, and orients children to varying views of the world. The area that a child can take in with one glance becomes much greater as the body climbs higher. For small children who spend so much time having to look "up" it must be an exhilirating experience to be in places where the view is "down." The resultant feelings of mastery have positive ego-building effects. Few experiences can make a child feel so important as sitting on top of a jungle gym—particularly if he is wearing an adult-type play hat that makes him even taller.

Very young children learn to negotiate climbing apparatus to get to various levels in their own way. Even the creeping child learns to turn around and go down steps backward in order to keep from falling face first.

For young toddlers who are just beginning to walk, steps made of pieces of wood one inch thick and twelve inches square can be an exciting challenge. Later he can tackle more difficult steps that he can walk onto and off of. Commercial plastic toys in the form of steps are available at very low cost which are interesting for beginning explorations. (However, some of these are poorly balanced. Have some children try the piece out before you decide to buy one.)

Toddlers who have been given the freedom to develop naturally, to sit up by themselves when they are able to do so—and not when someone artificially props them into sitting positions—and to creep and walk on all fours for weeks or months before walking upright develop confidence in their abilities to use their bodies at will. Such children are very adept at climbing gymnastic equipment, and some can climb before they are able to walk.

Most children, unfortunately, are prodded into performances before they are naturally ready for them, thus skipping many subtle stages of motor development. By the time they reach nursery school, many have to be helped to overcome fear of steps, climbing, and heights, much of which may have developed as a result of the reactions of overcautious parents. Help is best tendered by providing opportunities and encouragement gradually to become familiar with the climbing equipment and its uses. By holding a child's hand when he goes up or down steps, he soon learns to rely on handrails. I have never seen a child fall down on the steps when he is holding on to the rail. Steps and playground equipment that have no rails present a more difficult challenge. Here again, a helping hand gives children encouragement and helps them to find their own center of gravity and establishes the equilibrium needed to maintain balance. They will progress from a cautious, guarded approach at age 2½, to the daring hero of 3½, and the flying batman of 4½. (See photographs on page 72.)

Free-standing wooden steps have long been standard playground equipment for nursery schools. They can be used to reach high places, to form bridges and tunnels, and to help make hideouts and other special places. They can also be used in indoor play areas in inclement weather or where outdoor play space is limited.

Stationary equipment, such as a built-in jungle gym or a monkey bar can be used in coordination with movable equipment, such as the steps, ladders, planks, saw horses, boxes, etc. One advantage of the jungle gym is that several children can use it at the same time. Each child uses it in his own way while learning to be aware of not only his own space, but that being used by the others. The faces of happy children at the top of the jungle gym beam their feelings of accomplishment: "Look at me. I'm big!"

Slides, too, are great favorites. Even 1½ year olds can conquer their challenges. The challenge to the child is to get his body above ground level, to cope with the pull of gravity, and to find, as he achieves his own sense of equilibrium, that sense of self-worth that can only be learned—never taught.

The playground at our school includes an unplanned, but remarkable piece of climbing equipment—a brick wall with a fence built on top of it. From the time a child first sees this fence—and observes older children circling the playground by moving sideways along the wall, one step at a time while holding on to the fence—he wants to climb on it. Children are not helped up onto the wall—but if they indicate the need either by a direct request or by a look of coming fear, they are immediately and cheerfully helped down. A teacher might comment, "You can try that again later." Adults are cautioned not to say, "Oh, you're too small yet," or "Be careful, you'll hurt yourself," or similar such fear-instilling phrases.

An alternative to built-in climbing apparatus is portable gymnastic equipment. These pieces are made up of ladders that can be adjusted to various heights and can be used with cross bars that are both high enough to hang from and low enough to use as walking beams.

A climbing platform like that in the illustration on page 122 is another popular piece of equipment. This platform was originally built to provide shade for the sandbox. In the spring of each year, after the children have become accustomed to the intracacies of this particular climbing structure and the adjacent equipment, they help the adults create complicated hanging obstacle courses to provide ongoing new challenges as shown in the photograph in this section.

A hill is a "must" for toddlers. It doesn't have to be a large hill to offer daily challenges to them as they learn to climb to the top. A larger hill for older children is also desirable, but not always possible. Uneven ground levels are advantageous in any play area. If you are fortunate enough to have access to real hills of any kind, be sure to take the children on frequent "mountain climbing" excursions.

Children also love to climb trees. Although trees are rarely found in big city playgrounds, they do grow in parks and backyards. Children should be encouraged to explore them.

OBSERVATIONS AND CONCLUSIONS

Climbing is an ongoing challenge to integrate body, mind, and space. As children climb, they have to determine which *direction* to move—up, down, backwards, frontwards, sideways, or diagonally. They have to judge the necessary *distance* to move the hands, legs, and feet from one position to the next, and the amount of *strength* required for the hands to support the body's weight while it is moving to its next position. They have to judge the *size* of a space to determine if it is large enough or too small for the body to pass through. They also have to determine the *location* of the space they want to get to—above, below, in between, on the other side, the other way, in back, in front, etc. Not only do they judge these distances, but they need to judge the *time* required for one part of the body to reach from one section of the equipment to another and the length of time they can support their body in one position. And they are also learning to be aware of the

Conversations

Look, look! I'm bigger than the whole world.

I'm a monkey.

Let's be telephone men. I'm fixing wires. The phone don't ring.

Here comes the truck. I'm going to climb higher with that ladder. It moves like magic.

I like butterflies. They fly high like an airplane.
Yeah, and they get on flowers. But, I don't like butterflies. They might bite me.
Butterflies don't bite.
O.K. But they fly around too much.

I can stand like this for two hours. Did you do it?
Yes, two times.

I'm the strongest man in the world.
What about me?
You're the strongest girl in the world.

Teacher, teacher. Come quick. There are pirates in the palm tree. I hear them talking.
They are real mean. Oh, oh. He ate my finger.

I can see on top of the sky. I'm gonna touch it. See, see, I can reach the sky.

I'm the biggest one in the world. Nobody is high as me.

You can't come. There's no room. Wait, wait, I'll fall.

See me? I like it.

space they are occupying or intend to occupy in relation to where other children are and the direction in which other children are moving at the same time they are moving.

As they move around on various pieces of equipment, children continually need to adjust the angles of their bodies in order to accommodate to the pull of *gravity* and to maintain *equilibrium* and *balance*. This adjustment is made both through *kinesthetic sensations*, which tell them exactly where the various parts of their bodies are either touching or not touching another surface at any given time, and through the refinement of the ability to *coordinate* the position of the various parts of their bodies with the movements of their bodies as a whole. These changing positions also orient them to the changing *perspective* of the environment as perceived from each different location. They gradually learn that what they see remains constant, even though it looks different at each new level. They learn, too, that they hear *sounds* differently as they climb higher and higher. Sounds generally becoming sharper and clearer as the barriers between the sources of sounds and the hearer decreases. Children sometimes judge *heights* and *distances* in relation to some sounds and their body positions and movements.

Overall body control, especially of the large muscles, is continuously challenged as the child has to figure out what part of the body to move and what part to put his weight on in order to get from one position to the next. For example, a very complex movement for a two-year-old is to manage to get both legs over the top of the slide and the body into a sitting position to prepare for sliding down safely. Children learn not only to move their own bodies safely, but to be aware of the *safety* of others in relation to themselves. In addition to promoting physical and physiological accomplishments, climbing increases the child's own *self-confidence* and *self-awareness*, important prerequisites for building strong, wholesome *egos*.

ROCKING, TEETER-TOTTERING, AND SWINGING

In infancy, babies are rocked in their parents' arms. This rocking soothes and comforts the child, and it demonstrates the parent's love for the child. It not only provides a soothing effect on the person being rocked, but on the person doing the rocking as well. It is natural, then, that children should want to continue experiencing the good feelings produced by such movements. Therefore, it is important to provide opportunities for the child to have rocking, swinging, and teetering experiences in the play areas.

Swings are dearly loved by children. Unfortunately, they are often grossly misused by many parents and educators. Many infants are placed into swings at too early an age. Being in a swing forces them to sit in an upright position long before they have had the opportunity to allow the strength of their own muscles to develop to the point where they can bring themselves to a sitting position naturally. If not prodded, cushioned, and propped up by adults, the average child would not sit up until approximately seven or eight months of age. No child should be put into a swing before he is able to sit up without help. Until that time he should have the freedom to wiggle, crawl, turn over, move, and do everything he can under his *own* power to bring himself to a sitting position. If allowed to develop the ability without artificial prompting, he will have fuller control of the muscular structure of his body, a healthier and more positive postural development, and the serenity and self-confidence that accompanies natural growth.

Another disadvantage of a swing, aside from the temptation to use it too early, is that most swings are one-at-a-time playthings. Also, in a nursery school setting, swings require one adult devoting full attention to that activity alone to avoid the danger of the possibility that a child may run in front of or in back of a moving swing. For added safety, swings should have canvas seats.

Rope ladders, climbing ropes, and similar equipment can also be used for swinging movements by children who have reached the appropriate level of motor development. They save the need for investing in a traditional swing which has more limited use than these multi-use pieces.

I prefer swings such as the horizontal tire swing which can be made at a cost of only a few dollars (see the photos at the end of this section). It's advantage is that it can serve several children at one time and can be safely used by even 1½ year olds. It has wide implications for dramatic play: It can be a boat, a train, an airplane, a fling balloon, a circus wagon, and an infinite number of other imaginative things invented by the children as they use it. It is safe enough so that an adult does not have to stand nearby to protect younger children from running into it. It is also possible for a child to play in it alone. A rope swing is good for two- to five-year-olds. It requires a different type of balancing than the other swings, and it, too, needs a minimum of supervision.

The rocking boat is by far the most popular piece of apparatus used in our school, and I'm sure it has proven to be so by many others. The rocking boat has many advantages as a piece of play equipment. Physically, the movements are limited to sitting in one spot, holding on, and enjoying the rocking motion. But there is no limit to where the children's imagination takes them from there. Our rocking boat was made by a parent and has stood the test of hundreds of children using it over a period of twenty years. Occasionally it is turned upside down to make steps. However, since we have

59

Conversations

Hey. Watch us. Watch out. Don't go too fast.

Make it go.
You have to make it go. I'm too little.

Don't let go. I'm coming. This is hard.

This way. This way.

Let's put this board over here. You go get the big blocks. Not there! Here!

Get on. Now this is your place.
He's gonna get his rear end stuck.
No, that's not funny. I won't push any more if you keep doing it.
I'll wind you up. Okay?
I'm on the high part.

Let's go faster.

Puff the magic dragon lived by the sea.
Turn it off.
I turned it on. Puff the magic dragon lived by the sea.
I turned it off again. Turn it off.

I'm dizzy.
Let's push again. I'm falling.

I'm four-and-a-half.
Me, too.
I'm dizzy.
Me, too.

so many other steps around our school, we find the need for additional ones is minimal. Because of its popularity, we store the boat away for two months of each year to encourage the use of other equipment by those who spend much time in the boat.

As with other playthings in the school, specific rules apply to playing in the rocking boat to ensure that no one gets hurt: (1) No one outside the boat touches it while it is moving; (2) when someone wants out, the children stop the boat immediately to let that person out; (3) children must always hold on with both hands; (4) they must share the seats; (5) if one child thinks the boat is moving too fast, it must be slowed down—but if no one complains, the children may rock as fast as they want to. When children start to gather around the boat, an adult will come to supervise. The rocking motion of the boat sometimes inspires an impromptu song fest. The children might start out with "Row, Row, Row Your Boat." Other popular rocking boat songs are, "Down by the Station, Early in the Morning" "Old MacDonald had a Boat Ei-ii-ee-ii-oh. And on the boat he had a pig . . ." Sometimes to quiet down an overactive boat-rocking group, the teacher will suggest rocking slowly to the tune of "Rock-a-Bye-Baby."

The rocking pan or flying saucer and the barrel are additional equipment the children use to rock themselves with in the school yard. Inside, rocking chairs are always availalbe.

The traditional teeter-totter can be a dangerous plaything for preschool children because the child on one end may jump off unexpectedly, letting the other end drop. The most satisfactory kind of seesaw for use in a nursery school is one with rockers. However, the homemade wooden seesaw is also quite safe since the child's feet are always close to the ground. If the seat drops, its close enough to stop it easily. Children frequently make their own rocking boards.

When four- and five-year-olds are seen to spend much more time than most children using rocking equipment, further investigation may reveal some previously unnoticed learning disabilities. These are usually in the perceptual area, but may be of some other nature. The equilibrium brought about by the rocking motion and the effect of relaxed muscles may be giving the child a more acceptable view of his surroundings and more acceptable feelings about his own body.

OBSERVATIONS AND CONCLUSIONS

Equipment and activities that involve children in rhythmic, repetitive movements, such as in swinging, rocking, or seesawing, are important to the development of total dynamic body balance. Continuously changing positions require children to make constant bodily adjustments to retain their center of gravity in relation to the equipment they are using. This enhances the child's total sense of *equilibrium* as well as his ability to relate *visual, auditory, and kinesthetic adjustments* to the fact that even though his body is in motion, the body functions, size, weight, balance, and other aspects of being remain *constant.* This sense of constancy of self is very gratifying to children and they seek these kinds of experiences over and over again to recapture the accompanying feelings. They enjoy the visceral thrill (inside feelings such as *sinking sensation* in pit of stomach) of the rapid descent of the swing or seesaw or the forward thrust of the rocking movement, or the rhythm attained by swinging from side to side.

In activities that involve two or more children, such as using the rocking boat or the seesaw, they learn to make adjustments not only to their own bodies, but in relation to the position, size, weight, and number of other children. These adjustments require mutual *cooperation.* They learn that they can control the speed and movement of the equipment they are using, and that they must work out a system of mutual control when using it with others.

In using equipment such as the barrel or rocking boat, the child needs to consider *volume* and how much space his body takes up within a given enclosed area. From playing with the barrel, they learn that *round* is different on the inside than on the outside. All kinds of balancing equipment, from the seesaw to a makeshift rocker, made by placing a board on a block of wood, gives children basic scientific knowledge about the workings of *leverage* to cause the movement of a *weight* that is much heavier than the object causing the movement.

The repetitive action of swinging, rocking, and seesawing has a definite emotional influence on children, one that usually helps them achieve a strong sense of *relaxation.* Many of the physiological, physical, social, and emotional areas of growth that result from these kinds of movement activities can also be achieved from programmed body movement exercises like those experienced in creative movement activities.

TIRES, HOOPS, SPOOLS, AND OTHER THINGS THAT ROLL

A round shape is comfortable, basic, and full of intrigue. It has no beginning and no end. It can enclose. It can roll away. Wheels are round. They are one

of the earliest inventions—and children probably found ways to play with them even in ancient times. Hoops are also ancient playthings, and are still in use today. Before the automobile became common, children frequently played with metal hoops off of old wagon wheels. Modern toy manufacturers continuously market plastic hoops.

Small plastic hoops make an ideal plaything for two- to five-year-olds providing many opportunities to explore the concept of "round." Although they are not expensive, they are not an absolute requisite for the types of learnings their use can inspire. Bicycle tires and tubes, though a little more difficult to manipulate than the neatly manufactured plastic hoops, can be used in many of the same ways. I like to introduce hoops and bicycle tires together. Children enjoy the challenge of manipulating these two playthings that are similar in so many ways and yet are so dissimilar. They can be twirled, held over the head, balanced, crawled through, stacked, used as targets to throw things through, jumped through, placed in rows and other types of designs, and explored from every vantage point.

Closely related to playing with hoops and bicycle tires is playing with automobile and truck tires. Children find endless ways to play with tires on the playground. Some schools have created intricate play places out of tires that are bolted together. Sometimes tires are stacked up to make tunnels and crawl-through places. They can be places for children to be alone or for them to be together. They can be tunnels. They can be stacked, rolled, and climbed on. Even the three-year-olds can learn to roll the very smallest sized tires.

Wire spools provide another means of acquiring versatile, inexpensive (or free) play equipment. Both adults and children find endless uses for these spools. They provide supports for bridges and obstacle courses. Some are large enough to provide inside hiding places. Some are small enough to serve as tables. All have the delightful capacity of being able to roll.

Small wheels, discs of wood, lids, and other types of round objects can be used for rolling on edge, thus extending the skill learned through the play with hoops and tires.

OBSERVATIONS AND CONCLUSIONS

Children enjoy playing with anything that is *round*. It is the easiest shape for them to relate to, since it is the first shape they are able to reproduce by themselves as a symbolic representation. (This ability develops around the age of 2½ to 3, and comes at the time children develop the ability to control their wrist movements). Playing with tires, hoops, and wooden spools reinforces their concept of *round*, and the knowledge that round things never have corners. As they learn that

65

some circles and circular objects are big enough to fit themselves onto or into, that some are too small, and that some are big enough for several people, they reinforce the concept of *size* and *volume*. They extend their growing abilities to balance by learning to *balance* on circular objects, and by learning to balance circular objects against the force of *gravity*. They develop the knowledge that they can control the *speed* of the movement of these objects by a combination of gravatational control and force of body movement. They also learn that any rolling object will move faster, with less need for one's own strength to be involved, when that object is moving down an inclined plane. By the same token, they find that it takes greater effort to move such objects up *inclined planes*, and that the greater the incline the greater the effort. In addition, they learn about the *momentum* that can be caused by the weight of an object in comparison to the force causing that object to move.

Bicycle tires and inner tubes help children learn about *flexibility* and their own ability to change the shape of an object temporarily. They extend their knowledge of *positions* and *directions* as they either move the objects over, under, around, to the side of themselves, or as they move themselves over, under, around, inside of, or the other side of an object. By comparing the differences in the weights of plastic hoops and tires or tubes used as hoops, they enhance their ability to judge *differences in weights*. By comparing the differences in rolling various sizes of automobile tires, they also learn about differences in weights. Children who learn to twirl hoops around their bodies learn something about *centrifugal force*. All of these learnings are extended further through the children's play with balls, toy trucks and cars, bicycles, and other wheel toys.

BOXES, BOARDS, AND OTHER BUILDABLES

Packing crates were once common play equipment at all schools for young children. They could be acquired at little or no cost from many sources. With the growing scarcity and expense of wood and the substitution of cardboard, styrofoam, and splintery slats for crating, the one-time common wood crates are no longer so easy to come by. Today we often substitute cardboard boxes, plywood panels and other boards, sawhorses and other buildables. As long as the pieces are free of splinters, protruding nails, and sharp edges, and other such dangers, they can be handled and manipulated by the children at will. All you have to do is make them available, make space available for their use, and make time available. The children will do the rest.

Children are adept at building their own worlds out of boxes and boards (see photos at the end of this section). They will haul, pile, arrange, design, stack, connect, rearrange, enclose, separate, provide entrances, seal entrances, make roofs, bridges, tents, and tunnels. They will make places to be alone in and places that they think are secret. They will work together to make multilevel and multiroomed structures. They make closed places and open places, little places and big ones. As they develop their designs you should keep an eye out for safe connections and arrangements. You can also use your own ingenuity to suggest additional props when the design and the conversation seem to indicate a need for them. You promote consideration for others and in other ways help the play to be as meaningful as possible for all involved.

Although wooden or plastic sawhorses do not provide the same kind of enclosure that boxes do, they are useful for supporting various building materials, blocking out areas, and stimulating the imagination. The advantage of using sawhorses on the playground is that even though they are light enough for a 2½-year-old to move, they are strong enough to support the weight of several children at once. They are inexpensive and easy to make. To make one from scratch does require some ability at carpentry, however. For people who are not handy with hammer and saw, metal devices especially made to connect the legs and crosspiece of a sawhorse are available at a hardware store.

Plywood panels have endless uses on the playground. They can be hinged together to form a free-standing tent and all kinds of other structures. With round, triangular, or rectangular holes to look through cut in them they can be even more versatile. If cost prohibits the use of plywood, cardboard will serve the same purpose, although it will not last very long.

Ladders, planks, and two-by-fours, along with such things as pieces of canvas and braided rag rugs, also make wonderful building materials. Any kind of unfinished wood should be sanded to make it free of splinters and then covered with several coats of strong paint to protect it from weathering and to add to its aesthetic value.

OBSERVATIONS AND CONCLUSIONS

Children can apply what they have learned about *balancing* their own bodies through use of the various playground apparatus and other equipment to the way they use play apparatus that they construct themselves from boxes, boards, and other materials—even tables and chairs. By climbing in and out of boxes they find out that some have greater *volume* than others—in some boxes there is scarcely room for

67

Conversations

Let's build a fire station. You carry these blocks. I'll carry these.
Let's build a firehouse with the doors here.
O.K. You build the firehouse. I'm going to build a road here.

I'm not gonna play with you anymore.

This our sunny house and that is the rainy house. We better move the house over there so it can be a sunny house. Our new house is going to be in the sun and its going to be the sunniest house over there. We need a roof so we can sleep and close our eyes inside when its too sunny.

This is my house. Do you want to have something to eat in here with me?

We have to get on the fire engine. I'll drive down here. You drive up there.
This is a hook and ladder. You know that?

O.K. Get in. Don't anybody tell we're here. The cops 'r comin'.

Once upon a time I went with my dad. We went to the swap meet. The meat was good. I ate it. Mmm, mmm.

Let's play monster! Run, run, run. Oh, oh, I'm dead.
Oh, the monster's shoe came off. Can I play? Angie's coming after us.
Monster, monster, I'm a witch. You can't chase me.
We're cowboys. We have some food. You have to be asleep because witches sleep all day.
You have to give me the magic spell to sleep.

even one person, but other boxes have enough room for several. At our school we have a rule that permits children to build things no higher than the head of the tallest child involved in the play. Therefore, the children are constantly having to practice judging and comparing *heights*. They also learn to judge *widths* when their building space is limited or when they have a certain space that calls for something to fit "in between" or "across" or "over" or "under." This also helps them to learn to judge overall *distances* between objects, themselves, and other things in the environment. Each of these dimensions are not only judged by themselves, but in *relationship to one another*.

As they make their constructions, the children increase their knowledge of the meaning of *directionality* as they make decisions about whether to extend a structure upwards, sideways in one *direction* or another, at an angle, or in some other way. They need to use certain amounts of muscular strength in order to lift the various pieces being used. This gives them an opportunity to become familiar with the *weight* of various objects, and they learn that they sometimes need to enlist the help of others to control some very heavy objects. When several children are working on a structure, they learn to discuss their plans as they go along and to make *mutual decisions* in a cooperative manner. Although these plans are usually made as they go along, building projects involve continuous *decision making*. The total process is one of *solving problems* all the way from where to make the construction, what to use, and what to build, to how extensive to make the construction, and when to dismantle it.

As the children make their plans and carry them out, they are continuously practicing *eye-hand coordination* and all the mathematical skills required in *measuring*, which for them is all the more difficult because they are usually relying on *visual perceptions* rather than the more sophisticated measuring tools that older children or adults would use.

The completion of structures they have built themselves helps children realize an important sense of *accomplishment* and *self-sufficiency*, which adds to their *self-esteem*.

PLANKS, WALKING BOARDS, PLYWOOD PANELS, AND OTHER LEVEL RAISERS

Planks, two-by-fours, and other walking boards have endless uses in both outdoor and indoor play areas. Walking boards traditionally found in the classroom are an important means of providing ongoing opportunities for children to perfect their ability to maintain the bodily control necessary for laterality and balance. Any activity that requires equal use of both sides of the body, such as walking along a narrow board, promotes laterality. The child's ability to balance on the board with ease—or his lack of it—can give you a good indication of whether or not he is achieving laterality at a normal rate. Use of the walking board alone will not promote laterality, but combined with other movement activities including crawling, creeping, balancing, climbing, jumping, and other motor activities, normal development can be promoted.

Walking boards should not be too easy for the child to negotiate. Part of their value is in presenting enough of a challenge to ensure that the children cannot move too fast. If they move too quickly or run, the momentum of their body weight will help to keep them on course without the need for conscious control of their own balance mechanisms. It is sometimes necessary to hold a child's hand. In such cases say, "This is very hard," but don't take away the challenges.

After the children become more adept at using various walking boards, they will themselves start to construct bridges and other walkways that present increasingly difficult tasks. Planks can be used for creeping from one end to the other. At first they can be raised a foot off the floor at one end, then two feet, and later, for the more adept child, three feet or more. The child will creep both up and down these boards learning different types of balancing secrets from moving in each direction.

Somewhat similar to the walking boards is the teacher-made "skinny path." Although these pathways are usually on the ground or the floor, they present different kinds of challenges to the child's developing sense of balance because of the sides that shape the paths and the various angles at which the paths can be constructed. "Skinny paths" are basically paths or walkways formed by laying unit blocks or pieces of rope, wood, or board in parallel rows that allow just enough space for the child to move cautiously between them.

In addition to boards used for walking beams, a supply of planks and other pieces of wood should be available for making raised play platforms, bridges, tunnels, and other types of connections. These materials are safer and more versatile if they have previously been cleated at each end to help them grip onto whatever surface they are being used on. Boards can be finished with several coats of varnish to give them a longer life and smoother finish. An excellent place to buy boards and planks at little cost is the remnants section of a builders' supply house or a lumber company. Also, it is a good idea to watch for clearance sales at furniture stores where you may be

Conversations

Meow, meow.
I'm going to try balance.

Oooooh. I'm getting down.

Hold my hand. Hold my hand.

I can do it myself now. Watch me. I learned it.

This is an alligator.

Don't let it slip off. You can't go too fast.

We can be on the roof and all the other guys are
down there.
O.K. Let's fix this.

They're coming, they're coming. Quick, you have to
get to the forest.

able to pick up such odds and ends as table leaves for children to use as building boards. Their extra-smooth finish provides an interesting variety for the children.

Path walking and balancing need not be limited to boards, "skinny paths," bridges, and other wooden walkways. Pathways made from rug strips can provide new tactile sensations for the child who walks on them. Tactile messages from the strips help to integrate the child's total balance mechanism because they provide additional sensory stimulation. Sometimes the path can be a rope, a series of rubbery stepping stones or carpet samples, or any other material. From time to time, it is a good idea to challenge the child with a balancing walkway the minute he enters the school in the morning.

Along with planks, two-by-fours, and other walking boards be sure to keep a supply of supports to put under them. Bricks are good for this purpose. An even safer type of support consists of a cradle made of a few short pieces of wood cut from a two-by-four.

In addition to having raised areas for practicing balance, it is important to provide raised areas for other play activities. Dramatic play structures and playground apparatus usually take care of this need outdoors. Indoors, however, in the traditionally flat classroom, providing above-the-floor play space presents yet another challenge. Many adults are constantly saying to the children as they climb on benches and tables, "Feet on the floor." A deeper understanding of the basic needs of a child, however, leads to the knowledge that children need to climb. One way to keep children from climbing on the furniture is to provide them with materials from which to make their own elevated play areas.

For a school with an adequate budget and a handy carpenter, the popular multilevel carrels can provide off-the-floor places to play. Most schools, however, have neither the budget nor the carpenter for such a project. Also, anything used in many classrooms should be something that can be stored when it is not being used. With the limited storage space available at most schools, this is no small challenge. One solution is to set plywood panels on raised blocks, bricks, or other supports. When the platforms are not in use they can be stacked on the floor or removed.

Another way to use these play platforms is to add cardboard "sides" or "walls" to make enclosed areas. If you wish, you may put holes in the walls to see through. Masking tape is useful for providing temporary hinging for these cardboard walls. Even though cardboard is nowhere near as sturdy as plywood, the cost is so nominal—usually free—as to make it well worthwhile. Children who play within these enclosures are aware of their temporary nature and adjust their activities accordingly. This restriction is a positive one since there are plenty of other places in the school where the child can engage in robust activities to burn off excess energy.

OBSERVATIONS AND CONCLUSIONS

Children who participate in the play activities described in this section enhance their total *physiological growth* and develop some very important skills. As they walk along narrow raised structures, they are obliged to maintain their *balance* in *coordination* with a shifting center of *gravity*. This enhances the ability to perform in a bilateral manner and, even though one side of the body is dominant, to integrate both sides equally in order to achieve balance. By moving along these pathways backwards and sideways as well as forward, a child increases the ability to maintain balance and extends the awareness of *directionality*. If the boards are placed as inclines, the children are required to shift their body weight according to the degree of incline and to lean forward as they go up, or to lean backward as they go down, in order to cope with the shifting center of gravity.

One of the skills children develop from using these materials is to make body movements deliberately. Children learn very quickly that it is easier to run across a raised plank than it is to walk slowly and carefully. They easily accept the challenge of learning to move deliberately, seeming to sense that the ability to do so is an important and needed skill. These deliberate movements are coordinated with *visual, auditory,* and *tactile stimulations* that enhance the children's perceptions in all of these areas.

As children move across the various combinations of boards, they begin to acquire a sense of *timing*. They learn how long it takes to get from one end of a board to the other, how much longer it takes when moving across it sideways or backwards, and how much time elapses while they wait for a turn to use something that another person is using. This sense of timing is in some respects coordinated with principles of *measurement*. For example, sometimes the children, particularly beginners, place their feet directly heel-to-toe as they walk across a board. Gradually they learn to space their steps a little further apart, unconsciously measuring equal distances between one step and the next.

In addition to balancing on these boards, children learn to move them about and to balance them on other boards or supports. This provides further practice in judging *distances*, measuring *space*, and creating a balance. They sometimes make seesaws or jumping boards by balancing one board across another, learning that they usually have to find the *middle* of the board in order to find the proper balance.

Walking on these raised structures increases the children's *confidence* and encourages them to conquer other raised structures, such as fences and high bars. Developing these *skills* leads to increased *body awareness* and *self-understanding*, both of which are important ego builders.

CRAWL-THROUGH PLACES

The movement experiences in the Creative Play program are planned to help children relive the various movement sequences of an infant's normal growth and development. Since crawling and creeping are important aspects of these early movements, every play environment should include inviting, readily available places for the children to crawl.

Too much furniture in a room will discourage the children from moving about on the floor. Therefore, it is desirable to have as much open space as possible. One way to achieve this effect is to provide only the minimum number of chairs. From the beginning, the children should be encouraged to move about on the floor in all kinds of locomotor styles to encourage a maximum amount of crawling and creeping. Metal barrels, open-ended boxes, collapsible toy tunnels, and a variety of obstacle courses will all encourage the children to creep and crawl (see photos at the end of this section).

Children can create their own play tunnel by taping cardboard cartons together. These tunnels can be enlarged to any size the children desire, and can be made more attractive by painting them. Since their cost is negligible, you can easily afford to have several of these play tunnels about the school.

The "crawl box" pictured in photos at the end of this section was originally designed to provide therapy for a brain-damaged child. It was inherited by the school when the child outgrew it, and it has since become one of the favorite pieces of play equipment. We move it to different places from day to day, and the children do not hesitate to crawl though it whenever they come across it. Some children like to go through it again and again, some-times backwards, sometimes on their backs, during a five- or ten-minute period of time. It is sometimes used as an obstacle course through which children must enter or leave a particular room. It has also been the site of some elaborate dramatic play activities. Primarily, it is used as an adult-directed exercise aid.

The children are observed carefully from time to time as they go through the box for the purpose of keeping a record of their progress in developing a good bilateral, cross-pattern motion in crawling. (This is a motion in which the opposite arms and legs move in unison.) The ability to crawl flat on the stomach with a rhythmic bilateral movement indicates a well-established laterality, which is a prerequisite for reading and writing skills.

Other crawl-through places are frequently improvised by the children as they experiment with the various pieces of equipment, furniture, boxes, and other movable items that may be available. Adults in the school environment, as well as the children, are encouraged to build the structures. Obstacle courses spring up in various parts of the school, and everyone is suddenly crawling his way through them. Tables, chairs, and other furnishings can all be used for making crawl-through places.

Concrete conduits are valuable pieces of equipment on any playground. These pipes can usually be obtained free of charge from a construction company. However, some expense will be incurred in getting the pipe moved to the play area. Even so, the expense is well worthwhile because concrete pipe is practically indestructible, requires no maintenance, and will provide the children endless hours of fascinating play experiences. Many schools incorporate these pipes into manmade hills to make a tunnel under a hill. Free-standing pipe should also be available so that it can be climbed on and through and used in other imaginative ways.

OBSERVATIONS AND CONCLUSIONS

When children crawl forward on their stomachs, the peripheal (outer) vision of their eyes picks up the rhythmic movement of their hands moving forward in an alternating pattern. This helps them to develop in several areas. They learn to move each side of the body independently but in *coordination* with the other side, thus achieving *laterality*. They learn to coordinate their overall body movements with what they see and what they are thinking, thus increasing *visual-motor skills*. Because the body is stretched out lengthwise as they crawl, they develop a *time* awareness related to one part of their body reaching its destination before the other part. They develop a new relationship between *body and space*, learning that sometimes if a space looks like its really too small to get through, they can manage it by lying flat on their stomach, which makes their body take up less *vertical space* than when in any other position. They learn to recognize that outside sounds are somewhat muffled when they are heard in even a partially enclosed space. By the same token, they learn that their own sounds in an enclosed or partially enclosed space will sound very clear, even when spoken softly, and that people outside of that space might not hear them. Their overall *auditory perception* is enhanced.

Children learn many other things when they are crawling, especially flat on the floor or other surface. My observations indicate that they like being on the floor and are usually very cooperative in

almost any kind of crawling experience. Crawling may rekindle feelings of comfort and security that they had in early infancy, at a time in their lives that they were shown much approval for everything they did. This feeling of *comfort* and *security* is further enhanced by the *tactile sensation* of the surfaces over which they are moving, which are also reminiscent of infancy. Children usually become more relaxed when playing on ground surfaces.

The most important observation I have made is that when children have difficulty with reversals of forms, such as shaping letters backwards, crawling exercises temporarily help them to overcome the problem. Crawling movements and other rhythmic movements help develop laterality and *dominance*. It is my belief that these abilities are closely correlated with the ability of a child to learn to read easily.

JUMPING

Jumping is one of the most important motor activities for young children. It is an activity they use as a means of emotional expression. They jump for joy, anger, excitement, anxiety, impatience, and frustration when they can't have their own way. Children who appear to have learning difficulties of a perceptual nature, frequently have difficulty separating their bodies from the ground surface, as in hopping and jumping. Hopping and jumping help children to integrate the movement of both sides of the body at one time, an ability that is crucial to the development of visual-motor perception.

In order to jump off the ground, children must first feel secure in their relationship to the space around them on the ground. Much experience in crawling, creeping, playing on the floor, walking about rooms with furniture in a variety of positions (simple obstacle courses), climbing small boxes or steps, hiding in enclosed areas, and crawling under and climbing over things help children to orient their bodies to the space they occupy.

To help children learn to jump off of something, put them on a low bench or table, take both their hands, and "jump" them off in a sort of swinging motion. Most children like this activity and will ask you to repeat it over and over again. It helps give them confidence in being temporarily in midair, with no solid base under the feet. In performing this and similar activities with very young children, *be careful that you do not use violent jerking motions* that could injure their shoulder sockets. In addition to the actual physical skill and self-confidence this activity fosters, it also helps develop a close relationship between the child and an understanding adult. Any time you become involved in actually playing games with children, you

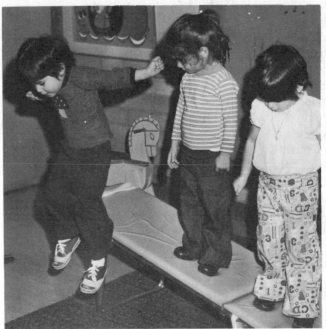

are helping them to meet their needs on a level that they can understand and cope with.

A desirable piece of equipment for every school is an innerspring mattress jumping pad on which children are free to jump and tumble. Innerspring cushions from old couches and chairs can also be used. Mattresses and pads are safer than trampolines. Since the children cannot jump quite as high on mattresses, they are better able to control their movements.

OBSERVATIONS AND CONCLUSIONS

Jumping experiences help children develop their overall *gross motor skills*. Some children, those with immature gross motor skill development, need extra help in learning how to lift their bodies off the ground. One way to provide this help is to give the children opportunities to develop good bilateral crawling and creeping ability and to practice walking on raised, narrow boards.

Once children do learn to jump, they develop new perceptions of *space, height, width, distance,* and *direction* in accordance with how high they can jump, how wide a space they can jump over, what direction they jump (forward, sideways, backwards), and how far they can jump. Toddlers first learn to jump down from a height of two or three inches. This is a big *ego*-building experience for them, one that emphasizes to themselves their need to be aware of using the entire body to achieve *balance* and maintain an *upright position.* As they grow older they enjoy the challenge of jumping off of higher and higher places. They seem to enjoy the *visceral sensation* of moving through space. *Bouncing up* and down on mattresses or other bouncy apparatus usually encourages poor jumpers to have more *confidence* in themselves in all kinds of jumping experiences, resulting in increased jumping skills.

Jumping is an activity that makes children aware of the necessity for *safety* precautions. They soon learn that it is not safe to jump down onto toys, equipment, people, or hard surfaces. They discover that it is easier and safer to land in sand, soft dirt, grass, or something that gives, such as a mattress.

Jumping leads to learning to hop, which is much harder than jumping with two feet. The child appreciates being told how difficult it is, so that he does not feel inadequate when he sees that some children can hop before he is able to. Usually, if a child is developing normally in other areas of movement skills, a few sessions of *hopping* while an adult holds the child's hand will lead to the ability to hop alone.

Sometimes children can more readily learn to hop if they start out by holding one foot up. Holding the foot out of the way is for many children a more difficult task than getting the other foot up off the ground. As children learn to jump and hop, and subsequently to *leap*, *gallop*, and *skip*, they develop a sense of *timing* and the ability to compare how long it takes to jump or to hop to a place instead of walking or running. They learn that jumping down goes very quickly, but that jumping up onto something takes a little more *time*. As they jump up and down they make rapid adjustments to the changing *perspective*, as they do when they swing, slide, and rock. They learn that even though what they see seems to be moving, it actually stays in place and only the viewpoint is changing. This further heightens the child's ability to realize his physical position in terms of *space*.

WHEEL TOYS

It is a great thrill for a small child riding a tricycle for the first time to realize that it is his own efforts that are making it move. Wheel toys are very popular, but no school should have so many that they are used to the exclusion of other equipment. Wheel toys can include tricycles, Big Wheels and other kinds of plastic vehicles, Irish Mails and other chain-driven toys, pedal cars, wagons, doll buggies, toy grocery carts, wheelbarrows, and miniature handtrucks. It isn't necessary to have all of these things, but it is a good idea to have some variety to enable the children to exercise different sets of muscles as they change from one toy to another.

By observing children at play with wheel toys, you can get a good idea of the kinds you might like to provide. Children like to ride on them by themselves and they like to give rides to their friends. They like to tow things. In fact, some manufacturers offer wagons that can be attached to a tricycle. Even without equipment specially designed for that purpose, children devise ways to tow things. The towed object might simply be a block of wood or some kind of toy without wheels. Sometimes it is a cardboard carton in which other things can be hauled. Children often haul things around just for the sake of the activity, but sometimes they haul things for the purpose of getting them from one place to another.

In purchasing wheel toys, be sure to look for solid construction because the wear and tear on these items when they are used by large numbers of children is very great. Select good-quality metal tricycles with front and back ball bearings. These will add years to the life of the vehicle.

The cost of the plastic tricycles is considerably less than that of a metal tricycle. The maximum life of one of these toys at our school is about two years, although the life can be extended by writing to the manufacturer to obatin replacements for worn-out parts. Plastic tricycles are available in several sizes, including very small ones for very small children. They are even popular with toddlers, for whom they are really too big. Even if they can't reach the pedals, these children like to sit on the plastic tricycles and push them with their feet. They become very skilled at controlling the movement of these vehicles.

In studying the movements required of children using the low-built plastic tricycles, it appears that they achieve a better visual-motor experience than they get from the traditional tricycle. Because of the child's position, he is better able to observe the movement of his feet. As the child's feet go round and round while he pedals to propel the vehicle forward, his eyes pick up the rhythmic movement of the feet, which helps to integrate his entire being with that rhythm, helping to develop laterality and the ability to use both sides of the body equally.

The wheel toys are frequently used to develop various dramatic play episodes, either by individuals or by small groups. Much of the time, however, the children use them to explore various ways of moving, various speeds, and other aspects of the environment.

Definite rules apply to the use of wheel toys:

1. They may be used only in designated areas.
2. They may be used for riding, hauling, or towing, but not for bumping into people or things.
3. They may not be driven at excessive speed.
4. They must be shared with others who want to play with them.
5. When several children are using them at the same time, they must all follow the same general pattern of traffic.
6. They must be parked in a specific place when the activity is finished.

Sometimes we paint diagrams on a paved area to encourage the children to develop various activities. They generally do not respond when an adult attempts to structure the use of these diagrams, preferring to find their own ways to use them. Sometimes we provide wooden ramps to give the children the experience of riding up and down hill.

Sometimes the limits of the area where wheel toys can be used are extended. One such special event is a parade. In some parades, the children simply ride their vehicles from one area of the school to another and then back again. A more elaborate parade is an excursion around the block. On some occasions, the children can decorate the wheel toys with yarn, tape, and other materials before they set out on their journey.

Conversations

Go save my bike.
I will.
It's not very nice to save bikes. It's not nice, you know.

There's just funny people following us all around. I bumped my chin, ouch.

Do you hear that noise? That's gas coming out.

Pretend I'm the gas man. That's five dollars please.
Thank you, mam.

I need gas to go all of the way to the freeway.

I still need some more, don't bump into other people.
Now I ran out of gas completely from sitting here too long. Beep-beep. Honk-honk.
I'm out of gas. I just came all the way from Mexico.

Here comes the ranger. Get out of my way everybody. I'm coming. Whooooo! Watch it.

I don't hold on.
That's not safe.

Thank you, Superman, for saving me. Is the plane all torn up?
Yes, I'll show you the plane.

Another special event involving wheel toys is a circus. Occasionally we ask the four- and five-year-olds to plan and present a "circus" for the two- and three-year-olds. At these events, the children perform intricate (to them) tricks on their wheel toys—like riding without holding on. They are, of course, always carefully supervised by the adults. It is interesting to note that some children play the role of clown, daredevil stunt rider, or racer. Each child always seems to play the same role each time, leading to the conclusion that a "circus" gives each child an opportunity to meet an individual need, even though the overall activity is highly organized.

OBSERVATIONS AND CONCLUSIONS

When children propel themselves around on tricycles and other wheel toys, they have a tremendous sense of *independence* as a result of being in *control* of the vehicle. They know it is their own effort that enables them to move so rapidly from one place to another, and that they can move more quickly or more slowly—also according to their own efforts. Realizing that manipulating the pedals is what propels the vehicle enhances many areas of learning. Children learn to coordinate their *body movements* so that they can steer their vehicles in ways in which they avoid accidents and stay out of the paths of others. The *rhythmic movement* of feet and pedals as they go round and round helps to coordinate *visual perception* with each side of the body into an integrated whole, thus promoting the development of *laterality* and, subsequently, *dominance*.

Depth perception is an innate ability. As children move about on their wheel toys, they increase the ability to judge *distances* between themselves and other points, as well as other moving objects. They also become aware that the sounds they hear change with their changing positions, and that as they move further away from others, they may have to use louder voices to make themselves heard. These same experiences help children learn to *judge how long it takes* to move certain distances on various kinds of wheel toys. They soon find out that those with larger wheels cover distance much more rapidly than toys with smaller wheels, and that much less muscular effort is required. They also increase their knowledge about different *directions*. They discover that they can go forward, backward, the other way, to one side or the other (even though they may not be able to identify *left* and *right* by name), and even in a *circle* if they so desire.

They realize when they are going the "*opposite* direction" or the "*same* direction" as other peddlers.

Children playing with wheel toys have to be *aware of others* who are nearby. They are obliged to make quick *decisions* when an unsafe situation arises.

When children pull or ride in wheel toys, such as wagons, they have an opportunity to observe the working of the *wheel and axle*.

In addition to *gross motor muscle development* and bodily control, wheel toys seem to provide children a sense of exhiliration and opportunities for emotional release. This type of activity also brings their imaginations into play and leads to many dramatic play experiences. Sometimes they *pretend* to be riding a horse—sometimes a train, a boat, an airplane, a police car, or a fire engine. Always, the experience is a joyful, wholesome, and invigorating playtime activity.

BALLS

Balls made of stitched skins filled with bran have been found in ancient Egyptian tombs built 4,000 years ago. Balls made of leaves wrapped around dry grass and other materials are used by primitive people throughout the world. Porcelain balls have been unearthed. Plato recommended balls as one of the few essential playthings for a young child. Today, the ball is still one of the most common playthings used by people of all ages.

Clutch balls are good toys for a child who is not yet ready to walk. They are usually made of a rubbery plastic or cloth filled with foam rubber. The slots make it easy to pick up and hold, but it is still a round object that will roll when it is dropped. In going after the ball, the baby will follow its movement with eyes and body working in unison (see photos at the end of this section). This important movement strengthens the child's visual ability. When the child grasps the ball, he immediately puts it up to the mouth, as he does with all objects he is able to pick up. Exploring with the lips and tongue give clues about the texture of the ball. And while it is so close to his nose, he is aware of the scent of the materials of which the ball is made. The baby quickly learns that adults and other children will more readily play games with the ball than with some of the other toys. Almost from the beginning, then, the ball takes on importance as a social toy.

In addition to the clutch ball, other kinds of balls enjoyed and used by children include rubber or plastic balls ranging from very small to very large, tennis balls, wooden balls—like croquet balls—to hit with a mallet, plastic ping-pong balls to hit with a small paddle, rubber golf balls to hit with a rubber mallet, basketballs, rubber or plastic footballs, and beachballs—the larger the better.

Where to keep the balls always seems to be a problem. Plastic clothes baskets, prominently positioned about the classroom or playground, make convenient containers for balls. They invite children to help themselves. In fact they might even inspire a self-invented game. (See photographs at the end of this section.)

In some of the photos at the end of this section several children are playing with large rubber balls in ways of their own choosing during a one-hour period. Each activity helps the child develop important, though different, skills. All of the children are acquiring information about a wide variety of concepts. They will be able to call forth this information to reinforce the same and other concepts they will learn in other ways. They can also use it to learn new skills. Other ways children might be observed playing with a ball include throwing it into or at a target from a distance, throwing it and then chasing after it, rolling it down an incline, kicking it, throwing it against a wall and watching it bounce back, rolling it under a table and other objects, floating it in water, sitting on it, rolling it on the floor to another child who rolls it back, or throwing it to someone who will throw it back.

Definite rules apply to ball playing:

1. If the ball goes over the fence, the child must tell an adult—a child may never leave the playground to go after a ball unless an adult tells him to.

2. When playing with someone else, throw balls *to* them, not *at* them.

3. When playing inside, children may throw balls only in open areas away from places where people or things might get hit.

4. The ball must always be returned to the basket when the children finish playing with it.

In addition to balls, other objects can be used for throwing. These include bean bags which are simple to make and easy to clutch. Every school should have some kept at various places. Children will invent many games with them. Because they are so easy to grab hold of, they may help a child to learn to catch more easily than play with a ball will.

Ring toss hoops are another favorite throwing toy. These are usually used for tossing at a particular target, but children will readily invent other ways to play with them.

Balloons are also excellent objects to use in learning to throw and catch because they are slow moving. As the balloon floats slowly through the air, the young child has plenty of time to position hands and body to make the catch. This activity can be done to music.

OBSERVATIONS AND CONCLUSIONS

Balls are one of the first playthings given to an infant. Children soon find out that balls are *round*, but that some are *small* enough to be grasped with one hand and that others are so *large* that they are difficult to hold with both hands. Children discover that many kinds of balls can be squeezed—that they have some "give" to them and that they vary in *tensile strength*. Other kinds of balls, such as those used for golf or croquet, are solid. Some are strong enough to sit on. Others, such as balloons, will pop under too much *pressure*.

They learn about *spatial relationships* as they push, roll, and toss balls. They observe that only a certain number of balls will fit into a given area, even though additional space remains. Children also make observations in relation to their own bodies as they hold a ball over their head, on top of their head, cradled in their arms, under them, at the side, and in other *positions*. They learn something about *weight*, finding out that it's easier to *bounce* a heavy rubber ball than one that is too light. They also learn that muscular *strength* can control the speed and force that makes a ball move. They also notice that the ball will descend in the same arc at which it ascends. Without an awareness of this principle—the *parabolic curve*—it would be very difficult to catch a ball. Following the movements of balls on the ground and in the air enhances children's *visual-motor* acuity. When a child has to adjust his stance to throw the ball and then readjust his position to catch it when it is thrown back to him, he undergoes a very complex process of accommodating to his own *center of gravity* in order to maintain his *balance*.

Children enhance their *depth perception* as they judge the distance between themselves and the place to which they want to throw the ball. The rhythmic *sound* of a ball which is being bounced up and down at a steady pace helps the bouncer to coordinate body movements with the ball's movements. Children become aware that the *sound* the ball makes when it hits the ground will depend on the force with which it was thrown, its weight, the material its made of, and how far away it lands, among other things. They develop many other *sensory perceptions* through play with so simple an object as a ball. They learn that some balls, when left in the hot sunshine, will develop a very strong smell, especially if they are made of rubber. They learn that plastic will develop a different *odor* when it gets hot, but not the same smell as rubber.

They observe that even though the entire ball is of one *color*, it has many different shades over its surface as the result of the various

Conversations

We can go back and forth.

Get it for me.
We got to throw it in the basket.
I'm tired of standing.
We'll sit down and we'll throw it.

You have to throw it in your own basket.
We'll have to move closer.

Here I am. Can't you see me. I'm right here, not there.

Here it goes way up high, high. Oh, I did a boo-boo.

Look. I throwed it there. I get it. Noooooooo! I get it.
'Smine.

Come on and catch it. Hold your hands up. Got it.
Good.
mmmmmmmmmmmmmmmmmmmmmmmmmmmmmm

This one's broken. Who punched holes in it? Hey,
someone punched holes in it.

shadows that are formed on it. They discover that some balls have a *smooth* surface and that some are bumpy or *rough*.

Eventually children observe that the air inside of the ball or balloon is what holds its shape. Sooner or later they will notice when a strong wind is blowing, the moving *air currents* will make it difficult to control the movement of the ball. I've seen children delight in throwing a ball in the direction of a strong *wind* and watch it literally fly as though a giant had thrown it. With experience, they learn to throw in a way that will compensate for the direction of the wind.

Rolling balls down an *inclined plane* leads children to the discovery that the force of *gravity* is stronger when a ball is rolled downhill rather than on a flat surface. They also learn that they must exert greater *muscular force* to roll a ball up an inclined plane.

Some of the things that children find out from playing with balls also come about from playing with bean bags and other objects meant to be thrown. Bean bags are excellent aids for helping children learn to judge *distances, muscular force,* and for improving *throwing and catching skills*. Throwing bean bags at a target also helps to improve *visual-motor perception*.

PUNCHING BAG

The child is always seeking ways to be in control. A typical group of four-year-olds at play will become involved in some kind of argument or controversy, however mild, ten or twelve times an hour. Most of these aren't serious. They usually involve some repartee about wanting to *have* something or to *do* something or wanting someone else *not to have* something or *not to do* something. A good motor program that offers many opportunities for using the larger muscles of the body with force will help children rid themselves of the tensions that build up as a result of ongoing aggressive interchange. One favorite play activity that serves this purpose is hitting the punching bag.

The play activities and relationships between children in a group will change continuously as a school year progresses. One of the things that occurs with regularity, is that in the spring of each year children are more apt to seek out bodily contact with one another. This can result in much rough-housing and this in turn can lead to fighting—so out comes the punching bag. The children are encouraged to attack it with all their strength. Sometimes it is left on the floor in a corner of the room. Sometimes it is hung from a frame. It enables children to swing their whole arms with as much force as they wish to use, thus relieving tension without danger of being hit back.

Instead of the punching bag, or even in conjunction with it, we sometimes set out a massive amount of wet clay and leave it for several weeks. The children have been instructed in the importance of preparing clay to get all the air bubbles out of it. And so, at any given time, it may be possible to find one or more children vigorously pounding away at a large slab of clay, releasing tense emotions and aggressive feelings. Gradually they settle down to kneeding and shaping the clay, which in itself is a very relaxing and calming experience.

An effect similar to that achieved by clay pounding and bag punching is brought about by the use of carpentry equipment, especially a hammer. Even when extensive carpentry play isn't going on, children can always use a wood mallet and pounding board to release excess energy.

Other methods of achieving these same kinds of results include digging experiences and hiking.

OBSERVATIONS AND CONCLUSIONS

The primary reason for using a punching bag during playtimes is to give children opportunities to release *tension*. Angry children and belligerent children will use up so much energy in hitting a punching bag, that they frequently will start feeling more *relaxed*, and forget their original anger.

When children try to hit the bag, they feel very strong and important. They also feel a certain amount of *control* of the situation because the bag doesn't hit back. As they aim at the bag, they usually keep their eyes on the target. They visually pick up the movement of their hands as they reach out for the bag. The combination of vision and movement again helps to increase the child's *visual-motor skills*. The noise, too, made by the hands when they come in contact with the bag, is part of the total *sensory* experience, as is the *tactile* sensation of the surface of the bag. As they adjust their stance to maintain their balance against the force of the heavy bag, they increase their skill at shifting their *center of gravity* to meet their changing needs. They also become more skilled at judging *distances*, and learn just how far away from their target they have to stand in order to make the physical contact they are attempting. They learn that their *dominant* arm can swing harder at the bag than the other, but that by shifting their *weight* around they can get extra *strength* in the weaker muscles.

Sometimes when children are playing war games and shooting guns, I try to get them interested in the punching bag as a means of allowing for the release of *violent feelings* through play, without role-playing war and killing.

93

VIGOROUS MOVEMENT GAMES

There is no need at this point to elaborate further on the value of movement experiences for young children. Some children need to move more than others. It is sometimes important to acknowledge this and to plan part of your program around these children rather than badger them constantly to stop running, jumping, climbing, and, in essence, moving. Some of the need to move a great deal is, of course, taken care of through the various playground and gymnastic equipment and the dramatic play games that they inspire. Sometimes, however, you might have to provide additional areas or opportunities for extraordinary amounts of vigorous movement.

One way this can be achieved is to set aside an indoor hallway or other area for a certain period of time. Tell the children that they can run there—or gallop, or jump, or roll over and over and over on the floor. Special games to encourage vigorous movement can be utilized to great advantage during periods when children who are accustomed to much outdoor play have to be indoors because of adverse weather conditions. We call one such game "How Did You Get There?" It is usually played outdoors on a large parking lot, lawn, playground, or any other place where there is plenty of room for everyone to move vigorously.

To play the game, all of the children start out on one side of the open area to be used. At least one adult is there with them, and another adult is on the other side of the area. The adult who is closest to the children can say, "Horse, horse, how did you get there?" The other adult shouts, "All of the horses galloped." At that statement, all of the children gallop across the open area to where the other adult is stationed. The first adult may then say, "All of the horses jumped." The children jump back to where they started. The game continues, with a wide variety of movements being suggested by various roles. Some of these can be similar to the following:

Car, car, how did you get there?

All of the cars went speeding away.

All of the cars drove on a flat tire.

Tiger, tiger, how did you get there?

The tigers leaped across the fields.

The elephant ran through the jungle, knocking the trees down that got in his way.

The airplane flew across the ocean.

As the game continues, the children like to add their own suggestions for roles to play.

This game can also be played by running around a block. At each corner the movement role is changed. Depending on the size of the block, once or twice around should be enough to satisfy the most urgent needs for vigorous movement on the part of most children. If parking lots and sidewalks are not available, or if you can't run around the block in your particular location, you can always clear the furniture out of an entire room temporarily to provide the opportunity for gross motor movements with a minimum of restrictions.

OBSERVATIONS AND CONCLUSIONS

Children are generally willing to participate in the vigorous movement games described in this section. They seem to enjoy the opportunity to participate in heightened muscular activity, release *pent-up tensions*, and express *emotions*. These games give them opportunities to refine their *gross motor skills* through walking and running, jumping, hopping, and leaping, and, for the more mature, through galloping and skipping. (Most of the types of things that children find beneficial from these activities are recounted under the observations section for *Creative Movement* at the end of this chapter. Therefore, they won't be listed separately here.) However, it is important to realize that even so simple a movement experience as running across an open courtyard or down the length of a long hallway and responding to *group directions* can be joyful learning experiences that lead to wholesome understandings of *self* and *space*, and of self in relation to space.

CREATIVE MOVEMENT

Creative movement involves the children in rhythmic activities. It contributes greatly to the child's growth and development and can prevent or lessen the development of learning problems.

The creative movement program includes simple, quiet activities, such as sitting on the floor swaying gently back and forth to some appropriate rhythm, as well as vigorous activities, such as running and jumping, that involve the use of the whole body. Simple tunes and rhymes, or a steady, rhythmic beat can encourage the child to participate in a wide variety of creative activities based on natural developmental movements and growth patterns.

Approximately twenty or thirty minutes a day should be spent on creative movement experiences. It is the only time during the day at our school that an entire class is encouraged to participate in the same activity at one time, breaking away from the free and open curriculum of the rest of the program. This gives the children positive experiences in functioning together as a group. The movement program ensures that whatever a child's other activities for that particular day, each one is certain to have opportunities for developmental movement exercises of a specific nature. Over a period of several days, the children will crawl, creep, roll, bend, jump, shake, wiggle, gallop, hop, tip-toe, stomp, and perform all of the other movements that can be observed when children are involved in their natural play activities. If any children have moved from one developmental stage of growth to another too rapidly during their early physical development, they now have repeated opportunities to relive those movement experiences that would have occurred with the greatest frequency at that particular period of growth.

The creative movement program begins with crawling and creeping games. A tambourine is helpful for establishing a steady, rhythmic beat—while still leaving one of the teacher's hands free to use for giving assistance where it may be needed. It can be soft or loud, slow or fast, according to the mood and theme of the particular activity. For beginning crawling games, we encourage the children to imitate creatures that crawl. The program includes stories and songs about such things as worms and snakes. Throughout the creative movement program, the teacher is closely involved with the play. Children respond to adults who are able to play on the children's level on occasion. Such adults are often able to encourage the children to perform at more advanced levels when necessary.

When we move on to creeping activities, we sing songs about mice, kittens, puppies, and other small four-legged animals. We play walking games, varying the tempo with the tambourine from a very slow walk to running speed. The children pretend to be babies learning how to walk. They pretend to be towering giants. Giants are fun to interpret. Ours are always "gentle" giants to discourage any disruption of the rhythmic aspect of the experience by someone's getting carried away with his or her new-found power. This activity is performed very slowly. It is very hard for children to learn to hold their knees up and patiently wait for the next beat, which indicates that it is time to put that foot down and lift up the other one. Such experiences, which are built into the creative movement program, help to integrate the child's auditory abilities with his motor abilities.

Another movement experience involves all kinds of jumping activities, including pretending to be frogs, kangaroos, grasshoppers, and even popcorn. Some games are inspired by examples, stories, or even photographs. Some are inspired by challenges from an adult who will tell the children, "This is very hard." Everyone is allowed to move in his own way, and interpret in his own style. If someone needs help in performing a particular type of movement, that child will be worked with individually to determine the problem. It might simply be one of interpretation, or it might indicate a developmental lag of one kind or another, usually very slight but sometimes of great urgency.

Resting is an important part of the movement program. Resting games can be short or long depending on how long a rest period seems to be needed. In one popular resting game, the children pretend to be little birds in the nest. Sometimes their "mother" sings or hums to them while they rest, to lengthen their resting time.

In another resting game the children pretend they are newly planted seeds that sleep the "whole winter through." This game can incorporate weed pulling, rain, raking, sunshine, and similar things to extend the resting period into a ten- or fifteen-minute experience. Or the seeds can quickly sprout, grow, spread their leaves, and "wave to the boys and girls down below." This type of game is acted out by the adult, with the children "mirroring" the activity. This presents them with a different response experience than when they are interpreting their own actions to the words and beat of a song. Chapter 7 deals more fully with rest and relaxation.

One favorite activity, and one that is very easy to use as a taking-off point for this type of program, is sung to the tune of "This Old Man."[1] Some of the favorite verses include:

> This old man, he can shake,
> He can shake while baking a cake,
> Nick-nack paddywack, give your dog a bone,
> This old man comes shaking home.
>
> This old man, he can jump,
> He can jump right over the bump . . .
>
> This old man, he can hop,
> Hop, hop, hop all over the shop . . .
>
> This old man, he can wiggle,
> He can wiggle while doing the squiggle . . .
>
> This old man, he can creep,
> He can creep without a peep . . .

The shaking and wiggling represent whole body movements in which the body moves but no locomotion is involved. These motions are important for developing internalization of auditory-motor responses. Besides shaking

---

[1] From Clare Cherry, *Creative Movement for the Developing Child* (Belmont, Ca: Fearon Publishers, 1971) p. 48.

and wiggling, these movements can include bending, twisting, stretching, knee bending, arm swinging, swaying, clapping, and other actions.

In creative movement activities, the leader can always make up suitable words to sing to well-known folk songs or other tunes. Words can also be chanted rather than sung. Therefore, people who have no singing ability can participate in a program in which the children develop the ability to respond rhythmically. The primary requirement is that the adult enjoy the experience, so that his or her joy and enthusiasm can be communicated to the children.

In addition to structured activities, children have many opportunities for free interpretation. The focus of the program, in fact, is to give the participants opportunities to find their own ways of moving while responding to different stimuli and motivational suggestions.

Many of the creative movement experiences are improvised on the spot. Sometimes there are scarves to explore, recorded music to respond to, and dances to create. The rhythmic activities also give the participants an opportunity to explore creative expression through dance. The creative movement program enriches the growth and development of young children.

OBSERVATIONS AND CONCLUSIONS

Children who are involved in creative movement activities increase all of their *sensory-motor abilities* and *locomotor skills*. All the things they have learned through other types of movement play are reviewed in the context of heightened *self-awareness* and *body control*. They learn to move in a coordinated, fluid manner in response to a wide variety of *visual, auditory, and tactile clues*. Reacting to the auditory clues enchances auditory perceptual abilities. The children acquire the ability to move their bodies in *rhythm* to the beat of a tambourine or other rhythmic accompaniment. As their auditory skills increase, they become able to respond appropriately to accents, rests, and *musical patterns* of musical accompaniment, and still be able to maintain the basic rhythm of the beat. Through these auditory skills, they develop basic understandings of the *tempo* and timing of music and movement. Both musical and verbal clues help children learn the differences between a slow waltz, a faster polka, or a running step in relation to change of tempo. With each change of tempo, they make the necessary postural adjustments for maintaining their balance in accordance with their own *centers of gravity*. These tempo changes also help them to understand the vocabulary of *time relationships* when they learn to move *slowly, quickly, slower, faster, slower than,*

Conversations

Worms are crawling.

Now listen. I'm the teacher.

Turtle, turtle, where are you? Oh you are so slow,
slow, slow.

Their leaves unfolded so.

The wind blew them all away.

I'm Kalamazoo the Kangaroo, see what I can do.

The sun came out and everyone looked around and
said good-morning.

faster than, hurriedly, as slow as, etc. They not only learn about tempo, but they develop an understanding of the vocabulary of the *duration* of time, such as a *long time, a short time, a few minutes, a few seconds, a minute, quicker than,* etc. And they acquire the ability to accelerate or decelerate their movements on short notice.

As the children move through a given space, they pick up many visual clues from the environment, both from the other persons who are also moving, and from stationary objects. Movement activities give children opportunities to adjust their *visual perceptions* to the rapidly changing visual stimuli and to relate their own *position in space* and the space around them in terms of *depth, area, location,* and *volume.* The number of participants involved in the activity also affects each child's experiences. Children increase their understanding of directionality as they practice movements in response to such clues as *up, down, forward, backward, across, sideways, the other way, in front of, in back of, below, in a circle, in between, on the bottom of, on top of, to the other side, to the opposite side,* etc.

They grow in their ability to understand, accept, and express *emotions* as they play games in which they respond to such directions as *move quietly, loudly, heavily, silently, noisily, sadly, happily, softly, angrily, joyfully,* etc. These clues help them realize that they can control *sound* with their own bodies and that they can use their *imaginations* to express feelings, ideas, and concepts. Children arrive at certain understandings about their own bodies in relation to these expressions, and in relation to *size* and *space* when they respond to directions that ask them to make themselves *very tall, very short, big, small, fat, skinny, tiny, teensy-weensy, great big giant,* etc. They have many opportunities to expand their *role-playing* and dramatic abilities as they play at being a baby, or very old, or a fish, animal, bird, important person, tree, flower, and myriad other things.

Another thing that children achieve as a result of creative movement activities is an understanding of *sequencing.* Sometimes they may progress from being an infant and toddler to being a little adult and then a big adult and finally a giant. Sometimes these may be reversed. Some games involve growing from seed to flower, or seedling to giant tree, or perhaps being built as a snowman, standing in the sun all day, and slowly melting down to nothing. As they become familiar with the various games, they begin to anticipate what comes next. With increased *anticipatory skills,* they also increase their *ability to improvise* and create new or added sequences. Children who have been involved in *creative movement* for several months are able to improvise their own creative movement dances in response to single word clues or complicated musical accompaniment.

As the children respond to the various directions, they manipulate their bodies into different positions in a continuing manner, which greatly increases the sense of *kinesthesia* and the ability to respond with each separate part of the body independent of other parts, as well as in coordination with the other parts.

They also react to the different kinds of surfaces on which they move and to the various *tactile effects* of the props that are introduced from time to time—the smoothness of a silk scarf as compared to the rough texture of a length of burlap or the furry softness of a piece of velvet. These props, and others, also require responses to *color, shapes, weights,* and other physical properties, all of which heighten the overall *sensory-motor effect.*

Because creative movement is usually a group activity, children are continuously *interacting* with the other participants, including adults. Sometimes this interaction is on a very individual basis, requiring no more than being aware of *where others are* in relation to one's self. In such instances everyone interprets the music and directions in his own way. Sometimes *mirrored activities* are called for, requiring *imitation* in reverse. Sometimes *group cooperation* is needed for certain dramatization games. Always, however, I observe increased *camaraderie* among all children involved in a creative movement session.

6 Movement Experiences: Fine Motor Activities

MANIPULATIVE MATERIALS

One of my favorite playthings when I was a toddler was the lid to my mother's enamel percolator. At about two years of age, according to my mother, I apparently enjoyed the challenge of taking out the glass top and then manipulating it back into the hole in the center of the lid. I also played with the lids to her other pots and pans, and I especially liked fitting some old sauce pans into one another, making stacks of three or four in graduated sizes. My mother remembers giving me pieces of real dough to play with whenever she baked, which was almost daily. She remembers me stirring the cake batters for her. I remember shelling endless pods of peas, removing the meat from cracked walnut shells, and polishing the silverware every single week. Also, there were my own shoes to button, belts to buckle, snaps and hooks-and-eyes on dresses to fasten. Out of doors, there were sticks, stones, gardens, mud pies, and scraps of wood to hammer and nail. No zippers on the clothes. No beautiful store-bought toys. No educational games or preschool puzzles.

Today's child does not have so many natural opportunities to develop manipulative skills. Peas come ready to cook, walnuts arrive in neat plastic bags already shelled. Clothes for children are designed to make dressing and undressing as easy as possible. Special mixes and flours have even shortened the stirring time for cake batter from minutes to seconds. Outdoors, children who have yards to play in can't dig up rose bushes or pull grass out of the carefully manicured lawns. In many urbanized areas, much of the outdoor space is paved, limited, and boring.

Natural manipulative experiences have been replaced by educational toys, which are manufactured to encourage exploration with hands and fingers. Experiences with these materials, or with improvised materials that will help the child to develop the same kinds of skills, promote the development of the small muscles of the hands and the use of the hands in coordination with the eyes.

Children's play with manipulative materials should be geared to provide a variety of movement experiences, and to develop visual-motor skills and fine motor control. While these things are being developed, the children gain in perceptual maturity. They acquire bits and pieces of information that gradually come together in various combinations to form concepts. Remember that you don't have to *teach* concepts. Children cannot comprehend concepts that they are not yet developmentally ready to understand. Understanding any particular concept requires step-by-step preparation acquired through sensorimotor experiences. Your responsibility is to provide the play environment in which these experiences can occur and to help the children develop habits of observation, planning, trying and trying again, and manipulating the materials until they can make them go where they seem to belong or where they want them to go.

Demonstrating manipulative skills to children will not teach them to manipulate anymore than watching a violinist finger the strings would make violin players of them. The "do it myself" approach is again called for. The child may not do "it" the way it was meant to be done the first ten or fifteen times.

Perhaps you have had experiences similar to this one: I once observed that Brian was having difficulty with a very complicated jigsaw puzzle, one that even most of the adults found hard to put together. He looked like he was just about ready to burst into tears. Knowing that Brian was extremely success-oriented, I felt that he needed help. "Brian," I said, "how high can you stack those pieces of puzzle?" He proceeded to stack the pieces. Several times the stack collapsed. On the fourth try, he managed to get all twenty-two pieces to balance one on top of another. I observed Brian doing the same thing with that puzzle several times during the next two weeks. Then one day he said, "Come and see. I did it!" And sure enough. Brian was the first child in the school to put together this extremely difficult puzzle. As a result of stacking the pieces again and again, he had apparently become familiar with each piece, and alert to its individual shape, color, and differences. With this success achieved, we were gradually able to help Brian to understand that using materials in one's own way is the right way for that individual. Children may play with many different kinds of materials that are provided *primarily* for the manipulation required, but which may serve many other purposes at the same time (see photos at the end of this section). These kinds of playthings include:

1. Puzzles of all kinds, with various degrees of difficulty, and made of different types of materials (cardboard, wood, pressed wood, textured rubber). These include puzzles with knobs on them, puzzles with magnetized backs, inset puzzles, and jigsaw puzzles).

2. Various lock devices such as lock boards and boxes with locks and keys to match. The older child enjoys the challenge of figuring out what to do with several locks with only one key, or several keys with only one lock.

3. Tinker toys, Lego bricks, and other connecting commercial toys.

4. Turn-a-Gears and the insides of old clocks with gears that can be moved with the fingers.

5. Paper, crayon, scissors, paste.

6. Paper punch and stapler.

7. Various commercial toys that snap together, such as snap blocks, snap boards, or snap trains.

8. Large and small beads with lacing materials to string them on.

9. Large and small pegs with appropriate peg boards.

10. Suitcases and purses with various kinds of fastenings.

11. Various sizes of nuts and bolts all mixed together.

12. Short lengths of pipe and various types of fittings with which to create different types of connections.

13. Record players, radios, old carburetors, and old typewriters to dismantle with the appropriate screwdrivers, wrenches, and other tools that may be needed.

14. Various types of nesting toys including plastic barrels, plastic and cardboard boxes, boxes and cans.

15. Dress-up clothes with belts, buckles, buttons, and other fastening devices.

16. Lacing boards, peg boards with yarn.

In providing manipulative materials, remain alert to the sequence of the child's growth. Full development of the muscles that control the use of the fingers, and especially the fingertips, does not occur until sometime between 5½ and 6 years of age. Thus, making bows, as for tying shoelaces, involves actual physical movements that are very difficult for most 4½- to 5-year-olds.

Yet those same children at age 5½ or 6 may find it extremely simple to tie bows. There is no reason for trying to coerce children into tying their shoes before full fingertip control is achieved. There are so many other movements and skills to learn, things to do, all of which will enhance the child's development.

Children should have all kinds of shapes to handle, feel, and become familiar with, all kinds of things to fit together and take apart, to connect and disconnect, to screw on and screw off, objects to arrange and stack, and holes to put things through.

OBSERVATIONS AND CONCLUSIONS

Up to this point in the creative play program, movement play has been primarily geared to the refinement of *perceptual* and *sensory skills* in coordination with the gross, or larger, muscles of the body. Simultaneously, however, the children are refining these same skills in coordination with their fine, or smaller, muscles. Although the development of both is ongoing from birth, the achievement of *fine motor control* develops more slowly than, and as an outgrowth of, gross motor control. The *manipulative* experiences with which the children are involved help them develop skills in the use of their hands and fingers in coordination with *visual, tactual*, and other sensory *input*. Fastening things together, *connecting, disconnecting, inserting, taking out, fitting, matching,* and otherwise *combining* or *manipulating objects* all require control of the wrists, hands, and fingers. As children make these movements, guiding themselves with their eyes and with their sense of touch, they refine their *eye-hand coordination* skills, their *visual-motor* and *tactile-motor abilities.* They not only learn to recognize differences in *textures* easily, but learn to use the *vocabulary* of texture with such words as *soft, hard, rough, cold, sticky, stiff, smooth, prickly, sharp, bumpy, furry, slick, slippery,* etc.

As they handle the various materials, they learn to recognize *likeness* and *differences* in *shapes, forms, sizes,* and *weights.* They discover that it is not always possible to tell the weight of an object by its size. Some plastic objects may be very large, but much lighter in weight than a smaller object made of solid wood or metal. Some kinds of *metal,* such as aluminum, are much lighter than other kinds, such as steel. *Solid* objects are usually heavier than those which are hollow, except foam rubber objects may be solid and also very light.

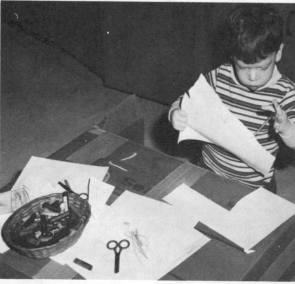

Conversations

Anyways I work here.

Now I have the gingerbread man.

Oh, this one's easy. Ha. Ha. Ha. Easy, easy, easy.

I wish you would move your chair over.

I've got a fire engine puzzle. I can put this together.
Whoops, I dropped it.

Put this one together. Eyes, eyes, eyes. I've got a belt
on. See my belt?

I'm making something for you. Here's a black
wheelie. I don't like it.
I don't like it either.

Bring me my calculator. More calculators! In case one
breaks. I have a special one in case one breaks.

Keep the box in the middle. Here, this is the middle.
No, this is middle.

If it goes this way, it makes a star.
Stars don't show in the sun. But they are there. They
only come at night.

I'm making the longest thing. I need all these things.

The papers blow away, don't they? You know why?
'Cause they flash.

I'm big. I can do it.

Whee! Whee! All pieces are in but one.

Look. I did it. Wow!

Their growing knowledge about size and weight relationships helps them to form basic ideas about *proportions*. They find out, for example, that some things that are different in size but alike in shape can't fit into one another because they are of different proportions. But if the proportions are the same, objects of different sizes and the same shape can be fit into or onto one another. Thus they learn about seriation. In handling these objects, they also learn that no matter which way they turn them, their shapes, sizes, and weights remain constant.

In addition to the manipulative skills and perceptual abilities that are enhanced with manipulative experiences, the children also have an opportunity to develop perceptual awareness that helps them *classify* and *categorize* things in accordance with the various means of making *comparisons*.

TACTILE MATERIALS

Tactile materials can include water and mud as well as fingerpaint and clay. Plastic clay (Plasticine) can provide children with challenging and rewarding experiences in exercising the muscles that control their fingers, hands, and arms. It should be kept where children have access to it whenever they want to use it. Manipulating clay is a soothing and relaxing activity that should never be discouraged. Keeping the clay in a maleable condition enhances its attractiveness.

Play dough is another material to use to encourage children to develop the muscles of their forearms and to practice finger-tip control—especially when they have the opportunity the make it themselves. Materials for preparing play dough should be made available from time to time for interested children to use as they wish. It is not necessary to give the children formulas or recipes. One way to make this activity manageable by children is to provide only small quantities of the various ingredients at one time. Set out a small bowl of flour with a scoop, a smaller bowl of salt with a smaller scoop, a small pitcher of water, and a plastic squeeze bottle the children can use to add small squirts of salad oil to the mixture.

Making play dough is one of the few activities that children should be required to finish once they start it. At our school we say, "If you make play dough, you keep making it until it doesn't stick to your hands." This rule is necessary because it takes a great deal of trial and error to make satisfactory dough—and some children give up too easily. Also, this rule encourages each child to persist until he achieves success—and the satisfaction that comes with discovering how to make something as though no one had ever done it before.

OBSERVATIONS AND CONCLUSIONS

Tactile materials stimulate the child's entire *sensory-motor* system, thus heightening his total awareness. Since the fingertips are the last part of the hands over which children gain full control (at approximately 5½ to 6 years of age), children respond well to opportunities to exercise them. As they manipulate tactile materials, children inadvertently release *emotional tensions.* This is a result of the combined effects of muscular pressures on and skin contact with the materials involved. This usually has a calming effect on an overstimulated or overactive person.

Finger painting, like scribbling, helps children become aware of the lines and patterns they are making on the painting surface. As they move their arms, shoulder, and upper torsos in *rhythm,* they become aware of their overall movement, which favorably affects *visual-motor perception.* The direct interaction between the child and the paint enhances the *sense of color and design* and the concepts of *transparency* and *opaqueness.* It also stimulates the child's *creative abilities.*

When children make their own play dough, they learn such expressions of texture as *floury, oily, too wet, sticky,* and so on. They will recall the meanings of these words later when they participate in cooking experiences, chemistry experiences, and other tasks that involve *mixing* various ingredients together to obtain particular results. They also learn to make comparative *measurements* as they can be overheard using such expressions as *too much, not enough, a little bit more,* etc. The concepts expressed, though only beginnings, will prove useful later on when the children are involved in solving *mathematical problems* and other tasks. Once they have made their play dough, they show great delight in their *accomplishment* and feel very proud of having made a particular product out of some basic ingredients. As they play with the dough, and with clay, Plasticine, and other manipulative and tactile materials, they become aware of their ability to create something new out of something that is already existing in another form. This is an introduction to both creativity and *craftsmanship.* These feelings build *self-confidence, self-awareness,* and *self-esteem,* all of which are important to the wholesome development of early lifehood.

Conversations

I made purple.
I want to make purple.

I get my shirt messy a lot, but that's O.K. Grandma
can wash it. She doesn't care. I get it in my hair a lot
sometimes, too, but it's O.K. Did you get your
clothes dirty too, Mrs. Smith?

Bobby eats clay. He's a baby. He cries. I'm going to
take all this clay and let Bobby eat it. He wets,
too. I'm bigger. I'm the biggest.

Uh, uh. Miss Sunny won't let you. She'll clobber you.
Teachers don't clobber. Only kids.

I can make it go 'round and 'round and 'round
soooooooooooo goooooooooooooshy, goooooooooooshy,
. . . . blue!

Yellow is faster than red. It goes in the shaving
creme faster and washes faster.

I can make two holes with two fingers. See that. All
at the time!

I'm going into the swimming pool. There, I go into
the ocean. Be careful, don't get in the water. I'm on
the boat. Come on the boat.
It's too far for me to swim.
But I thought you were Superman.
I am. And I'm on the other boat.

On, no. There's spiders. Come on up.
And there's a lot of rattlesnakes. Come on up here.
Hurry!

WATER PLAY

Playing with water should be an integral part of the play program. Water is soothing, clean, and full of surprises. It splashes. It moves. It bubbles, gurgles, spills, runs. It brings one back to those earliest months of life when playing in water while being bathed was one of the highlights of almost every day. It was the time, really, for first learning about play. It was a time for laughing and touching and close human interaction. It was a time for being held close, for being warm afterwards, and for being fed. And the buoyancy of the water offered a bodily sensation that was different from those experienced during any other waking activity. This sensation brought about an unusual sense of freedom, security, happiness, and well-being.

There are many ways to provide for water play even if low sinks, water tables, or even running water are not available. Plan ahead of time to provide protection for any surroundings that might be damaged by splashes. Also, make any necessary preparations to protect the health and safety of the children. Plastic "coverups" or aprons can be used to protect the children's clothing. They can be easily made by hand, or they can be purchased at small cost from discount stores.

Large sheets of cardboard cut from appliance containers will protect the floor, if such protection is needed. These can be additionally covered with layers of newspapers if you wish. Plastic cloths can also be used to protect table and counter tops when needed, and, if you plan a vigorous play session, you may wish to protect the walls.

The simplest types of containers are ordinary plastic household dishpans, washtubs, bowls, pitchers, and similar items. Baby bathtubs or other rectangular containers should be interchanged with round tubs for differing learning experiences through similar kinds of play. These containers can be used on tables or boxes indoors or out. They can also be put on the floor or even in the sandbox.

Most of the time you should use just ordinary tap water. In cold weather, warm water is desirable. In hot weather, cold water can be used for its cooling effect.

Whatever the container, wherever the location or the placement, the type of play the children become involved in will depend largely on the types of equipment you provide.

Very young children usually prefer the kinds of things they are most familiar with. The 2½- and 3½-year-olds greatly enjoy dolls they can fully immerse in the tub and scrub vigorously with soap and washcloths. Be sure to provide drying towels and drying places. Also, care should be taken to keep nonimmersible dolls (such as cloth-bodied dolls or rag dolls) separate from those which can be bathed.

Although older children will occasionally enjoy bathing dolls, they seem to prefer working with things like plastic funnels, cups, ladles, plastic meat basters, rubber or plastic syringes, and similar items. They may share the common water supply and tools with each other, but they are usually deeply intent on their individual experiments.

Children enjoy play fishing poles. They need no other accessories except water—their imaginations will provide the rest. Older children enjoy games that challenge their eye-hand coordination. One such game is "Catching a Fish." The "fish" are made by cutting shapes from waxed cardboard milk cartons. The shapes are then glued to small pieces of wood. A paperclip is attached to each "fish," and the child attempts to snag it with the paperclip "hook" on the end of his line. The pole should not be more than 12 inches long. If it is too long the string swings, producing a pendulum effect that makes it difficult for the children to direct the string. For the younger children, provide just a string with a paperclip hook on the end of it. This game can also be played with magnets.

Washing dishes is another favorite dramatic play experience. Although children "wash dishes" quite imaginatively, and frequently without actual water, do provide water and suds once in a while. They might even decide to use it for washing clothes.

Children also like to whip soapy water with eggbeaters to make soapsuds. A rotary eggbeater is best for this type of activity. Using an eggbeater involves complex muscular movements. Once the soapsuds have been made, you can give the children sponges and turn the activity into a furniture-washing party. Be sure to accompany this activity with lively music to establish a party-like atmosphere. Provide plenty of towels and don't worry about spills and splashes.

Bicycle pumps make delightful bubbles. These too, should be used with music. Play slow-moving music to help the children discover that pumping slowly will create larger bubbles than pumping fast. A small amount of glycerin added to the water will help the bubbles retain their shapes. Children can learn to make bubbles with their hands too.

Painting pavements and fences with large painter's brushes and water-filled paint buckets is a pleasant activity on hot, summery days when things dry out so fast they can be "repainted" many times. Indoor painting should not be overlooked either. Find some surface that really changes color when wet and can be gone over many times without causing any damage to it.

Put water in portable plastic swimming pools—but be sure not to leave the water in them after the supervised play is finished. Make-believe streams, or actual streams made by the children themselves, can lead to long hours of exploration, learning, and play. The children can make dams. They invent all kinds of bridges to get from one side of the stream to the other.

Children also like rain puddles. They like to wade in them, see reflections, and sail paper, wooden, or plastic boats. Sometimes they find earthworms or insects in them.

A water hose with a spray nozzle is an excellent piece of equipment for outdoor water play. It is often desirable to keep the water pressure low to prevent water from squiring out with too much force. In warm weather, outer clothing and shoes can be removed, and the water turned up for whatever kind of play develops.

Water play can also include scientific experiments. Water can be turned to steam. It can be frozen to make ice. Snow can be melted back into water. Children can spend many interesting play times experimenting with the arrangement and rearrangement of stones and rocks in clear water—two or three in a bowl, or fifty or more in a tub. Adults also get caught up in this activity. They exchange observations with the children on how the water changes the various colors of the rocks, how it makes them look larger, what arrangements are more pleasing, and many other things.

The soothing effects of playing with water, especially with soapy water, should be taken advantage of. The simple procedure of prolonging the soaping portion of handwashing routines can turn this necessary activity into calming play experiences. On days when the children are tense, have a bubbly hand-washing session. Give the children bars of soap or bottles of liquid soap (not detergent). You may have to give them some assistance by way of demonstrating how to get a sufficient quantity of bubbles—e. g., wet the hands first, then apply the soap; add more water if needed, but not enough to wash off all the soap. Then rub the hands together to build up the suds.

Other forms of water play include watering plants, mixing powdered paints, and sand and dirt play.

Water play should not be without rainbows. After children have observed real rainbows in the sky, show them how to create their own rainbows with water sprayed from a hose. If the sun is shining behind the source of the spray, a rainbow will appear in the spraying water. If you don't see it readily, manipulate the position of the spray until you do.

OBSERVATIONS AND CONCLUSIONS

Most children enjoy playing with water. They often comment on how the water feels. They learn that they can move it, control it, capture it, touch it, but it is difficult to hold it in their hands. It never resists them, but they can't make it stay still no matter how hard they try. They are very much aware of the *temperature* of the water with which they are playing, and verbally express such reactions as *warm, too cold, hot,* etc. I like to have them play with water that is as close to 98.6° as possible. Their reaction to the *wetness* that they can barely feel because it is the same temperature as their bodies, is a valuable learning situation. In playing with water, they learn that they can cause it to make various noises by *splashing, pouring, dripping,* and *gurgling.* They learn that it dries very slowly on cold, damp days, but very *quickly* on hot, dry days. They also learn that the water dries more quickly when the wind is blowing.

They learn that they can *control* how much or how fast they *pour* the water or how hard they *splash* it, by the amount of muscular effort and force they use in manipulating it. They lay the foundation for learning about *volume* when they pour water from a container of one size into one of a different size. Until they are developmentally ready to grasp the concept that volume is not dependent on shape, they will usually reason that the taller the container, the more water it will hold and will expect it to hold more water than another container that may be much larger but flatter and wider. They can, however, grasp the concept that two cups of the same size can fill one cup that is twice that size. With the help of others to show them what to look for, they discover the phenomena of *magnification* and *refraction* by studying how things look when they are in water, as in an aquarium. They also find out that they can see *reflections* in the water. They can see light and colors. And they learn that water is usually transparent, but that soap and other ingredients can make it lose its *transparency.* They reinforce their knowledge of *gravity* by noting that water always flows downward. They discover that some things will *float* and that other things will *sink.* They learn that some kinds of very small objects will always sink, but that some kinds of very heavy objects, such as a block of wood, will always float. They learn to *classify* objects by whether or not they can float or sink.

When it rains, they compare the wetness of the *rain* with the wetness of the water they've played with. They notice that rain doesn't always fall straight down, but that it sometimes falls at an angle. They find out that sometimes the falling rain is very cold and at other times it is not.

When several children play with water together, they usually *cooperate* with one another, *sharing* the utensils and other toys. Sharing when playing with water is very easy to do, because this activity provokes *relaxed feelings.* At 2½ they pay no attention to whether they get water all over themselves when playing, but by 4½ they learn that they can keep themselves dry if they want to.

Conversations

I need more soap. It's not clean.

You let it go in there and then you can tell how much there is.

My mom said I can cook her supper.
You got to share. Everybody gots to.

Squeeze it, squeeze it, squeeze it.

My hands are cold.
Can I have some. I want to take it home.

Let me see. I can't see. Miss Alyce, tell him to let me see.

This is how you make a big ball. I know how.

The water makes it melt fast. Get some more. Stir it. Stir it.

I know how snow comes. The water makes it.

Wheeeeeeeee! It's snowing now.

I'm swimming, I'm swimming. This is funny.

I like it.

When children make *bubbles*, they discover that they can cause the water to change into something different. Playing with bubbles reinforces various things they have already found out. They find out that bubbles, too, are reflective and transparent, that touching usually makes them pop, and that they also float, but in air rather than in water. They learn that bubbles are very quiet, but if they listen very carefully they can sometimes hear the noise they make when they pop.

When children are moody, tense, or overexcited, they become very *relaxed* and calm after a few minutes of playing with water, especially soapy water.

SAND PLAY

Sand has long been a basic element in children's play environments. It almost seems to be a fluid, like water. It can be poured from one container to another, somewhat like water. But unlike water, its movements are slightly more manageable. Once placed somewhere, it will stay pretty much where you put it unless the wind blows it away. Unlike water, it can be held in the hands. Children can shape it, whereas water only takes the shape of its container. Sand can be further controlled by mixing it with water. But dry or wet, it helps satisfy a need in children to make changes in their environment.

Sand play usually takes place in an outdoor sandbox or an indoor sandtable. The outdoor sandbox should be located so that it will receive both sun and shade during the course of the day. The ideal situation is to have the sandbox in a sunny area of the play yard with some type of covering to provide ever-changing areas of shade as each day progresses. It is easier to provide shade than to warm up areas that are never in the sun. A platform built over the sandbox will shade the sand and provide an elevated play area.

Some sandboxes have seats around the sides for children to sit on or use as surfaces on which to make the traditional sand cakes and other goodies. Children also like to sit right in the sand. Temporary sandbox seats for use in cold or wet weather can be made from 2″ x 8″ pieces of wood planks. During warm weather, these same pieces of wood can be used for "tables."

Sandboxes can be made of cement or boards. The sides can also be made from railroad ties or telephone poles. A shallow pit with cement sides that are level with the playground surface makes a convenient sandbox, especially when it comes to sweeping spilled sand back into the box. No matter what the sandbox is made of or where it is located, it is important to consider drainage.

Locating it in a place that is somewhat higher than the surrounding areas will facilitate drainage.

The type of sand in the sandbox will influence, to some extent, the ways the children use it. Sand that is used for making plaster is clean and dustless, although it is expensive. So is silicate (#30 is recommended). These types have rounded edges and are good for very young children and for home use. The least expensive kind of sand is the coarse sand used in making concrete. However, if it is too coarse it won't compact for shaping. Beach and creek sand are both excellent. Those who live in areas where such sand is available, can pick it up at no cost. Fine beach sand can also be bought, but it's very expensive. Those who live near a beach or a creek can collect it on field trips with the children. It is, of course, important to make sure it is obtained from a clean, unpolluted area.

Whatever type of sand is used, it should be about twelve to eighteen inches deep in an outdoor sandbox. Indoor sandpiles can be from two to twelve inches deep, depending on the size of the container. Sand used outdoors should be replenished every year or two.

The types of play that will take place in the sand will be influenced by the kinds of play materials provided. Basically, digging and pouring equipment is needed—bowls, spoons, empty cans, funnels, sieves, plastic bottles, scoops, strainers, and similar items will probably be the most commonly used. Wooden salad bowls and spoons are especially good. How the children play with these things will vary, depending on how many are available at a particular time, and on whether the sand is dry or damp, and if water is available to mix with.

Toy trucks, construction vehicles, and similar items can also be used in the sandbox. Children will use them for hauling, digging, and shifting the sand from one area to another. On some occasions, one or two of these items can be used with a very small selection of other types of toys.

On other occasions, wet the sand in the sandbox and give the children small cars and small balls to play with. The balls should be at least as large as golf balls, but no larger than tennis balls. To utilize these, they usually create roads, dams, hills, and tunnels. Sometime, you might wet the sand before the children come to play and heap it into a large pile in the middle of the sandbox. You can also scoop all the sand out of the middle of the sandbox or push it to the outer edges—or push all of it up against one side.

Water for use in sand play can be supplied in several ways. One way is to fill sprinkling cans and plastic bottles with water, which the children can refill from nearby buckets. If you have a garden hose, you can let a small amount of water trickle from it. You can also put plastic tubs or buckets of water right into the sand.

Conversations

No, we don't need more sand. We're making a big
hole. Do we need anymore water.
No.

I love you guys.

I'm making soft sand.

Everytime my daddy takes me to the liquor store, he
gets me a candy ball with chocolate.

Can we pour the cake in?
Not yet! It's heavy, Oh-oh. It went down on the
stove.
I'll cut the cake and what piece you choose I'll give it
to you.

Back it up here so I can dump it in here. I'm gonna
make a big mountain.
O.K. No, I want to get the dirt out, did you hear me?

Look at the hole. Oh, you dummy.
I'm not a dummy.
Not you. Her. She stepped in the hole.

Guess what's under my sand hill. Don't anyone tell
her. It's a car.

Quit that. This is where I'm putting my cake.

Don't get all of my sand. You're taking too much
stuff.

I'm going to dig, and dig, and dig, and then I'll dig to
the other side.

For indoor sand play, put the sand in dishpans, washtubs, baking pans, and similar containers if you do not have a sand table. Small, individual containers to be used by just one child are preferable because the child will usually take care not to spill the sand. When two or three children use the same container, they are sometimes careless about keeping the sand from spilling. Wet sand is easier for children to control than dry sand, but they should have the opportunity to experience playing with both.

Children don't always need utensils for use with the sand. Playing with wet sand, using only the hands as tools, provides an excellent sensory experience. It is important that children have frequent opportunities to use natural materials without artificial tools.

In some situations, it may be necessary to keep outdoor sandpiles covered when they are not in use. This precaution will keep stray animals out of them.

Sand play requires certain safety standards that the children must be aware of. These should include:

1. Never throw sand, either at another person or from one place to another.
2. To keep dry sand from blowing into someone's eyes, never fling it into the air.
3. Don't hit people or things with sand toys.
4. Don't eat sand.
5. If you play in the sand with your shoes on, empty the sand out of your shoes before going indoors.
6. Do not remove sand from the sandpile without permission from an adult.
7. Put sand toys away when you are through with them.
8. Never remove sand from the indoor sandbox.
9. Do not put clay, paint, or any other such material into the sand.

OBSERVATIONS AND CONCLUSIONS

Children enjoy feeling the *texture* of the sand in their hands. They sometimes comment on the way different kinds of sand feels. They like to hold the sand in their hands and let it run through their fingers. They like to throw it in the air and watch it fall. What may seem to be random play, is their way of finding out about *gravity, texture,* and other related facts. For example, they find out there is a difference

124

between what can be done with *dry* sand and what can be done with *wet*. They like to cover themselves with dry sand. They like to pour it from one container to another, which is a foundation for *measuring* activities. But they like wet sand so that they can make cakes, and hills, and other *shapes*. They sometimes construct hills with roadways for rolling cars or marbles, which leads to further understandings about *gravity*.

Children find it difficult to walk in sand because their feet sink down in it. They literally have to lift their feet up as they move, which develops different muscles than ordinary walking does. Some kinds of sand stick to the body, especially if it is wet or if the body is perspiring. When children study sand with magnifying glasses, they observe that it is made of many different *sizes* and *shapes*. Some of the pieces may look like broken shells, some like tiny pebbles. Some are *transparent*. Some of the sand is very white, some grey, and some pieces are often very dark brown or black in appearance.

They notice that wet sand appears darker in color than dry sand. Also, when sand is wet, they can use their fingers or a small stick or other tool to make designs in it. Wet sand is *heavier* than dry, and doesn't blow readily in the wind. Dry sand sometimes blows even in very gentle wind.

Children like to dig holes in the sand, make tunnels, use it as pretend food for cooking, and sometimes they just transfer it from one area to another. When children dig in sand they develop their *awareness of other people* and learn to be careful not to get it on other people.

All the time they are playing with sand, they do a great deal of talking. From their *verbalization,* it is easy to tell that they are usually imaging all kinds of *make-believe* situations, some involving *role play* and others involving *fantasy*. It is easier for them to *share* the sand than the sand toys because there is usually plenty of sand for everyone. Extended play with sand, especially wet sand, is very *relaxing*. After playing with it for a while, even sharing the toys becomes easier.

DIRT AND MUD PLAY

Dirt and mud are probably the most natural play materials that exist. The inclination to play with them is also one of the most natural of children's play impulses. The colors are interesting, and the textures vary. Children who are allowed to play with dirt and mud are lucky. Many children find this kind of

Conversations

No, real people don't push trucks, so don't push it.
Let's go. Go this way, Danny. Beep, beep, beep.

Stop. Make it straight.

No, don't make it go in there. No don't go through
that crazy road. This way.

O.K. I'll be the fixer. Wait, I'll get my tools. You give it
to me.

It's too much dirt. Don't throw it. Hey, not like that.
O.K. that's right.
Everybody get in line. Here we go. Got to move it.
Move it, I say.
Pretend we have to move all the things for the
people.

First you have to get it loose. See, like this. I can do it
good.
Make it straight. We have to go that way.
I'll try it out.
O.K. It's your turn now.
If we put water on it, it would be better.

play soothing in the same way as water play. It can encourage 3- and 4-year-olds to overcome earlier inhibitions developed by their parents' demands for fastidious cleanliness when the children were 1 or 2.

A pile of dirt on the playground can enable children to have satisfying digging experiences. An expanse of open ground where children can scoop up the earth is even better.

Digging tools should be real ones and not toys. Good quality gardening tools, both the hand variety and the short-handled type, are easy for children to handle. A child who uses them can really see something happening. The child's play will naturally be influenced by the tools that are available.

Children will dig, pile, haul, dump, and generally rearrange the dirt they are playing with. Such toys as dump trucks, scrapers, diggers, and other construction vehicles will encourage them to play in various ways. If the dirt is damp enough to hold its shape, or if water is available to dampen it with, children will make ditches, streams, dams, and hills with tunnels running through them. They will drag boards over dry dirt to make roads and paths.

Children involved in this type of play will dig for a while and then turn to some other kind of activity, usually one that is less strenuous. Later they will come back to dig some more. Children are obviously able to pace themselves according to their own interests, abilities, strength, and need to rest.

Even when natural soil is not available, it is possible to offer containers of dirt and water for the children to mix. They will form the mud into pies, cakes, cookies, loaves, and other familiar shapes. Mixing the dirt and water by stirring them together with some type of stick or spoon is beneficial to the child's visual-motor development.

Mud can also be used for finger painting on windows, as shown in the photograph on page 118. It can also be used on paper. If adults show playful attitudes, washing the mud off the windows can be just as much fun as applying it in the first place.

OBSERVATIONS AND CONCLUSIONS

Sometimes children use their hands and fingers to play with available dirt and mud. As they manipulate the material, they find out that its *texture* is much different from sand. It is *smooth* rather than gritty. It can be rubbed and broken down between the fingers to form a very fine powder. When sand is put into water, it sinks to the bottom. Dirt, which is lighter, will *dissolve* in the water, *float* around in it, and only the very heavy pieces *sink* to the bottom. If soil stands in water for a couple of days, however, it will eventually sink, too. Children observe that dirt sticks to their skin more readily than sand, and that it is much harder to get off. Dry dirt sometimes sticks together in *clods*, which are usually easy to break up with the fingers. It can be mashed still further, sometimes using tools.

They discover that dirt found in different places varies in *color* and texture. Some dirt is very dry looking and light in color. Some is darker, and some looks reddish. Some dirt is very moist and sticky and looks and feels like *clay*. Water added to dirt can make *mud* out of the dirt. Mud can be manipulated like clay if it isn't *too watery*. Children learn that they can play on a dirt surface, but that it is difficult to play on mud because it is usually *slippery* and wet. Even so, mud can be formed into pies and cakes, and can be used to build hills, dams, and other things. Designs can be made in both dry dirt and packed mud. Mud can also be used like fingerpaints to make *designs* on windows and other surfaces.

Children like to dig in both dry dirt and in muddy areas. They discover that although the surface of the ground is sometimes *loose* enough to dig into, it may get *harder* as they dig deeper. They also learn that mud sticks to their clothing even more than dry dirt does—but, in most instances, this knowledge doesn't affect how they play. Children seem to experience a certain good feeling in playing with mud and dirt that transcends worrying about the clothes. They seem to have an *affinity with the earth* that satisfies certain innate feelings and needs. Some children may even eat the dirt. This can be an indication of a need for iron in the system, but it may be simply that they want to find out what it tastes like.

7 Rest and Relaxation

Children frequently find some quiet corner to relax in, alone or with a friend. One minute, they may be running out of doors, vigorously engaged in fast moving games. The next minute, these same children may be seen quietly working a puzzle indoors, listening to a record, looking at a book, or just lying down on a mat. The child coming in from active outdoor play will often engage in some kind of familiar and easy indoor play before tackling new ideas. The natural rhythm of the play environment is one of continually changing patterns of movement and energy.

Involved teachers will sense this pattern and will sometimes reinforce it when the need arises. For example, if a group of children have been for a long walk, they will be tired when they return. This may be the time to play some resting games, quiet finger games, and pursue other relaxing activities.

The secret of creating restful, relaxed situations is to consider resting as part of the total movement program. Nonmovement enhances the understanding of movement. In order to relax, children need to become aware of their ability to control the degree of tension in their muscles. This awareness is just as important in periods of rest as it is during vigorous physical movement.

An open, relaxed environment helps children relax. Many techniques can be employed to promote activities that will help children enjoy being still, being quiet, relaxing. In practicing any of these techniques, it is important to be totally involved with the children. It is also important to be free of tension, and to have a relaxed posture. A quiet voice, gentle movements, and a serene expression will also help set the mood for the children.

Tell a quiet story. The children can lie on their stomachs and cushion their heads with their folded arms. The story can be about quiet sounds that people hear while they are trying to go to sleep, or about animals saying goodnight one by one and then closing *their* eyes and going to sleep.

Sing or play records of soft lullabies. Move quietly among the children, stroking each one's head gently in turn.

Some days, ask everyone to sit on the rug and quietly look at books. They may exchange books with each other, but they must do so without speaking.

On other days, play finger and arm-movement games.

Make up a story about a snowman who stood in the hot sun until he began to melt, and melt, and melt. Soon he is nothing but a puddle on the ground, lying so still in the sun. The children can perform the story—first they "melt" and then they get smaller and smaller as the puddle slowly dries up.

A similar activity involves asking the children to be rag dolls, first walking, then dropping in a heap and lying still.

They can also play "Little Birds Asleep in Their Nest." After they "sleep" for an appropriate length of time, they can wake up and fly *quietly* away. Then they come back to the nest to sleep again.

They can pretend to be frogs sleeping in a pond through the long winter.

Play "Think of Something Quiet." In this game, everyone thinks of something quiet, but doesn't tell anyone what it is. Each child tries to move like what he is thinking of.

It is especially important to sit quietly just before going home for the day. This time can be used for quiet conversation with the children. You might want to review some of the highlights of the day or talk about some anticipated event for the next day. It can be a good time for more finger games or word-rhyming games.

Once you have developed some good techniques that work for you, try to use two or three different areas for resting and relaxing. This helps children to practice their skills and to recognize that, ultimately, relaxation comes from within. Keep your repertoire of activities fairly simple. This is one time when familiarity, repetition, and simplicity are more important than novelty and change.

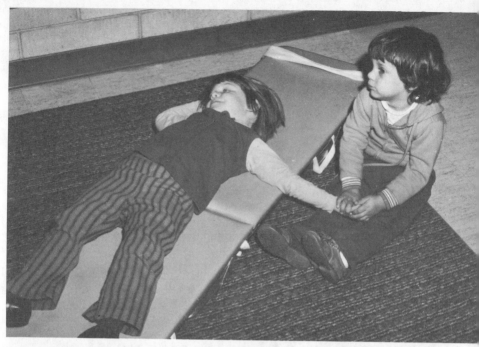

8 Construction Experiences

From infancy, children spend a great deal of time just moving objects around. In the beginning, this is their way of finding out about the objects themselves. They pick a thing up, put it to their mouth, examine the texture with their lips and tongue, and then drop it or leave it. Later they learn to control their grasp so that they can hold on to a thing or drop it at will. At this point they seem to enjoy doing exactly that, except that instead of "dropping" the object, they deliberately put it down in either the same spot or in a different one. This behavior keeps building until soon they are deeply involved during much of their play time in simply moving things from one place to another.

This activity enables children to explore environments and to develop the skill of picking things up and putting them down. They learn that they are able to control certain objects, at least to a small extent. They also learn that some things are easier to grasp than others, that some things need to be held with the entire arm or with both arms, that some things are heavier than others, and that some things are just too big for them to move. They learn that some things are slippery, pliable, wiggly, or top heavy, all of which influence the way they can be moved. They also learn that an object can be hot or cold, wet or dry, and, to the hope of their parents, whether it is a "touchable" or a "no-no."

Unfortunately, children are forbidden to handle many of the things they would like to touch, pick up, and move. And even more unfortunately, they have no way of comprehending why one item can be touched, but another, equally enticing, cannot. "Too hot" may be a reason they can learn at a fairly young age. But such reasons as, "That's Mama's best china," or "That will break if you drop it," are a little too complex, and can only add to the children's confusion.

They often don't even know exactly what the "no-no" is applied to. If a child is standing on a chair and reaching over a plate to grab a glass of water and hears an excited "no-no," he doesn't know if it's because he is standing on a chair, reaching, touching the plate with one hand, or touching the table top with the other hand. He may not relate it to the glass of water because he hasn't reached it yet.

Because this urge to move things around is so important, it is common practice to provide young children with many toys and empty containers and the freedom and time to do just that. With practice, they eventually learn that not only can things be moved from place to place, but they can also be rearranged to create private little environments to their own liking. And so they begin to arrange "spaces" for themselves in a corner of their play area, the center of a room, or wherever they may be using their playthings. At this point, they like to play with materials that they can use to build things with—and to knock down, too.

Small blocks are frequently among the child's first toys, along with the rattles, balls, and dolls that are given to older infants to play with. At this stage, they are still primarily interested in whether or not they can *grasp* the block. They will later be used for beginning experiences in stacking and will be hauled from one place to another.

Square-shaped wooden blocks, with pictures of animals, numbers, or letters of the alphabet, have long been common playthings. In recent years plastic blocks have become available. In addition to the various block-building materials, children are frequently provided with commercial educational toys or building sets with which they make small-scale constructions.

Using blocks and other building materials helps children meet their need to restructure the environment and to try to understand the world.

CARDBOARD BLOCKS

The child's first blocks should be cardboard or plastic so that they can easily be handled by one-, two-, and three-year-olds without danger to themselves or others. Beginning building blocks should be large enough to enable young children who are operating primarily at the gross motor level to pick them up easily, using the entire arm if necessary. Also, projects with these blocks will show quick results, an almost necessary requirement for early block play. Since the cardboard blocks we use are all the same size, the children's building attempts are not complicated by the need to judge comparative sizes in forming their structures. They are inexpensive, durable, safe, and quiet. They do not make a lot of noise when they are knocked down, which is a feature that adults appreciate. Painted cardboard boxes can be used with these blocks. (Seal the flaps shut with tape, and then paint the boxes with one or two coats of rubber-base or acryllic paint. It is best to paint them all the same color, so that the colors do not distract the children.)

One-and-a-half-year-olds, like to carry cardboard blocks from one place to another. Sometimes they will stack two or three blocks if encouraged to do so, but they do not find that experience very interesting. They would rather be moving around.

Two-year-olds are more interested in making some kind of structure with the blocks. They too like to carry the blocks around, so they may make the structure some distance from the block supply. They typically find a "space" which they adopt for the time as their own. In that space they will pile blocks as high as they are able in one stack. Sometimes they will make two stacks, and sometimes the "stack" is a horizontal row on the floor. They respect each others' constructions and do not knock down someone else's stack, although they do knock down their own. Frequently two children will cooperate on a building project. Very rarely you will see three working together. When three children do build something together, one usually loses interest and by the time the structure is finished, there may be only two left or sometimes only one. To them the blocks can be used for walking on, dumping in a big pile, or sleeping on, as well as for building things.

Three-year-olds are more involved in symbolization and are more interested in the result of what they construct than are twos. Sometimes several children will get together and create a rather complex arrangement of cardboard blocks, supplemented by other building materials they may find or other kinds of blocks from the various play areas. Usually they have determined that they are building a spaceship, a fire truck, a diesel engine, or an airplane. Sometimes it is a house, but more often it is something that can be excitingly dramatized.

Four-year-olds and five-year-olds are even more apt to build a predetermined structure when they are using blocks. As they build, they verbalize their dramatic play ideas with such comments as, "This will be where the ladder goes," or "We need two seats for the drivers," or "I'll pump it up and then we can get going," or "Here's the dumper. We need to dump everything." A building project by this age group may go on for some time. Sometimes it may even be left up to be worked on even two or three days. The children continue to add one thing or another to elaborate on the play they are dramatizing. This activity requires the mimimum amount of adult involvement. When children have the freedom to build what *they* want to build, and when

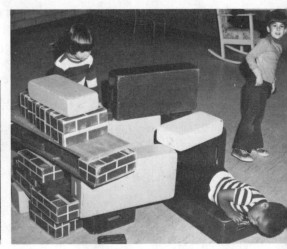

Conversations

It's a jail. A big one.

Get out, don't sock me. I'm gonna tell my mom,
know something, I'm gonna tell my mom.

No, it goes on top. Stack 'em up, stack 'em up.

Can I play?

Put the flying ghost up here.

Look, you knocked this down. Pick it up.

Hey, watch it. You do that side and I'll do this.

Come an help me. I need help. Let's move this. This
way. Oh, noooooo.

Let's have one door.

Over here. This is our hourse.

I'm helping you. Here's our roof.

We're making our own house. Neat-O.

Yeah, is that the garden?
Yeah, and here's the telephone.

sufficient space and materials are available for a number of children to meet their urgent need to make constructions, they cooperate readily and play harmoniously. The children have fewer disagreements than they do in many other play activities. Some children who do not play with the unit blocks very often become quite involved with cardboard blocks. Some of those who do play with unit blocks seem to be quite confident in transferring their abilities to this medium and will often be the ones who take charge.

Children of all ages frequently use the blocks to make private enclosures where they can stretch out and relax, look at a book, have a quiet time with a special friend, play with a toy, or whatever else they may choose to do.

OBSERVATIONS AND CONCLUSIONS

Children first begin to play with blocks by moving them from place to place, arranging them in various orders, and making enclosures and constructions with them. Through these activities, children discover that they are able to *rearrange* things, which gives them some degree of *control over their environment*. Playing with blocks obliges the child to control his *muscular movements* in order to *balance* one block on another without knocking the whole stack down.

After they become familiar with some of the simpler structures they can make with the blocks, children begin to expand them into more and more complex arrangements. With each new arrangement, they add to their knowledge about the use of space, *spatial relationships, size* relationships, the *weight* of the blocks, and related concepts. When they build a structure with blocks, they usually assume *dominance* over the particular space they are using. The unwritten "law" is that others must ask permission to enter into that declared space. However, since we have a plentiful supply of blocks to use, the children soon learn to *share* them, and also to build *cooperative* structures. In building cooperative structures, one child will often make the *plans, supervise,* and give *directions* to one or more others.

Block structures become *symbolic* of towers, walls, houses, fences, garages, apartment buildings, caves, schools, etc. As the children talk about what they are building and what actions they are going to perform, they exercise their *vocabulary* skills and their abilities to *verbalize* about what they are doing and what they plan to do. They also practice using their *imaginations* in developing the accompanying dramatic play.

UNIT BLOCKS

Wooden blocks in graduated sizes are ideal materials for the play activities of very young children. The two-year-olds will use blocks primarily for hauling and toting and transferring to other locations. I once watched a two-year-old laboriously pick up one 12″ block at a time, walk across about twenty feet of floor space, set it down, and walk back for another. He did not set the blocks down in any particular order or style. He was just "dumping them in this new location, one at a time. After he had moved all twenty-four blocks that were on the shelf where they were kept, he began the process of taking them all back, one by one. When someone tried to play with a few of the blocks that had been moved, he ran back very protectively shouting, "Mine." Even though he had not "built" in the way we think of building something, these were the blocks he was playing with and that was the way he had arranged them.

Six months later, I observed the same child, who was now three years and two months, building a structure by stacking the same blocks in four piles, right next to one another. It might have taken him longer to reach this point of maturity if an adult had given him the feeling six months before that carrying and dumping the blocks was not an appropriate way to use them.

In creative play, children must be allowed to explore at their own paces, use materials in their own ways, and be given the opportunity to learn on their own terms. The adult's role includes the responsibility of knowing where children are in terms of growth and ability in order to give verbal encouragement to progress to each new stage of understanding.

Most three-year-olds start playing with unit blocks by stacking them. Usually they start out with small, individual stacks, balancing each piece as they go along and starting over patiently if the stack falls down. Falling down, in fact, is part of the game. Gradually they will get involved in more complicated structures, often with a friend. Even though the children put considerable time and effort into putting a structure together, they still consider knocking it down to be fun.

Four-year-olds are more apt to start building large space enclosures either as their basic structure or as one within which to put the structure they subsequently intend to build. Children's first structures may be nothing more than a simple tower made from one block stacked on top of another one. As they continue to play with blocks, they continue to master new patterns which they are eventually able to combine in order to create more complex structures.

Five-year-olds may get involved in building multifaceted structures— whole communities, in fact, with intricate systems of connecting tunnels, doors, bridges, and secret passageways.

Conversations

This is the planetarium. You have to make the bridge
to get there.

You fix the city and I'll make the freeway come to it.
You need the city first, silly.

This will make it bigger. Acccch! It just won't stay.

This is just like a real house. This is a window. Hey
this is knocked down. I can fix it.

This is where you buy your packages . . . You have to
give us money.

Over this way. Push it, push it.

Your mommie's pretty strong!
Yes, she could *bing* you like that!
Don't talk like that. 'snot nice.

My mama bought me earrings and my sister a turtle
pin.
What's so great about that? I have a mouse pin.

I'm going to stay at school all night.
You are not going to stay here. You'll go home when
your mother comes after you.

By placing certain types of props very obviously in the same area where the blocks are, adults can sometimes motivate different types of dramatic play. A box of plastic animals might encourage the children to build a zoo or a jungle. A shoebox full of toy airplanes, may inspire an airport, especially if the children have ever been to an airport. Cars, a miniature gasoline pump, and similar props might encourage the children to build a service station or a parking lot.

OBSERVATIONS AND CONCLUSIONS

Children playing with unit blocks increase their *perceptual skills* as they judge the *size, weight, length, width,* and *thickness* of each block they pick up to use. They may start out by picking up any block at random. But after they have started to develop some kind of construction, they begin to evaluate the available *space,* the available blocks, and make a *decision* as to what they are going to build. Some children build one particular plan over and over again. Those who do so, have a basic construction process which they are familiar and comfortable with. But even they will eventually begin to elaborate and expand their basic structure into a more complex one.

How they *plan* their building frequently depends on how many children are involved in the activity. If several children are working on one construction, they may build just one structure *cooperatively* or work together on a multi-unit structure. On multi-unit structures, they may develop each unit cooperatively, or each may work on an individual unit, but eventually they see to it that the individual units connect with the other units that are being built simultaneously. These various types of experiences require the children to assess the *area* of the space on which the construction is being erected. They must also solve problems involving how *high* the structure is to be made, how to *balance* one block on another, how to bridge an open space, how many smaller blocks must be fit together to *equal* a larger block, and similar things. They notice that even though the blocks may differ in length, they are all of the same width and thickness except for a few planks and boards that are not unit sized. They know that they can place the blocks in a long row, but the row can be no longer than the space they have in which to use the blocks. They practice using blocks with the flat sides down or standing them *horizontally* on the narrow side. They also use some of the blocks *vertically,* and discover that they are a little more difficult to balance in that position. They like the *challenge* of the more difficult vertical positioning of the blocks and experiment with many ways to play with them in that form. As they experiment with the blocks, they discover that they can combine two or more to create new *shapes* for different types of connections and forms. Sometimes these shapes are *symbolic* of something they are building, and sometimes they are just part of the overall abstract or free-form *design*. Sometimes the buildings are very symmetrical and sometimes they are asymmetrical. But always the children have to contend with *gravity* in working out their patterns.

Both in creating the structure and in putting the blocks away after playing with them, the children are in an almost continuous process of *classifying* them according to their various dimensions, frequently grouping them by size. Even when they are playing by themselves they like to *verbalize* what they are making or doing with the blocks, and where they intend to put the different pieces. Sometimes they name what they are building. Sometimes they talk about the structure with their friends who may be helping them. They may discuss each step as they go along. But as they near completion, they begin to talk about how the construction will be used. They may play with various accessories, either miniature toys or symbolic forms, to act out the use of the construction. They like to answer questions about their buildings, and respond readily to new ideas given them by an adult. Sometimes, when they have worked hard on some particular construction, they like to *describe* it to interested people, often recounting exactly how they went about building it.

Older children (some 4's, most 5's and 6's) like to have signs made to label various parts of their more complex constructions. This helps to make *reading* a practical skill for them. They sometimes practice *counting* when they want to figure out how many blocks they have used, or how many they have in comparison to one of their peers. They may even practice *dividing* when, to build two separate constructions, they divide the available blocks between two people.

Children usually show satisfaction when they are working with blocks, and are usually very pleased with their finished product. They feel especially *important* when their building is allowed to stay up for two or three days—or even just for one day. This is an important booster to *self-esteem*.

HOLLOW BLOCKS

The traditional hollow wood blocks, which have long been part of the nursery school and kindergarten environment, provide play opportunities

Conversations

One of our blocks fell down.
This will make it bigger.

Who's the wise guy?

This is just like a real house.
This is a window. Hey, this is knocked down. I can't
play in here.
Get out.
No.

We're making a bigger one. We'll put something here
so we can get up on here.

Bum, de bum, de, bum.
Wait, don't hurt yourself.

I suck my thumb. It's going to fall off. My mommy
told me.

My mother said my daddy is ugly.
Oh, no. He is handsome. Girls are pretty and boys are
handsome.
My daddy is handsome and a boy, too.

You get to come to my birthday.
I know. I like ice cream.
Today when I went to the store, there were candy
hearts.

that know few boundaries. They are fun to use because they are versatile, imaginative, and durable. Expensive, but fairly satisfactory plastic substitutes that serve much the same purpose are available at a much lower cost. The bright, strong colors of plastic blocks sometimes seems to overwhelm the children, perhaps limiting their imaginations somewhat. If purchasing them, select the less brilliantly colored ones.

Three-year-olds playing with hollow blocks spend most of their time just making platforms, seats, and one-layer enclosures. Or they may use them as building blocks and stack them as high as they are able to. But if another child uses the blocks to set off an area or to create a setting for some dramatic play activity, the children will recognize the fact that they are in use and will not move them until the activity or play is over.

Four- and five-year-olds make specific things (see photos at the end of this section). They use the blocks for vehicles, boats, houses, grocery stores, shops, garages, hospitals, restaurants, hiding places, rocket ships, television sets, stages, orchestra pits, tables, chairs, jumping hurdles, and sometimes platforms to raise themselves off the floor.

Because of the limited number of hollow blocks available, the children frequently combine them with other "buildables." Sometimes props of one kind or another are used with the block structures. Sometimes these props might be suggested by the teacher.

OBSERVATIONS AND CONCLUSIONS

Because hollow blocks are heavier than the cardboard blocks and the unit blocks that the children play with, children are obliged to make different types of *movements* in transporting them from one place to another. This necessity increases the children's *gross motor skills* and also helps them learn about *similarities* and *differences* in weight. They also develop their muscular *strength* when they carry the blocks around. Since hollow blocks are sized by units like the smaller wooden ones, the children learn something about *size* relationships, how many blocks it takes to *equal* the next larger size, how many of the smallest blocks are equal to the largest size, etc. They find out what happens when they set a block in *rectangular,* upright, or *horizontal* positions, how high they can be stacked before it becomes necessary to climb on something in order to reach higher, and how many blocks it takes in the different positions to make a structure of a particular size.

Children frequently make very *symmetrical* constructions when they play with hollow blocks, which enables them to learn a great deal about making balanced designs. They find that because the blocks are

146

heavy, they are easier to balance on one another and that they hold their *balance* better than lighter weight cardboard blocks. Also, because these blocks are heavy, they help children learn about the *distance* between two points. They learn to judge just how long they can carry a block in a certain way to get it to the desired place without dropping it. Children sometimes comment on how hard or how far it is to carry the hollow blocks.

Children frequently use the blocks to *solve problems,* such as when they want to raise themselves up high enough to reach or to see over a certain place, or to barricade themselves from the rest of the environment, or to *divide* a play area between two or more children. They also use the blocks as *symbolic* representations for various types of play activities. Primarily, however, they use them in their dramatic play games to form houses, garages, vehicles, business establishments, or whatever else the particular game calls for.

CARDBOARD BOXES

Ordinary cardboard cartons are valuable motivational toys. Their uses are limited only by the children's imaginations. They can become trains, houses, cars, rockets, ships, airplanes, beds, caves, garages, airplane hangers, tables, stoves, sinks, stores, offices, cages, telephone booths, or any other place or object the children want them to be. Sometimes the boxes themselves lead to the development of some dramatic activity.

Mainly, children want to get into the boxes. Just setting out some empty boxes in an area where no other type of play is going on will motivate the children to explore and investigate. They will climb in and out of the boxes, turn them on their sides or upside down, share them, close the flaps while they are inside, peek in and out, change places, change partners, rest, and even become very possessive of the particular box in which they feel most comfortable (see photos at the end of this section).

Boxes should always be on hand for the children to play with. They can be used for entrance ways into classrooms. They can be used for partitions, area dividers, easels, roofs, and hiding places.

Serviceable boxes can be strengthened by gluing reinforcing layers of cardboard over the sides and by gluing strips of lathing onto the ends and centers of each side of the box.

Carpet samples, pillows, stuffed animals, rag rugs, pieces of fake fur cloth, and similar soft materials add to the luxury the child feels when using these very private, too-small-for-adults places.

147

Your cardboard box collection should include as many shoe boxes as you can store. They can provide several weeks of building-block play. If they are reinforced inside with solid-packed paper, sealed with tape, and painted, they will last much longer. If the tops are not sealed, they can be fitted inside of one another, which provides yet another type of play experience.

Whether a child is alone in a box or sharing it with others, the experience seems to satisfy his fantasies, appease his fears, and enables him to be separate from what the others are saying or doing—yet conscious of the security of being part of the group.

You can get appliance cartons from most department stores or stores that sell appliances like stoves, washing machines, and refrigerators. One such box should always be available for an "alone" place—preferably marked with a sign reading "One at a Time." The children will respect the occupant's right of privacy because they will expect (and get) similar respect when it is their turn to use the box. There should be no limit on the length of time a child may stay inside the box. Each person has different needs. If one box is not enough, use two at a time.

Colored Cellophane taped over the openings of an "alone" box will add another dimension to the experience.

Cartons used in the classroom can be painted by the teacher or by the children. Painting the boxes with acryllic or latex paint makes them both attractive and more durable. The children tend to respond to the colors by handling the boxes with greater care than they do unpainted ones. Other painted boxes can be kept on hand to use for carrying and hauling whenever a particular play activity requires.

OBSERVATIONS AND CONCLUSIONS

In playing with cardboard cartons, children discover that they can *control* the amount of *light* in a box by opening or closing the flaps. They notice that after they stay in a *dark* box for a while, their eyes adjust to the light and they can see in the darkened area. They also learn that noise coming into the box from outside is somewhat muffled, especially when the flaps are closed. And they learn that the *sounds* they make inside the box bounce back to them very clearly, even though people outside of the box may scarcely be able to hear them.

They discover that cardboard may be softer to sit on than wood or metal, but that it is not as *soft* as cloth or some other materials. They notice, however, that the cardboard is resilient, which causes it to give slightly under their *weight*. I have heard children comment about the

149

smell of the cardboard, especially when it is torn or wet. They find out that when it is *cold* outside, it can be *warmer* in a box. On hot days, they notice, the *darkness* of the box makes it seem *cooler*, but when they close the flaps the air becomes stifling and breathing is difficult.

As they explore boxes of different *shapes*, children develop an awareness of *comparisons* between *size, volume,* and *proportion.* They find out that they *fit* more easily into some boxes than in others, and, because of proportions, more comfortably in some than in others. They also find out that some boxes are large enough for several children to fit into, but others are scarcely large enough for even a tight fit by one person.

When children play with boxes, making *private* enclosures in which to seclude themselves, they enjoy the feeling of *seclusion.* They know their friends are nearby and they usually feel *safe* and relaxed. Sometimes being inside a box gets a little *scary,* but that is a part of the challenge of the experience. It helps children handle such *feelings* in situations where they know that just one or two moves of their body will get them out. And while they experiment with how to keep their places private, and still let in some light, or how to prop up the side of a sagging box, they acquire many basic *scientific principles* that they can later relate to other phases of their play and to life in general.

CARPENTRY

Young children who have had an opportunity to observe carpenters at work are always intrigued by the activity. The swing and blow of the hammer, the buzz of the saw, the magic of things being put together or taken apart look important, exciting, and tempting to children. Two- and three-year-olds enjoy playing at carpentry with toy tools. As early as possible, children should be introduced to real tools. The wood they use to saw or to hammer nails into must be a soft wood. The saw must really cut and the hammer must be heavy enough to drive the nail into the wood.

Certain rules should accompany the use of tools:

1. Tools are used only in the carpentry area unless an adult has made other arrangements.
2. The wood must be either fastened in a vice or nailed with *two* nails to the top of the carpentry bench before the saw is used on it.
3. Do not place hands too close to the saw.
4. Only two children at a time may play on one side of the carpentry bench.

5. Carpentry tools must be put away when not needed anymore.
6. Tools are only for woodworking and are not to be used for any other kinds of play activities.

For introductory experiences, provide only hammer, nails, and pieces of soft pine wood that can be nailed together. Allow children to use the hammer and nails for as long as they are interested. Provide help in learning to use the hammer if help is needed or wanted. You might try slowly hammering a piece of wood of your own next to where the child is, so that he can move his hammer to the rhythmic sound of yours. For beginning sawing experiences, provide lengths of 2" x ½" pine. Either place the wood in a vise or put two small nails through it to fasten it to the table surface, so that it will be held steady while the child is sawing it

In carpentry, even the three-year-old may be likely to name the object being constructed. The most usual object is some type of vehicle. Things the children have constructed can be painted and used as play materials.

OBSERVATIONS AND CONCLUSIONS

Children feel very important when they have opportunities to use carpentry tools and materials. As they become skilled in doing so, their feelings of accomplishment boost their *self-confidence* and *self-esteem*.

The use of carpentry tools requires children to *integrate* their muscular movements with their visual reception, thus developing *eye-hand coordination* and *visual-motor perception*. They develop the ability to use their muscles to control the force with which they use hammers, saws, and other tools. They learn to position the nonactive hand in such a way as to protect it from harm, but at the same time assist in the task being performed. For example, the child may use one hand to hold an object into which he is driving a nail. Or he may rest one hand on the piece of wood he is sawing in order to provide *leverage* to the body. Boys and girls later learn to obtain another type of leverage, the kind needed when they pull a nail out of a piece of wood with a claw hammer.

As their perceptual skills increase, children are able to *compare* the *size* of one piece of wood to another. They also learn to judge *thickness, length, width,* but probably not volume. They discover that it takes more *time* and effort to get a nail or a saw through a thick piece of wood than it does a thin one. They find out that the thicker the wood, the longer the nail must be in order to go all the way through.

They also learn that if a piece of wood is thin, they need to use a narrow nail to avoid splitting it.

Children using carpentry tools need to be aware of how close they are to other people, how much *space* they have to allow them to move their tools without hurting anyone, and how far away they need to be from another person in order not to be in their way.

As children become adept at using various tools, they discover that they can hammer or saw more efficiently when they use the same *speed* and *force* for a period of time rather than frequently changing *rhythm*. They also learn that they can accomplish more by a slow, steady rhythm than by quick, sporadic spurts of movement.

At first, children enjoy carpentry just for the activity itself, without feeling a need to make anything in particular. But as they acquire experience, they become interested in making things that are *symbolic* of particular objects or the actual objects. In creating these objects, they must develop the ability to make plans and to *sequence* the steps of the activity to achieve the intended results.

When children are given several varieties of wood to use, they learn to make *tactile discriminations* among the different kinds. They find out how to use sandpaper to obtain a smooth finish. When the *scent* of the wood they are sanding or sawing is very strong, children may develop a perceptual awareness of the smells of various kinds of wood.

Children usually talk very little while they are intent on their carpentry, but after they have finished they do like to talk about what they have done. This helps them develop the ability to recount the actual steps they took.

WOOD GLUING

Wood gluing is a realistic preliminary to woodworking with carpentry tools. It gives children the opportunity to explore the properties of wood by handling small scraps of many different varieties, sizes, shapes, and textures. Young children show great ingenuity as they create their designs and gravity-defying structures. Each piece is glued on for the joy of the single action, the next piece and next action flowing from the first, and leading to the third—but without preliminary planning or structured design. This is creative expression in action.

When presenting wood and glue to two-year-olds, it is important to limit the quantities and shapes to three or four so that they can concentrate on the act of fastening the pieces together. As they reach the age of three, children will respond to the surprise element of varying shapes and can easily handle the challenge of selecting from two or three dozen pieces.

Four-year-olds become very innovative and inventive in their handling of the wood gluing materials, and will sometimes cooperate on very large, long-term projects. In these cooperative structures, each child works as an individual, but amazingly, the finished project always evolves into a cohesive whole. When the constructions are finished they are sometimes painted with either tempera paint or a shiny water-based enamel. Sometimes they are painted all one color. Other times many colors are incorporated into one construction.

By the time children have reached five- or five-and-a-half, they frequently become interested in making symbolic representations in their creative products. These children may choose to structure their wood gluing to make an identifiable object—a house, doll bed, airplane, truck, or other such item. However, many children of this age are intrigued by the design possibilities of make-believe buildings and other structures, and do not try to label the thing they are making.

A variation of the wood gluing experience is in making wood collage designs. Provide flat wood bases and many small flat chips of wood with which to cover or partially cover the base. Again, for two- and three-year-olds, limit the number of pieces from which to choose and provide a small base on which to do the gluing. The older children will respond to the challenge of having an abundant choice.

OBSERVATIONS AND CONCLUSIONS

Creativity is very much in evidence when children use their ingenuity to build constructions by gluing small pieces of wood together. They develop *eye-hand coordination* as they pick up one piece of wood, put glue on it, then pick up another piece of wood and press it carefully against the glue, and then repeat the process until they decide they are finished. The children find it necessary to consider *size* and *shape* of each piece as they fasten the various pieces together. They discover that it is easier to glue a small piece to a large one than the other way around. When they have attached one piece to another, they find out that it takes a certain amount of *time* for the glue to set, and that usually the piece of wood that has just been stuck on needs to be held for a little while until the setting has taken place. They find that *thicker* glue holds better than *thin* glue but that it takes longer to set.

Children sometimes make very large wood constructions that they work on as a group. In these situations each child develops his ideas in reaction to those of other children. Cooperative construction generally starts out in a spontaneous manner, but leads to the children's growing ability to *cooperate* on a planned construction from the design to completion.

They learn that they can *change* the appearance of the entire construction by the type of paint they apply to it and by the colors they use. Sometimes they paint the whole thing a single color, which calls attention to the construction as a *whole*. On other occasions they decide to paint individual pieces different colors, which accentuates the separate forms that make up the whole.

CARDBOARD CONSTRUCTION

Closely related to the wood gluing is cardboard construction. It is harder for the child to do than the wood gluing because it involves larger pieces, a variety of fastening materials, and more intricate problems of balance and design. Two's and three's don't usually choose to participate in this activity, although they may do so if they wish to. The older children enjoy it, and can be very creative. To prepare for this activity, provide all kinds of cardboard boxes. Sometimes the children can paint all of the boxes different colors, and then select the ones they want for fastening together. Other times they build their sculpture first and then paint it, usually with just one color. This presents the problem of getting into all the little corners that were formed when the boxes were fastened together. In addition to white glue, provide Scotch tape, masking tape, wire, string, stapler, and paper clips.

In providing cardboard for this kind of activity, include roll paper tubes, box lids, very small boxes, and some pieces of cardboard scraps. It is advisable to limit the sizes of boxes to no larger than a shoe box. Breakfast cereal boxes are usually too flimsy. However, by judging the capabilities of the children who are using the materials, you may determine that they can handle the flimsier boxes satisfactorily.

OBSERVATIONS AND CONCLUSIONS

Although gluing cardboard is similar to gluing wood, the problems each variation presents are different. Wood constructions seem *permament* and durable, which is an impression children fail to get

155

from using cardboard. The great variety of *shapes, sizes, colors, textures,* and even the lettering on the boxes, all influence which boxes the children *select* to use and how they make a construction with them. I have rarely seen a child use the same type of construct pattern twice with this material. Since the boxes are never quite the same, children do not seem to relate the present experience with previous ones.

After the children select their boxes and start gluing them together, they are faced with numerous problems that require quick *decisions.* They find that some surfaces don't stick to each other very well because they are too *slick.* They discover that their construction suddenly becomes *topheavy* or gets thrown *off balance* because the last box they added is not positioned properly, or is too heavy, or is out of *proportion* to the other boxes. They generally find ways to solve these problems, such as using masking tape or string to hold the boxes together. To improve balance, they may decide to add another *support* coming up from the surface rather than reposition what they have already glued. They learn that through these and other means they can create different ways to achieve balance than those they used in playing with blocks.

The act of painting cardboard constructions *challenges* children to use their brushes in ways that will enable them to get into all of the intricate *corners* formed where the various pieces connect with one another. They have to figure out how to paint the bottom part of the construction without getting paint all over their hands which would happen if they held onto a part that has already been painted. The new positions in which they have to hold their brushes and move their hands exercises their *visual-perception* and *eye-hand coordination* skills.

STYROFOAM

The children who are involved in a program of creative play are always eager for new materials to experiment with. Offer them a tray with a variety of things that will stick into Styrofoam, such as stiff wire, hairpins, thin wooden dowels, toothpicks, pipe cleaners, artificial flowers, thin twigs, nails, and feathers. You might also put out some things that look like they would stick but won't go through the Styrofoam surface, such as straws and some flexible trimmings such as yarn, ribbon, string, telephone wire, scraps of cloth, and bits of cotton. In a box nearby, keep pieces of Styrofoam scraps, some

Styrofoam balls of different sizes, and some finished pieces cut into different shapes such as circles, triangles, rectangles or squares.

It is a good idea to give two- and three-year-olds only a small choice of items. They spend their time mostly sticking things into the Styrofoam and taking them out, over and over again. Four- and five-year-olds become very creative with these materials. They may decorate one piece by creating a very intricate pattern, using ribbons and yarn to weave in and out of the various things they have stuck into the surface. As the children become more familiar with the properties of these materials, they become more ingenious in using them and more imaginative in creating their designs. They experiment with the many ways in which the pieces can be fastened together to form stabiles (free-standing sculptural designs, as opposed to *mobiles*, which hang suspended) and other types of constructions.

By supplying different kinds of materials to use with the Styrofoam, the children can be led into other problem-solving situations. One day, as an experiment, I only placed toothpicks and Scotch tape on the tray for the Styrofoam. Immediately, one inventive girl (four and nine months) taped several toothpicks together, joining them end to end, to make long sticks on which to balance the "roof" as she called it. She made several such supports, and was very proud when the piece that she balanced on top, although it was twice the size of the base, stayed in place as a result of careful positioning before the girl inserted the toothpicks into the material.

OBSERVATIONS AND CONCLUSIONS

Children like using Styrofoam because it is so easy to fasten together. They respond, too, to its various *textures* and they like to rub their fingers over the surfaces. This activity tends to heighten *tactile awareness* which intensifies any other learning that may be taking place at the same time or immediately following. Some of this learning involves recognizing *similarities and differences* of various pieces of Styrofoam that are available for the children to make constructions with. Sometimes, after someone has completed a particular type of construction, other children like to try to duplicate it. However, the available pieces are always slightly different in shape and size from those used previously, so reproducing a construction with Styrofoam is not as easy to do as it is with building blocks that always retain the same shapes and sizes. The result is that children find themselves obliged to *create* new *patterns,* since they do not have the appropriate pieces needed to repeat any previous construction. The entire *problem-solving* experience involves figuring out how to *balance* the lightweight Styrofoam to keep it from tipping over as it is being worked with, how to make use of the *fasteners* that have been provided, and how to elaborate on the construction even though the pieces provided are very limited.

As the children figure out how to use different kinds of fasteners, they learn to cope with the differences between *flexible* pieces that can be bent into various shapes and pieces that are *rigid*. They also determine how to use pieces that can be stuck into the Styrofoam but are too light to support another piece.

⑨ Natural Science

Through the process of classifying and reclassifying, children learn about the physical properties of the things in their environment. As they become aware of different colors, sizes, shapes, forms, weights, textures, tastes, odors, and other physical properties, they constantly reclassify or modify what they have previously learned to make it agree with their new observations. Things a child learns as a result of responding to his natural curiosity provides the foundation for his intellectual development. The child's perceptual abilities are gradually refined, enhancing his ability to form concepts and to appreciate the value of those concepts.

It is important to help children realize that through their own investigative efforts they can make discoveries about the things in their environment. With each new time-saving, work-saving process and device, we take away from children one more opportunity to know how things are made and how they work. Scientific exploration should be based on a "do-it-myself" approach. Preschool children acquire much of their knowledge from their own sensorimotor experiences rather than from abstract thought. They learn more from their own movements than from observation. Still, they should be shown how to handle materials and tools safely. They should also be given preliminary clues as to what they are likely to find out as a result of certain experiences. Depending on their previous experiences and knowledge, different children need different amounts and kinds of verbal or other support during the various experiences. They should usually have an opportunity to evaluate what they observed or accomplished during the experiences.

159

PLANTS AND GARDENS

Growing plants and raising gardens, both indoors and out, help children expand their knowledge of nature. Children look upon preparing the soil for a garden as an adventure when they are given plenty of time and are included in the planning. Children who have the opportunity to watch their own seeds grow to maturity will have greater respect and appreciation for all growing things. It also provides important experiences in following through a specific plan to achieve desired results.

Use outdoor gardening space if it is available. The plot doesn't have to be large. If an outdoor area is not available, use garden flats. You can get them from a nursery or you can make your own. Children can also plant seeds in individual containers, such as flower pots or empty cans with holes punched in the bottoms for drainage. Styrofoam boxes in which cassette tapes are packed make good individual seed beds.

Plant both vegetables and flowers if you have enough space. Children should harvest and eat any vegetables they raise. They should also pick and arrange the flowers.

The tools they use should be real ones rather than toys. Use either the short-handled garden tools, which are available at most hardware stores, or use the small hand-gardening tools. Children should always follow a few simple rules when they use tools:

1. Do not leave rakes with the teeth sticking up, even for a moment. Always stand them against a wall or fence.
2. Do not swing, hit, throw, or run with any tool.
3. Put all tools away as soon as you have finished using them.

In preparing an outdoor garden, the children can first spend several days loosening the ground and removing all weeds, rocks, and other debris. The next step is to rake and level the area to be used. Children can perform these tasks as long as they are allowed to pace themselves, although they may need your help to see that they don't become overtired. Teams of three or four children can take turns digging and hoeing for five- or ten-minute periods. Each child should have a choice of participating or not participating, as in other play activities.

Plan *with* the children how to use the plot. If possible, take them with you to buy the materials for the garden. Arrange for the children to water the garden. Watering should be as much a part of the entire procedure as is the planting. Set up charts to ensure that everyone who wants to participate gets an opportunity to do so. Children also enjoy house plants and flowers grown indoors. Give them an opportunity to take care of these items too.

OBSERVATIONS AND CONCLUSIONS

The development of an *appreciation for nature* and for *growing things* is the most valuable result of gardening. Even so, children acquire a great amount of other knowledge from this experience. To begin with, they learn to *classify* the various things that grow as to whether they are food or flowers or weeds or other type of plants. They learn about the processes involved in growth and the *sequence* of growth from seed to sprout to plant to bloom and then to seed again. They learn that plants need *food* and *water* to grow, just like people do, and that the *sun* and other *lighting* also affects how they grow. Discussing these things with children helps them develop habits of *observation*, and encourages them to look for new growth, not only in the things they have planted but elsewhere as well. They observe that some things take longer to grow than others, and they expand their awareness of the passage of *time* by *comparing differences* in how long it takes various seeds to sprout, blossom, etc.

When children actually plant a garden, they have the opportunity to find out that there is more than one kind of *soil*, and that different soils vary in *color, texture, moisture, content,* and *density*. They are able to measure *distance* when they lay out equally spaced rows and to measure *depth* as they make the holes for the seeds. They learn that the *tools* they use have specific *purposes*, that they need to be handled in ways that are *safe*, and that the *rules* that govern their use make sense.

Children seem to experience a sense of satisfaction whenever they are close to the soil. This feeling makes it easier for them to *cooperate* with others and to *share* the tools and space, as well as the responsibility. They develop a sense of *group responsibility* that is lacking in most of their other play experiences. Perhaps they sense that it is too difficult to make a garden alone. All children involved feel very important when they see the things they have planted start to grow, and they all share in the *esteem* that is evident when they eat the foods they have planted or show others the flowers they have grown.

ANIMALS

Pets and other living creatures are important to children. They enjoy talking about them, including them in dramatic play incidents, and making up stories about them. This seems natural in view of the fact that animals, real or imaginary, are not as demanding on children as the humans they know are.

The care and safety of any living creature brought into the classroom must be given careful consideration. They should be adequately housed, protected from mishandling by the children, and, if they are dangerous in any way, caged. In schools, it is necessary to provide for weekend and vacation care when it is needed.

To provide week-end and vacation care for school pets, simply give the children an opportunity to take them home. With their parent's permission, children may "check out" a pet for a particular date. The pets are usually signed up for many weeks in advance. Two weeks ahead of time, the appropriate family should be reminded of the animal's impending arrival and given an opportunity to change dates. One day ahead of time a final reminder should be sent, still leaving time to arrange for a substitute. The pet is then sent to the child's home in a portable container along with enough food and simple written instructions for its care. This system can be used for week-end care as well as for short vacations and the long summer vacation.

Guinea pigs, rabbits, and white rats can all be handled safely by children. They are easy to care for, and children like them. Guinea pigs are particularly good because the young child can hold one without hurting it.

Fish, snails, salamandars, reptiles, and turtles may not be handled by the children, but they can provide opportunities to acquaint youngsters with the various needs of different types of creatures. Children should be encouraged to observe and imitate the movements of these creatures.

Chickens can best be introduced to the children by hatching some eggs in a classroom incubator. Two or three of the baby chicks can then be raised in a coop. It is a little more difficult to find families to take care of chickens during vacation periods than it is guinea pigs. They are best cared for in an outdoor coop in a permanent place, but it is possible to make arrangements to fit your own needs.

Silkworm caterpillars and butterfly caterpillars are also interesting to have in the classroom. Their presence may enable children to learn about the phenomenon of metamorphosis. Silkworm moths will live only for a brief period after emerging from the cocoon. Monarch butterflies might live two or three years, even in a cage.

Children are also interested in other kinds of insects. Try to have cages available for insects the children might bring to school. You can buy inexpensive insect cages at variety stores, or you can make your own from two plastic gallon-size bottles and some window screening. Cut the bottoms off the bottles, leaving a 2″ rim. Use a piece of window screening about 12″ high and long enough to be made into a circular cage that will fit snugly into the plastic bottle bottoms. Then secure the screen at top and bottom to the plastic pieces. The children should be allowed to observe a caged insect for one or two days, and then they should release it.

OBSERVATIONS AND CONCLUSIONS

Children generally appreciate the wonder and value of *living creatures* as an integral part of the entire world. As they gain experience with animals, their interest in them grows. They become aware of the many *likenesses and differences* between the various kinds of animals, and learn to *classify* them in appropriate groups, such as fish, fowl, insects, rodents, and mammals. Within these groups they learn to identify particular types and to *categorize* animals with which they may or may not be familiar.

In caring for animals at school, the child learns that other living creatures may depend on his own actions, thus leading to a sense of *responsibility* toward these animals along with feelings of *tenderness* and *love*. They learn that there are *right and wrong* ways to handle animals, both in regard to *safety* and comfort of the animals and the safety of the children.

10 Physical Science

Curiosity is one of the driving forces during children's play. Play gives children many opportunities to explore basic scientific concepts in a natural way. Traditional science programs for young children generally incorporate demonstrations and explanations rather than giving the children opportunities to explore and discover. If you do want to conduct some experiments for the children to demonstrate certain scientific principles, they will enjoy them. They accept them as magic. However, science is not magic. Neither is learning.

Giving children natural materials and tools will enable them to conduct their own research. Give careful thought to the preparation of the play areas in order to minimize the need for too many restrictions and directions, which can only inhibit investigative processes. Also be sure to set realistic goals for your science play activities. The important thing in preparing a science program for small children is to give them the opportunity to develop their innate abilities to find out for themselves how things work and what the things in the world are like. They should be encouraged to ask questions and to look for answers. They can learn to make observations and to discover how to respond to their observations. In addition, adult interaction helps them sort out the information acquired from these observations, which will enable them to form basic concepts. Later, they should be offered additional experiences that will permit them to test, verify, expand, or build on to those concepts. They gradually become able to recall previous observations that help them anticipate what will take place next. Eventually they become able to make predictions.

Children should have opportunities to learn the basic principles of simple machines: the wheel and axle, the lever, the inclined plane, and, if possible, the pulley. They have already been learning about simple machines in a variety of ways. For example:

Wheel and axle   Wheel toys and paint rollers.

Inclined plane   Slides and ramps; rolling things down hills; sliding bottle caps through paper tubes; structures built with boards and planks; screws and screwdrivers. Children seem to learn more about inclined planes if they work with materials that they can manipulate in order to change the angles themselves rather than if their experience is only with a stationary object, such as a slide.

Levers   Seesaws and claw hammers. Screwdrivers can also be used as levers.

Pulleys   Toy construction trucks (such as Tonka toys) that have a scoop operated by a crank. If it is possible to set up a block and tackle in one of the play areas, you can point out the relationship between the toy truck and the real pulley.

The adult's role is to motivate the children to play with the science materials and to be alert to their individual needs for help. Questions, demonstrations, observations, and responses to children's questions and observations are secondary to their freedom to use the materials as they wish.

Whenever it is necessary to set up special rules to govern the use of science materials, it is important to explain them in firm, simple terms to meet a specific need.

MAGNIFIERS

Magnifiers of all kinds are exciting and informative things for children to play with. They provide immediate feedback about the world. Children want to, within reason, and for however long they are interested. (See photographs at the end of this section.)

Along with the magnifying glasses, provide various special materials to look at from time to time. For example, mix water with table salt, epsom salts, and sugar in separate containers. Apply the mixtures to some colored paper and wait for the salts and sugar to crystallize. Then ask the children to examine the crystals under the magnifying glass and to report what they observe.

Magnifiers on stands are appropriate for the classroom, and they can provide ways to share many interesting observations. However, using them does not call for much movement on the children's part and they are apt to become teacher controlled. Being aware of this possibility should help prevent it.

Magnification instruments include telescopes and opera glasses. Real instruments are better for this type of play than toy ones—even if the real ones are old and battered. The lenses will be easier on the children's eyes. Toy magnifying instruments are often rickety and poorly made.

The use of different kinds of magnifiers can provide the background for other magnification experiences, such as observing water in a fish bowl. Children can make their own magnifiers by filling heavy, plastic transparent food bags with water, sealing them with rubber bands, and holding them over objects to be magnified.

An important word of caution: Because of the danger of fires, do not keep magnifiers in places where the sun might shine on them. Children of nursery school age should not be shown how fires can be started with a magnifying glass. It is also important to remind children that the magnifiers are made of glass and can break if they are dropped on hard surfaces. A simple check-out system will help keep track of them to make sure that one is not accidentally left out in the sun. It also provides an opportunity to remind children of the necessary precautions.

For storing magnifiers, it is important to keep in mind the changing patterns of the sun through the day. A place that is safe in the morning may not be safe in the afternoon.

OBSERVATIONS AND CONCLUSIONS

Using a magnifying glass is a wonderful *eye-hand coordination* experience, in which children become aware that they can move the magnifier to locate it where their eyes can *focus* properly on the object they are investigating. They realize that they can adjust their focus by moving the magnifier, rather than by moving the thing they are looking at.

As children observe the various things they see through the glass, they learn about differences in *sizes*. They finally understand that even though the size of an object appears to increase when it is magnified, the object does not actually change in size. As they look at things through a magnifier, they learn that *textures* vary greatly. They find some things that look like they are made of a single piece are actually a combination of many miniscule pieces that can be seen only when magnified, or that some things that appear smooth to the naked eye are actually very rough in texture or irregular in shape.

A more difficult realization comes about when they understand that various seemingly separate parts, as seen under *magnification,* actually make up a single entity. This perception leads to an understanding of *whole-part relationships.* Children also learn to make *comparisons* between two or more objects that appear the same to the unaided eye, but look entirely different under magnification, such as two different kinds of leaves or the grain of two different kinds of wood.

They learn that they can *discover* many things for themselves through the use of certain tools, such as the magnifying glass and that they can make things seem to change by how they *control* it.

Looking through telescopes and binoculars encourages the child to incorporate the concept of magnification with that of *distance* Children become aware that things that are actually *far* away can be made to appear very *close,* even though they are still in the same place. They learn that even though they are in *control* of the instrument, it is the magnifying glass that *causes* the changes in appearance.

MAGNETS

Magnets should be presented in ways that will enable the children to use them on their own terms. It is not necessary to show them that the magnets will attract certain items or will adhere to certain surfaces—the children will find these things out for themselves.

Esther, age five, was walking around the school with her teacher and a magnet, which was a new object to her:

Teacher: Why do you suppose it didn't stick to the brick?

Esther: Because the brick isn't painted.

Teacher: Why didn't the magnet stick to the painted wood?

Esther: It just didn't.

Teacher: Why did it stick to the metal window frame?

Esther: Because it's painted.

Fortunately, the teacher, trained in ways to encourage individual growth, did not tell Esther she was wrong. For the time being, Esther had achieved success. After exploring many surfaces of the walls and other fixtures in the room, she had found a place where the magnet would adhere. The fact that she deduced the wrong reason is not important. When she's ready, she'll know what magnets stick to or attract and that whether or not the object is painted is irrelevant. But her feeling of success at the moment will give her the encouragement to experiment further, not only in regard to magnets but in other areas as well.

Children can be shown how to extract iron by rubbing the magnet in dirt or the sandpile. The iron thus collected can be placed in the lids of shoe boxes. By moving the magnet around under the lid, the bits of iron can be made to move correspondingly. Miniature metal cars or plastic cars to which magnetic strips have been glued can also be made to move in this manner.

Play areas can contain two or three boxes, along with some boxes with various sized magnets and metal objects. These objects might include paper clips, washers, nails, screws, bolts, nuts, miniature metal cars, and similar items. Show the children how they can make the little cars roll by holding the magnet slightly in front of the car.

Children can be shown how to rub a nail back and forth on a magnet to magnetize the nail. They can pick up a paperclip or straight pin with the nail. Try using both an iron nail and an aluminum nail and see what happens.

Magnetic strips, available at stationary stores, can be used for hanging art work on metal file cabinets, metal window frames, and on other metal surfaces.

By mixing a variety of types of materials in one box, children will discover that magnets do not stick to paper, glass, plastic, wood, cloth, and many other materials. You can mix some pins and small nails in with a box of Styrofoam pieces and let the children extract the metal with a magnet.

Although you may introduce the children to some of the games and experiments that can be done with magnets, always keep in mind that the main reason for supplying the magnets is to stimulate play and self-discovery. Be sure not to allow your own fascination with magnetism to interfere with the children's freedom to make up their own games and experiments.

A favorite magnetism game is to make a pretend fish pond. Cut fish from cardboard milk cartons. Clip two or three staples into the fish. Use a magnet on the end of a string to "catch" the fish with. Children of four and five years can catch "fish" that are numbered from one to five or ten. The same idea can be used to "fish" for other metal objects such as washers and bolts. These can actually be immersed in a tub of water. The water will not affect the magnetism. Be sure to remove the iron objects from the water when the children are through playing with them. They will rust if they are not dried off.

Children can use small magnets less than an inch long to build miniature structures, learning as they go along how to manipulate each piece.

In addition to small hand magnets, it is desirable to have one or more very large magnets to experiment with. If you have access to a firm that deals in surplus electronic equipment, you might be able to locate a very large industrial magnet. Because of the weight of this magnet, it is usually kept either on a table or on a piece of wood that is mounted on rollers so that it can be moved. The magnet is of great interest to children—and to many of the adults. Anything that you can supply that will really encourage such involvement will increase the total value of the play environment. (If you do obtain such a magnet, be sure to warn people wearing wind-up watches to remove them because the magnetism could break the hair-spring. Electronic watches are not affected.)

Children can acquire additional experiences with magnetism by taking apart old radios. Children who are using a screwdriver on the speaker area of the radio will notice that the tool seems to adhere to the speaker. With further investigation, they will uncover the magnet that is at the center of the speaker. Magnets can also be extracted from the electrical motors of battery-operated toys.

OBSERVATIONS AND CONCLUSIONS

Children are fascinated with the effects of magnets. Using them gives children a great deal of practice in *eye-hand coordination*. They find the hand-movements are influenced by the pull of the magnet if they are holding the magnet near an iron or steel object. They soon learn to exert extra *muscular control* to control the magnet. At first they are confused by this force, but they soon learn that it is the magnet that is causing the change of movement, not their own lack of control.

They learn about short *distances* as they find out that the field of magnification extends a certain distance from the magnet itself. For example, they find out that they can roll a small toy car close to the magnet and when it reaches the *magnetic field* it will be drawn to the magnet. They expand their concepts of time when they see such magnet-caused movements occur almost *instantaneously*.

As they explore the environment with small hand magnets, they find out that the magnet will only adhere to certain kinds of materials. They try to figure out why it will adhere to some and not to others. When they reach the age at which they can use *logic*, they are able to discover that the difference is in whether an object is made of *metal* or not. If it is metal, they have to *classify* it further according to whether it contains iron or not.

When children dig in dirt or sand to remove metal filings, they form the basis for a future concept of the value of *minerals* and other substances that are extracted from the soil. When they play with these in a box lid and move them around with a magnet held under the box, they develop their *visual-perception abilities*.

DRY-CELL BATTERIES

Today's children accept electricity as a matter-of-fact phenomenon but they are highly interested in exploring it. One item that most children are very familiar with is the battery-powered flashlight. Flashlights should be provided without the batteries, but batteries should be available. Help the children learn to insert their own batteries when they want to use the flashlights. Since batteries become outdated, be sure to check the supply frequently and replenish them as needed. The size is not important but small flashlights with the small batteries are desirable because of the expense. But when you do buy batteries, get the best ones you can. The cheaper ones may leak. Before discarding a run-down battery, try putting it in the sun for a while. This will recharge, to some extent, batteries that are not too badly run down.

One activity that children enjoy with flashlights requires the children to cover their flashlights with pieces of colored Cellophane. The children are fascinated with the various colors they can produce when they turn on their flashlights. Usually two thicknesses of Cellophane are necessary to produce a distinct change in color. If you don't have a room that can be darkened, the children can play with these lights by rigging up a closed cardboard box with small holes to stick the end of the flashlight into and peepholes to look through. Two or three sets of holes in the same box will allow two or three children with different colors on their lights to use the box at the same time.

Six-volt batteries are also fun to use when children experiment with old motor-operated toys. Look for broken, motor-operated toys at the Salvation Army store, Goodwill, or similar shops. The motor in such toys is usually still good, but either the battery has rusted or the connections have corroded. Take the toy apart by removing the cover. You will find two wires connected to the motor. Lengthen these by fastening to them two additional wires about 18″ long. Remove about one inch of the insulation at the end of each wire. Connect these wires to each terminal of the 6-volt battery, and the motor will operate. This activity is safe and will lead children into many other experiments. Four- and five-year-olds can connect two or three broken toys together by the use of wires and operate them with one battery. Tape the wires to the motor with electrical tape to prevent the children from pulling them hard enough to make them come loose. See photographs at the end of this section.

If you take the time to paint the toys' gears with acryllic paint, the children will play with them even more. If there is more than one gear, paint each one a different color.

Other simple electrical games involve the use of light boards and buzzers. Naturally, as in all areas of the play environment, an adult should be nearby to give assistance, suggestions, and answer questions when the need arises.

OBSERVATIONS AND CONCLUSIONS

Further development of children's eye-hand coordination skills occurs when they play with batteries and wires. They have to move their hands carefully and deliberately in order to make the connections properly. While they are doing this, they have to keep their eyes focused on the point where the wires and batteries will contact. The children learn that they can make a motor work when they touch the wires to the two terminals on a battery and they can make it stop by disconnecting the wires. But they also learn that the battery caused the actual movement, not the person who touched the wires to it. After much experience, they learn that they can reverse the direction of the motors by reversing the terminals at which the wires are connected.

When children watch a motor go round they keep their gaze intent on the mechanism. This combination of the movement of the motor and the visual process intensifies each child's visual perception. They form a basic concept of electricity, which they will expand on as they mature and become able to handle abstract thinking.

Children who take motors apart in other play activities discover that there are magnets within the motors and realize then that there is some relationship between the motors and magnets.

With flashlights, children extend their concepts of the use of batteries for functional purposes. They delight in discovering that they can control the light by manipulating the on-off switch.

STETHOSCOPE

Some inexpensive play stethoscopes do work, but more often than not they are a waste of money. Purchase only the kinds that are actually used by physicians. Though these items are not very expensive, we do caution the children that they are very sensitive and tell them to handle them carefully

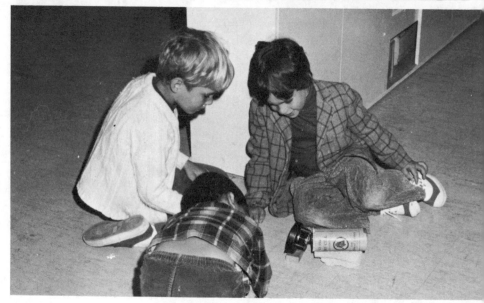

the way the doctor does. As a result, we're able to keep two or three working stethoscopes around for the children to use whenever they want to play with them.

Sometimes we may place a pocket watch on a tray with a stethoscope, so that the children can take turns listening to it. When this activity is offered, it is a good idea to have another stethoscope readily available for any child who is interested in it but does not want to listen to the watch.

Children can learn to listen to each other's heart beats, to various clocks, and to the guinea pig, or any other living creatures you may have.

OBSERVATIONS AND CONCLUSIONS

Stethoscope play is a valuable aid to increasing the *auditory-perceptual skills* of children. They actually hear heart beats with the aid of the stethoscope, and can learn to identify other sounds with it too, such as the ticking of a watch, the buzz of an electric typewriter, or the hum of a piece of electrical equipment.

In addition to the perceptual development, the ability to become *familiar* with the stethoscope as a harmless instrument helps to reduce some children's fears of doctors and nurses.

Children who have the opportunity to use real instruments, such as a stethoscope, in dramatic play activities become much more enthusiastic with their play and much more realistic in their *role playing*.

COOKING

All children are aware of the need to prepare food, even if it's just to wash or peel something or to put it in a serving dish. In their dramatic play and make-believe games, most children spend one or more phases of growth deeply involved in pretending to cook. This activity might take place in the sandbox, mudpile, housekeeping area, or doll corner.

In the creative play program, the children are given many opportunities to create their own formulas and recipes, such as in making play dough or in mixing their own tempera paint. In cooking, they are introduced to the concept of following a precise procedure.

The more freedom and experience children have had in creating their own procedures, the easier it is for them to be very precise when given exact directions to follow. They have already learned that they are able to be creative, imaginative, and inventive. They are learning that they are free to be individuals and that they are both trusted and respected as individuals. With this type of learning being emphasized, they are well able emotionally to attend to a very structured process such as is required in cooking.

The cooking we do in the creative play program falls into two categories: (1) Individual, one-serving recipes in which each child makes the full recipe for personal use. (2)Group-cooking recipes to which each child contributes equally for use by the group.

One-Serving recipes

For the one-serving, individual recipes, the ingredients of a traditional recipe are broken down into the number of servings it is intended to make. Thus, if a recipe calls for 1 cup of milk, and is meant to serve 8 persons, the individual recipe will call for 1/8 cup of milk. Since three tablespoons are equal to 1/8 cup, the recipe card which shows the recipe pictorially, can indicate 3 tablespoons of milk.

Individual recipes are frequently mixed in paper, Styrofoam, or plastic cups, or in small bowls. Cereal bowls are a good size for most recipes. We try to break most ingredients down into either tablespoons, teaspoons, or a fractional measuring-spoon size. If appropriate measuring cups are not available, we sometimes place a piece of colored tape on a graduated plastic measuring cup to indicate to the child how far it should be filled. This is good for eye-hand coordination, but does not allow the independence that an exact-size container provides.

When using eggs in individual recipes, the eggs are beaten up in a bowl and the required amount is indicated by tablespoons or teaspoons, as needed. One egg is equal to 4 tablespoons.

If a stove is not available, use an electric frying pan.

Jello

One 6-ounce package will make approximately 12 individual (3½ oz.) servings. Prepare cards for each of the following ingredients, with a drawing of the required number of tablespoons on each card.

1 Tablespoon Jello
3 Tablespoons hot water
3 Tablespoons cold water

Place the appropriate quantity of each ingredient in a separate bowl—enough for the entire group. Put a tablespoon in front of each bowl and place the appropriate instruction card behind each bowl. Give the children a 6-ounce Styrofoam drinking cup in which to put their individual ingredients. They may stir their mixtures with a teaspoon. Then place the cups in the refrigerator until the Jello sets.

Biscuits
One pound of prepared mix will make approximately 12 to 14 biscuits. Prepare cards for the following ingredients:

¼ Cup (or 6 Tablespoons) of biscuit mix
1 Tablespoon cool water

Use a container that holds exactly ¼ cup. If you don't have one, use tablespoons instead. Give each child a bowl for mixing the ingredients and forming them into a ball. Using a wide spatula, each child places his biscuits in an electric frying pan (400°) for baking. (The frying pan is, of course, carefully supervised by an adult.)

Pudding
One 3 3/4 ounce box of instant pudding mix will make 7 individual servings. Your "recipe" cards should read as follows:

1/3 Cup milk
2 Tablespoons pudding mix

Stir ingredients together in a 5-ounce paper cup until firm enough for spoon to stand upright in center of pudding.

Applesauce Pancakes
Use either canned applesauce, or have a group project of applesauce making beforehand. Prepare "recipe" cards as follows:

1 Tablespoon applesauce
2 Tablespoons beaten eggs
1 Tablespoon flour
Salt (Indicate that only a pinch is needed by showing just a few grains on card.)

Mix the ingredients. Bake in lightly greased skillet.

Conversations

How come these carrots are round? We always have
them long.
They don't look like carrots.

Do you eat dirt?
No, I like to eat things that taste better, like apples
and ice-cream.
Well, I eat dirt, because it's gooshy.

This orange looks like a baby cradle.
Rock-a-bye-baby.

It has to get cooked. Then you mix it up.
You just mix it. It's hot. Careful Oooooh.
I can smell it.

You can't cook it until you make it.
I know how to do this. My mommy showed me.
First you don't spill it. See, like this.
I'm going to have the biggest one.
Uh, uh. They're the same. Everybody has the same.

Count your pennies before you give it to me.
Juice is only two pennies. I have three pennies.
I can have three carrots for one penny.
I want a cracker. Can I have two crackers? I have two
pennies.

Oatmeal Cookies

> 2 Tablespoons brown sugar
> 2 Tablespoons flour
> 3 Raisins
> 1 Teaspoon oil
> 2 Tablespoons beaten eggs
> 3 Tablespoons oatmeal

Stir in individual bowls. Bake in lightly greased electric skillet.

Group Cooking

Group cooking requires each child to contribute something to the dish being prepared. Two examples follow:

Fruit Salad

Each child brings a fruit from home. Suggestions may be given to include 1 peach, 3 apricots, 1 apple, 1 orange, 1 banana, 3 tangerines, 20 seedless grapes, 10 strawberries, and so on. Each child washes his own piece of fruit and, under adult supervision, actually peels or cuts it and puts it in the salad bowl. This may be followed up by having everyone take a turn with the beater to make some whipped cream to go with the salad. Vegetable salad can be made this way, too.

Stew

The stew we make is sometimes made with meat and sometimes with just vegetables. The children bring the ingredients from home, such as 1 potato, 1 onion, 2 carrots, 2 single stalks of celery, 10 string beans, 10 green peas, and so forth. Each child prepares the vegetable he has brought from home, and puts it into the pot. An adult prepares the seasonings, giving the children equal turns to add the seasonings, liquid, and any other ingredients. If meat is included, it is first braised in an electric frying pan. Then the children slowly add the prepared vegetables. They take turns "supervising" the cooking and testing with a fork to see when the meat is cooked well enough. While the stew is cooking, the children set their tables, butter bread, and do whatever else is required for the "meal."

Other cooking ideas for the classroom are "make-your-own" hot dogs, popcorn, open-face sandwiches, and your own favorites. Vegetables grown in a school garden are especially appreciated.

OBSERVATIONS AND CONCLUSIONS

Cooking has many possibilities for important learning if children are allowed to cook according to the abilities of their own age level. When they make the individual recipes, they learn to follow written *directions* in a prescribed *sequence*, to *measure* accurately, and to carry out any accompanying verbal instructions. They learn that there are valid reasons for knowing *numbers* when they read a number in a recipe and then relate it to the act of *measuring* what they need.

They develop better concepts of *time* as they learn to judge how long it takes for different items to cook, bake, or otherwise become ready to eat. They observe that most things change in both *color* and *texture* as a result of the cooking process. When they have made something themselves, they are more aware of how it tastes, and thus increase their ability to evaluate differences in how things *taste*.

Children learn many of the same kinds of things when they prepare group recipes, except that more *verbal directions* are usually involved than written ones. They learn the value of *cooperating* doing an equal share of the work in order to achieve a desired result, and to get an *equal share* of the food. When they make the larger amounts than were called for in the individual recipes, they begin to learn to judge differences in *quantities* and measurements. They also learn that *large* quantities usually take *longer* to prepare and cook than *smaller* amounts, thus enhancing their perception of *time*.

When foods are in the process of cooking or baking, the children are soon aware that the smells come from the food. They get practice in identifying various *odors*. Part of the food preparation process involves such related learning experiences as *cleaning up* afterwards, *serving, manners,* etc.

11 Letters and Numbers

LETTERS

We attempted to find a wholesome alternative to pressuring children to read at an early age that would prepare them to learn to read in a natural way. This has led to the development of a program called "How-to-Make-a-Word." It is logical and it is free of any artificial pressure. It is an outgrowth of methods used in the remediation of reading problems with seven- and eight-year-olds. We use it with five- and six-year-olds.

From the first day of the school year, the children find, along with the commercial "educational toys," puzzles, crayons, books, miniature cars, paints, clay, and other classroom materials, an abundance of alphabet letters of many different sizes, colors, textures, and materials. Some are very small and others are as high as the average child in our school—approximately 36". (These can be cut out of 3-ply cardboard or plain cartons. By gluing together five or six thicknesses of cardboard, you can make letters that are 1" to 2" thick and have a strong textural quality.

In addition to having many alphabet letters to play with, children also have many opportunities to paint alphabet cut-outs. They also have opportunities to write letters with crayons and with thick pencils, as well as opportunities to trace the letters, outline them, and color them.

We refer to the letters by their sounds only, not by their names. Its very difficult to learn to always call an "M" by its sound, "mmmmmm," instead of its name, "Emm." It's very difficult for an adult to learn to say just the sound, without tacking on an "uh" or "eh" at the end, but it can be done.

We deliberately avoid using vowel sounds during the first five or six months of the year to discourage overeager parents from pressuring the children into making words. When the approach to the alphabet is slow, steady, and natural, the achievement seems to fall into place when the child is ready. Usually, about March of each year, many of the older children start writing words on their own. Or they start asking how to spell particular words. This does not take place during any formalized "reading" period. The materials are always available as one of several activities available at any given time for the children to participate in.

One rather difficult game the children really like to do is to form letters out of "puzzle pieces." For this game, curved and straight pieces to form letters of the alphabet are cut out of a piece of construction paper. We place them on a small tray or in a basket, and the child puts the pieces together to form a letter.

In all these activities, capital and lower case letters are used interchangeably. The point is for children to learn that both forms represent the same sound. When and how to use each can be taught much later.

After the children have used the letters for various activities for about six months and after they have learned about ten or twelve sounds very well, dictate to one child at a time the letters of a simple word, such as "fat" or "can." Then ask them to read the letters they have written. They easily realize that they have written a word. This realization may come at once, or it may take a while to sink in. After the child has learned the principle of putting the sounds together to make a word, the rate at which he progresses in actual reading depends only upon how much time you care to spend on it with him.

We don't spend too much time on it. We put out flannel boards and let them all play at making many words, changing the first and last letters to form different words. Sometimes the vowels are changed. They actually "play" with these letters, as we had hoped they would, and soon they begin to "instruct" each other. It would be easy at this time to introduce regular primers and other readers. Instead, we continue to encourage the children to engage in the many school experiences that have brought them to this great enjoyment of "how-to-make-a-word." We continue to emphasize how letters sound. And we continue to encourage talking, moving, building, dramatizing, creating, and all of the other play activities described in this book. For it is not any one experience or just "learning the sounds" of letters that has made this natural ability to read come about. It is the juxtaposition of all of those experiences that are appropriate and natural for the development of each individual's full potential.

NUMBERS

We present numbers in a somewhat similar way as letters. They are mixed in with the other play experiences and play materials and are treated contin-

Conversations

Do you know what 3 and 3 is?
Yeah, nothin'.
No, it's six. Hear that. Six.

When I'm five I'll go to my cousin's school. In the
same class.

What's after one hundred? Infinity, that's what.

I was sick yesterday. I had a temrature.
Me, too. I'm sick.
And I'm sick, too. Everybody's sick.

I went to Disneyland yesterday and got a hat.
I went, too, and the pirate shooted at me. I was
scared.

One of the fish croaked.
But fishes bodies are not like ours. They don't have
legs. They don't have arms. They don't have hair. But
they have fins.

What does she do around here?
She's the boss. She bosses the teachers.
That's not much. I never see her do anything.

uously, but casually. Our primary interest is to provide a foundation for acquiring an understanding of quantity, comparative relationships, and one-to-one correspondence. To count by rote has no value except as a "parent pleaser." But to be able to match the number "3" with three objects, to count how many chairs are needed to enable each child to sit down, or to comprehend the symbols on a card telling how many carrot sticks and how many cups of juice each person can take from the "juice table" are all useful. To recognize which object is *larger* or *smaller, thicker* or *heavier, longer* or *shorter,* or *closer* or *just the same as* is also useful.

So throughout the school day, and throughout the children's play, they are constantly being given opportunities to use numbers and comparisons to figure out answers. They are also given many different kinds of games to play using numbers. Play numbers of various sizes, thicknesses, textures, and materials (like the alphabet letters) are to be found in various play areas. Sometimes the children use them to make designs. Sometimes they play games such as "Find all of the 5's," or, "Now find two 4's."

Sometimes they find squares of paper on a collage table with numbers written in each square. An adult may suggest that the same number of items that are represented by that particular number can be glued onto the paper. Sometimes a slip of paper might have on it the numbers from one through six, with matching dots beneath. Nearby is a paper punch. The children who use these papers punch a hole on each of the dots, and then count to see that the holes equal the numerical symbol. Later they are able to punch the appropriate number of holes without previously marked dots.

Numbers are also cut out of large pieces of construction paper for painting designs on. Small numbers are supplied for pasting onto pieces of paper. Sometimes they are just mixed in with other items for the design effect. Sometimes they are used in conjunction with an equal number of other items.

Children enjoy using all kinds of measuring devices. They like to check each other's weight on bathroom scales. Height charts, which the children check and recheck for each other, are also important centers of interest. Tape measures, or sometimes just pieces of string, are used to measure the length of an outdoor play area, or a cupboard, or to find out whether or not something can fit through a particular doorway. Older children like to play with balance scales. They should be supplied with like objects of different sizes and weights to use on the scales.

During all of the months that the children are "playing" with numbers, they are also being given opportunities to learn to write them. Templates, numbers to trace, and numbers to copy are all set out in the various play centers from time to time. Sometimes they use real money when we have the Giggly Grape Store (described in Chapter 13).

By the time the children in the creative play program are ready for elementary school, they are also ready to do simple addition and subtraction in a natural manner since it has been a natural part of their everyday play experiences.

OBSERVATIONS AND CONCLUSIONS

The primary purpose of using letters and numbers in any form in the creative play program is to *familiarize* children with them. In playing with the letters, the children learn to recognize them by *sound*. They learn to use them to *symbolize* various sounds. They learn that they can create these symbols themselves on paper. By the time they are 5½ or 6 most children learn that they can combine these symbols to make words although some may learn this at an earlier age. The discovery that they can *make real words* by combining the sound symbols excites even the children who may have only learned seven or eight letter sounds during the school year.

Children who are not yet mature enough to read, will play with the letters, learn to reproduce them, and *may* learn to combine three sounds to form simple words, but they generally show little interest beyond that. Those who are ready to read indicate it by recognizing their own *accomplishment*, by displaying their feelings of *self-esteem*, and by looking for words in the books that they had previously only "picture-read."

In addition to becoming familiar with numbers, children in the creative play program become able to relate numbers to such concepts as *how many, more, the same as,* and *less* in ways that are useful to them at their particular age level. Two-year-olds learn to bring *one more* chair to the table. Three-year-olds learn to *divide three cookies between three persons*. Four-year-olds learn to *get enough cookies so that each person can have one*. And five-year-olds can learn to handle such complex tasks as *dividing* seven cookies between three children, or vice versa.

12 Creative Expression

Throughout the creative play program, children are encouraged to move freely, make choices, and use their imaginations. They find out that they do not always have to conform as long as they show consideration for other people and things and do not endanger themselves or others. Originality is applauded. Independence of action is given positive reinforcement. For example, the two children who invented the double-basket ball game (see photos at the end of the section on Balls, Chapter 5), were playing in the hall when it was not being supervised, which is not permitted. Instead of being reprimanded they were asked to take the game into their classroom and show it to the other children. Playing in the hall unsupervised was not made an issue of by a long lecture on it. The children, two five-year-olds, already knew that rule. But demonstrating the game to others reinforced the principle of invention and independence as well as the expectation that they play in a supervised area.

Children should always be given enough time and encouragement to handle their own wraps and other belongings. If a child is unable to put on a sweater, someone shows him how to slip his arms in first and bring it over his head. This helps the child develop independence of action, which is a prerequisite for creativity.

In any discussion of creative expression, it is important to recognize that a person can be creative without any particular kind of talent and that a person can be talented in one or several areas without being creative. A person may have unusual or extraordinary ability in some area, such as auditory awareness, eye-hand coordination, dramatization skills, overall body coordination, musical awareness, and similar things. This talent sometimes lies untapped throughout an individual's entire life for a variety of reasons. It may be that whatever that person does in the area of his particular talent is done in an outstanding manner, but with little orginality or inventiveness.

By the same token, children can be helped to develop habits of creativity that will serve them throughout their lives. Even if people have no natural talent for various artistic skills as we know them, creativity is needed for new ideas, new approaches to life, and for ventures into the unknown. Continued human progress depends on the fact that some people have the ability to think and act creatively. One of the factors that facilitates this type of thinking is an individual's freedom to express her or his own feelings and emotions. Some people have suppressed their feelings to such an extent that they often need to retrain themselves before they are able to recognize them. Unless we are able to recognize our own feelings, we find it difficult to recognize feelings in others and to help children learn to express some of these feelings through creative arts, such as music, dance, sculpture, language, drama and graphic art.

The experiences for creative expression presented in this chapter are geared toward helping children feel free enough and independent enough to enable them to allow their own ideas, emotions, and feelings to influence their actions. The activities are all approached in the context of play. As in other areas of the creative play program, the children are free to participate, or not, for whatever length of time they are interested. In their participation, within the limits of simple guidelines necessary for health, safety, and courteous behavior, the children are trusted to express themselves freely. In fact, the adults involved in the school find this same trust and encouragement because creative people and creative environments in themselves inspire creative expression.

Creative expression through art is enhanced by occasionally inviting a professional painter or sculptor to use our premises for a day or more as a temporary studio. This enables the children to observe professional watercolors and oil paintings taking form and to see a lump of clay gradually formed into a piece of sculpture. When these things are a part of the children's everyday play experiences, each child learns to be comfortable with the principle of creativity and to accept creative expression as a natural part of life.

ART EXPERIENCES

When children make their first exploratory marks with crayon or pencil on paper, they probably do so in imitation of what they see others doing. However, they soon become aware that through their own efforts they are able to change the appearance of the paper or other surface they are marking on. Even though they don't realize it, they are being introduced to the personal satisfaction that can come from creative expression through the use of art materials. The magic of making something appear where there was only a blank space has a gripping effect on young children and they are eager to experiment with more and more ways of creating that magic.

The earliest scribbles made by children are very important in the development of control of the movements of the hand in coordination with what the eye sees. As the child moves his hand all around the paper, his eyes pick up that motion along with the marks he is making. The eye movements follow the hand movements, and both motions are fed to the brain, which records the integrated action of eye and hand for future reference. Each additional experience of this type, as well as other movement experiences, enhances the child's potential for developing additional skills in the future.

The developing child should have frequent opportunities to scribble. Paper and crayons should be available in many play areas. Large pieces of paper should be spread out on the floor in one area or another each day so that children can scribble on them while they are in a kneeling position. Being on their knees gives them an additional sensory impression as a result of the pressure on their knees and the movement of their torsos caused by their hand movements. This position adds to the number of muscles that are moving at the same time, thus giving the children another opportunity to perfect their ability to integrate movements of the entire body at will. Playing music during this activity lends yet another dimension to the experience.

Crayons for the child of nursery school age should be thick so that he can grip them with his entire hand. Different kinds of paper should be available. Crayons leave their marks best on paper that has some degree of texture. Very slick or fragile paper should be avoided. The child should also have the opportunity to use paper of different sizes, shapes, and colors. These changes can motivate the child to try to use the materials in new ways.

Tempera painting should also be treated as a play activity. The painting experience can be varied in numerous ways (see photos at the end of this section). The colors can be varied weekly, according to the season, holidays, special events, or whims. The kinds of surfaces the children paint on should also be changed from time to time.

Pieces of Celotex are useful for putting painting paper on. These pieces can be placed flat on the floor, on blocks of wood, on table tops, or they can be propped up against the wall like an easel. All of these ways of painting should be used in order to challenge the children with the different types of postural requirements that each new position calls for.

Changing the shapes of the paper will increase the child's familiarity with such shapes as circles, triangles, rectangles, squares, free-forms, big autumn leaves, and valentine hearts. Use small pieces of paper and large ones. Sometimes, give the children oversized pieces of paper that two or three people can work on at the same time. Large rolls of colored Kraft paper or colored butcher paper can be used to provide a variety of shapes, sizes, and colors and it is less expensive than construction paper or art paper.

Another interesting thing to do with paper is to cut holes of various shapes in it for the children to cope with. Cut one or more circles, triangles, squares, or free forms into the paper. Give the paper to the children to paint on, but do not comment on the fact that the paper is different. Children will make their own observations according to their particular stages of development.

When two- and three-year-olds first see such openings, they may at first ignore them and go on painting as though the hole was not there. Soon, however, they begin to realize that the holes are shaped differently each time and that they appear in different places. They begin to take notice of them and then are faced with a problem-solving situation. What to do about it? Some will ignore the side of the paper to the left or right of the hole. Others will attempt to get to the other side of the hole by following its outline with the brush on paper. Some will actually lift the brush off the paper to avoid the hole completely and start painting on the other side of it. Eventually they become accustomed to such challenges and will begin to incorporate the holes into the total painting. The "negative space" then becomes just as important as the rest of the paper. Some three-and-a-half-year-olds will incorporate the shape of a hole into the type of shapes they paint. Many four-year-olds do this, and most five-year-olds do so most of the time.

Another novel way to prepare children's painting paper is to make some marks on the paper itself with crayon or felt marker. For example, for one week you can have all the painting paper marked with such symbols as three little circles in the lower right hand corner, or one big X in the middle, or one circle in the upper left corner and a square in the lower right corner. Use your own imagination and make no comment about the marks. Allow the children to make their own selections. Observe how they will start using their imagination to incorporate *your* marks into *their* paintings. Many children will ignore the marks. That is their right, since the paintings they are creating must be completely of their own design.

Still another excellent type of painting experience can be provided by offering only pennant-shaped pieces of paper for a three- or four-week period. In most art projects, the children select and position their own paper. For this project, however, it is a good idea to position the paper for anyone who wants to use it in order to ensure that the wide side of the paper is to the child's left. This placement encourages left-to-right movement of the brush or crayon. Most people, whether child or adult, automatically start painting or drawing on the widest section of the paper. As the design progresses, they work toward the right to the narrowest side of the paper.

In addition to varying the shape, color, texture, size, and proportion of the paper on which the children paint or draw, the texture of the paint can also be changed once in a while by adding various things to them. Sometimes the additive can be an ingredient that the children can smell, such as a little cinnamon in the red paint, for example, or some lemon juice in the yellow and green paints. (In using these types of paints, watch out for those occasional children who can't resist tasting anything that smells like food. Even with frequent reminders, some can't resist taking a little taste. This should be discouraged, even though the paints are not toxic.)

The consistency of the paint can also be changed by adding such items as Karo syrup, whipped soapsuds, or salad oil. Let the children explore the possibilities of mixing the paint with various ingredients themselves. They may not paint pictures with the resultant mixtures, but they will increase their knowledge that there is more than one way to achieve a goal. And any mixing movements by the child is an important aid to the development of visual-motor skills.

Another good thing to do is to give the children an opportunity to mix their own powdered tempera paint as often as possible. This is easy to set up as an independent activity by controlling the amounts of materials that are made available. Provide three- ounce-size paper cups or the plastic tops from spray bottles in which to mix the paints. If the mixing containers are small, children will only mix enough paint for themselves to use. The dry tempera powder is set out in clear plastic glasses along with scoops that will measure half a teaspoon of powder. Use eye-droppers or small ear syringes to add water to the powder. These materials not only give the child a controlled squeezing experience, but they limit the amount of water used. Once the powder and water are in the container, the child stirs the mixture together with an ice cream stick until it is the right consistency. Recipes are not provided. Each child learns through direct experience, and as a result of telling each other how to thicken or thin paint until it feels "just right."

Sometimes the beginning attempts at paint mixing result in colors that are very light and watery. We keep a supply of printed notes on hand, for the benefit of parents, to staple to the paintings on which all child-mixed paints are used. The note says, "Your child made the paint that was used on this picture." This reminds the parents to comment on the paint the child made rather than wonder why this wishy-washy painting was ever sent home.

Soon the children become adept at mixing brilliant, creamy colors. Invariably, the paintings they create when they mix their own paints show several things that may not occur in their ordinary paintings: (1) The colors seldom overlap one another—apparently they want every bit of it to show, and none of it to be covered by another color; (2) the paintings are much more symmetrical in design than previous paintings—perhaps the stirring movement puts the entire body into harmony; (3) The entire paper will usually be covered, even though the painting may be by a child who has never covered all of the paper in any previous painting.

The most remarkable thing about the paint-mixing experience is that it increases the verbalization of the children involved. In an experiment with twelve children under three years of age in which the participants were given various excercises for one week to help them develop a good wrist movement, we noted several interesting things. First, all of the children were able to stir the paint with a circular motion of the wrist, instead of using the up-and-down motion for mixing that is normal for that age. Second, the children's vocabularies increased temporarily. Children who had never been heard to speak at school were using words that their parents insisted their children didn't know. Finally, for approximately fifteen or twenty minutes following the brief stirring session, these children interacted in dramatic play activities, using conversations similar to those of children 3½ or 4 years old. In spite of these results, two-year-olds should not be included in paint-mixing activities. Stirring is an activity that children will naturally develop the ability to perform after they are approximately three and a half. Until that time, artificially teaching children to stir may speed up their abilities to use their wrists, possibly causing them to skip over an intermediate step of development.

Finger painting is an excellent way to help children appreciate the possibilities of expressing feelings and moods through art materials. Although it is frequently presented as a tactile experience, finger painting is also a rhythmic movement activity and an important means of emotional expression. It also helps to integrate the body and mind as the eyes follow the patterns of the hand movements and the resulting designs. Children should usually stand up when they are finger painting so that they can involve their entire bodies in the activity. Playing music while the children are finger painting can be exhiliarating for them, but it should not be done everytime they paint. Group singing can also enhance the experience.

The easiest kind of finger paint to prepare is the commercial variety, of course, which is usually more transparent than most preparations made from home made recipes. However, it is possible to make a good paint by mixing liquid starch and powdered tempera. Cooked starch made from plain cornstarch or a prepared mixture produces an even better quality of finger paint. Another way to make finger paint is to mix liquid tempera with a little library paste. Adding glycerin to the starch and tempera mixtures helps to keep it transparent and it provides a really good, slippery consistency that children like.

The colors of the finger paint affect children, as well as other people, in various ways. Once in a while ask them to think about the colors while they are painting. Then, when they have finished, ask them to tell you how the colors made them feel.

To enhance the children's appreciation of the use of art materials, show them that you value their efforts. Display their pictures and ask them to give you one of their art projects to keep.

OBSERVATIONS AND CONCLUSIONS

Art projects give children a special opportunity to use their hands and fingers and the small muscles of their arms. This exercise develops overall *fine motor control* and their *visual-motor perception*. One of the important learnings that results from doing two-dimensional art work is that children become familiar with the many ways in which they can *divide* up *space*, balance that space so that it is pleasing to the eye, and relate the different spaces to one another. They develop an awareness of *similarities* and *differences* of *colors, shapes, lines, textures, symbols,* and art materials. This increases their perceptual awareness, and helps them to learn to classify and put things into various categories.

They become aware that there are many ways to achieve *balance* in their art project. They learn to utilize lines, colors, *color contrasts,* and shapes, as well as *placement,* to achieve balance. As they become more skilled in handling the materials and in making pleasing-to-the eye art works, they grow in the ability to make *aesthetic* judgments.

Through their various art projects, children learn that it is possible to express *emotions* and *feelings* both through the way they handle the materials and the colors they select. They learn to use their *imaginations,* invent new shapes and ideas, and as they grow in maturity, they learn to use art as a means of *communicating* with others. All of these achievements culminate in increased *eye-hand skills* and growth in *self-esteem* and *self-awareness.*

Children who have an opportunity to use a wide variety of art materials learn many elementary concepts related to each particular material. For example, when they use starch and tissue paper to make collages they learn about *transparency* and about how two colors can *combine* to make a completely different *color.* When they make their own paint, they also learn about the relationship of one color to another and how to create *new colors.* When they add various ingredients to paints they learn still more about *textures, odors, cause and effect,* and *changes.* Because different types of paints take different lengths of time to dry, children learn to compare *wet and dry.* They also formulate more mature concepts of *time.*

When they use crayons to fill in solid areas or to make scribble pictures, or when they move their arms around to apply paint to paper, their eyes pick up the movements, again enhancing *visual-motor perception.*

Through collage projects they learn still more about *textures, balance,* colors, and *likenesses and differences.* They expand their knowledge of such concepts as *thick* and *thin, heavy* and *light, wide* and *narrow, hard* and *soft,* and *big* and *little,* as they use the various collage materials.

Actually, there are so many things that children learn through art experiences that are appropriate to their age, that it would be close to impossible to enumerate them all. Therefore, children should have many opportunities to participate in art experiences of all kinds.

MUSIC EXPERIENCES

Music is an important element of the creative play program. Musical instruments of many kinds should be available to the children in various areas of the school. Drums, tambourines, and other percussion instruments that are used during organized music times should also be available when a child feels like using them. Only a few things should be put out at any one time or in any one place. But some instruments should always be available for children who are interested. A two-octave miniature electric organ can sometimes be used to play songs by ear. An autoharp should be placed on a convenient table that is easily supervised. Children can then explore it when they wish—either with a pick or with their fingers.

A piano with the front panel removed will enable the children to see the insides. The children should be allowed to play with the piano whenever they wish, although, as in all other school activities certain rules should govern its use. At our school, the children are reminded to use not more than one finger on each hand at a time. They are allowed to feel the strings while someone is playing in order to feel the vibrations. But they may not pull the strings or poke them.

Spontaneous singing may take place at anytime. Sometimes it may be started by a child at play. Sometimes an adult may introduce a song that seems appropriate to what the children are doing. Sometimes a few children will stop what they're doing and ask an adult to play some musical "circle" games with them. These games should incorporate the appropriate tune and words, but they do not have to be played in a structured circle, which is too inhibiting and too complex for most preschool children. In the creative play program, the children have many experiences with painting, drawing, pasting on round-shaped paper, and playing with circular objects, which makes understanding the concept of "circle" comparatively easy for them. However, to respond to the verbal and musical calls of the circle games is enough of a task at one time, without the added restriction of staying in a circle. Children are more creative in their expression if they are allowed to move freely during the game. There may be occasions, however, when the circle form seems to fall into place spontaneously. Like standing in lines, it's something that doesn't need to be *taught*. It's a basic human grouping form. When it happens naturally, and the group is in a harmonious mood, let it be. But avoid punitive attitudes and tensions if one or two have difficulty staying with it. If it starts to get out of hand, break up the circle altogether and use the free approach. I use the word "scramble" for such a purpose. If the group is too large to move together easily, you can try breaking it up into two circles.

Not all music in the creative play program is spontaneous. Frequently, during the period just before going home, the children will join together with their teacher for a kind of unwinding time. During this time they may have quiet conversations, evaluating what has taken place on that day or what is planned for the next day or some other future time. They may play some quiet games, and they usually have about five or ten minutes of group singing. It is amazing how large a repertoire of songs they acquire from these brief daily sessions.

Parents who can sing or play musical instruments can be invited to help the children become familiar with various aspects of music. In our school, one talented parent comes twice a month to conduct fifteen-minute singing sessions with each age group. Her style of teaching is very structured. Since the children have so little pressure in their everyday play, they respond well to this experience. The structured, patterned lesson becomes a novelty rather than the other way around, as is usually the case.

For the child to enjoy *both* movement experiences and singing experiences to their fullest, do not try to combine the two very often. Two- and three-year-olds are only confused by the need to respond with both expected song and expected movement. It is too complex an activity for them at this age, and can only be accomplished through rote training, continued drill, and emotional pressure. Then, at best, the performance will be artificial and stilted.

Children of this age can perform simple hand movements in accompaniment to simple songs they know how to sing, but usually they will sing better and more clearly without the hand movements—or they will follow the hand movements better if an adult does the singing. Some four-year-olds can fairly easily combine hand movements with singing, although many children of that age will also do only one or the other at one time. By the time the child is five, he enjoys "acting out" some of the songs he sings, and many children can both sing and move together at this age. Most six-year-olds are well able to do both.

Musical experiences for children should include many opportunities to explore pure sound. For example, occasionally put out equal-sized glasses with different amounts of water in them for the children to strike with a light mallet or small stick. Music boxes, toy xylophones, wind chimes, and similar devices will also enhance the children's awareness of differences in sounds. Point out to them the source of any unusual noise. Listen for sounds on group excursions, or even while in the play yard. Ask the children if all cars sound alike. Do all birds make the same sound? Do all dogs bark the same way?

OBSERVATIONS AND CONCLUSIONS

As a result of musical experiences during the creative play program, children have many opportunities to develop *auditory perception* and *auditory-motor control*. They also become able to *coordinate* the musical sounds and rhythmic beat of what they hear to different ways of moving. *Listening* to and producing music, intensifies the awareness of such words as *slow* and *fast*, *soft* and *loud*, *happy* and *sad*, *softer*, *louder*, *the same as*, and other concepts. They learn to identify various sounds, *rhythms*, and *tunes*.

Children frequently use their imaginations to create their own songs, to *express* their *feelings* or *moods*. They learn to enjoy singing, being in an orchestra, and listening to all kinds of music. They become interested in musical instruments, in where the sound comes from, and in the musicians who play them. This sometimes results in a wholesome *appreciation* of good music, whether the child has natural talent or not.

DANCE AND BODY MOVEMENT

Dance and body movement give the children another kind of opportunity to express themselves emotionally. One way to make a change of pace after a period of movement activities is to say, "Let's play like you're all beautiful dancers on a television show, and you're all wearing beautiful clothes and twinkling shoes. I'll play like I'm turning on the television to see the show, and then you start dancing all over the stage. The whole room can be the stage. Does someone have some more ideas for the show?" When this suggestion is made with great enthusiasm, the children respond with enthusiasm. "I'll be the announcer," one child says. "I'll dance on my toes," says another. "I'll be a giraffe," declares Kevin, who simply cannot bring himself to imagine that he is a real dancer. We put a waltz on the record player and the show begins. Children who have had experience in responding to the rhythmic beat of a tambourine are able to move interpretively to the rhythm and melody of the dance music. Sometimes props, such as scarves, streamers, hats, or other items are available to wear or wave as they dance. Sometimes children take one-at-a-time turns and other times they perform in groups. This activity is always festive, almost party-like.

Sometimes body movement is combined with dramatic expression to give children experience in showing emotions. Here is one way to create this kind of experience:

Everyone think of something quiet. Don't tell me what it is. Just think about it inside you. Are you thinking about something very quiet? I can't even hear you move. Now, stay right where you are and play like you're something very, very tiny. Ohhhh. You're so teensy-weensy I can hardly see you. O, my goodness! All of a sudden you're something very fat! And now you're very strong. Now pretend you are something very, very wiggly. Now you are something that doesn't move at all. [Continue with other movement suggestions such as *shakey, upside down, sideways, bent over.* Then gradually move into expressions of "moods."] Now you're very angry. Someone was very mean to you. Now *you're* the one who is mean. Let me see you look mean. Meaner! Now you're very funny. And very important. And very, very smart. Now something very scary is coming, and you look like you are afraid. Now you look all alone. [Continue with as many different types of emotions familiar to the children that you can think of.]

It is a good idea to start this kind of game with everyone sitting on the floor. If the play is going well and everyone seems to be enjoying it, the activities may be repeated with everyone standing while the leader encourages a greater amount of mobility. For example:

And now you're someone very mean and you are moving all around the room looking for someone to be mean to. Now you are so happy you just can't stand still.

Everyone present, whatever their age, should be included in all dance and body movement experiences. No one should be on the sidelines watching. Even visitors to the program are encouraged either to participate or leave the room. In creative experiences, the differences between adults and children are only relative.

OBSERVATIONS AND CONCLUSIONS

Children in the creative play program have many movement experiences, which help them make the transition from goal-directed creative movement to dance movements very easily. They learn to *pretend* that they are performing dancers, and show great *self-awareness* in *coordinating* their movements with the music, and in *interpreting* the music to the best of their ability. They realize that they may interpret the music in their own way, however, and that they have the freedom to *express* their own *ideas, moods,* and *reactions.* They move softly when the music is soft, quickly when the music is fast, vigorously when the music is vigorous, and to make other appropriate responses. They learn to incorporate the whole body when they *respond* to the rhythm. This is a very great accomplishment for young children because the control of various body parts develops at widely differing rates.

As they move about in response to the musical accompaniment, they become skilled at evaluating *spatial relationships*—that is, to comprehend where they are in relation to other people. They must determine quickly not only how to move but where to move. These movements help them refine their abilities to pretend to be other beings than the ones they are, and thus extend their entire concept of *symbolization.* They learn to use all aspects of *body language* to communicate various ideas and expressions, including sounds made by using various parts of their bodies, facial expressions, postural expressions, and other aspects of their being. Using props helps to extend even further their awareness of *spatial relationships,* the utilization of *available space,* and their own *position* in that *space. Kinesthetic perception* is increased, along with general musical appreciation.

DRAMATIZATION

By *dramatization,* we mean the acting out of stories and plays for an audience, rather than the dramatization that is a part of children's regular imaginative play. Children in the creative play program are free to express their emotions, under controlled conditions. They are encouraged to be honest about their feelings, and the adults who are involved with them try to reflect back to them what they may not be able to express. Children are not told that they should not cry. Instead, they should be told, "It's all right to cry.

You must really feel bad to need to cry like that." If you know the reason the child is crying, you might say, "I bet you really feel mad because Jason kicked you. That would make me feel very angry. I might cry, too." With this approach, you can say to this child on a future occasion, "I know you're feeling very angry. Bobby won't let you have the car you wanted to play with. Show me on your face how angry you feel." If you are patient and persistent, children will respond to this type of assistance in acquiring control of their emotions without suppressing them.

Games, dance, and movement activities can all be used to help the children practice expressing emotions and feelings. When emotional expressions can be accompanied by movements, the release of tension and emotions is greater.

With these kinds of opportunities to practice emotional expression, most of the children in the creative play program become very good actors. Sometimes, after an adult has told them a story, they will act it out while she repeats it. At the beginning, this acting out may just be pantomine. But after it has been repeated a few times, the children begin to take over the lines themselves. They don't need costumes or other props because these children have had many opportunities to develop vivid imaginations. However, if props are introduced, they take them in stride.

On one occasion at our school, a teacher and a few children started to act out "Billy Goats Gruff." When other children heard the threatening noises of the Troll, they came to join in the game. By the time the game was over, thirty-four Billy Goats had crossed the bridge, and each one stopped to talk to the Troll saying that his brother was bigger and would be better to eat (see photos at the end of this section).

The children's all-time favorite story is "The Three Bears." Other favorite stories for play acting are "The Three Little Pigs," "Humpty-Dumpty" (complete with a story explaining that he fell off the wall because he was so lazy that he fell asleep), and "Little Red Riding Hood."

Another favorite dramatic presentation is a movement activity that we call "Rainbow." It begins with about nine or ten children all holding balloons. They pantomine the following:

One day the sun was shining brightly. [Children holding yellow balloons cluster together to form the sun.]

A big cloud came and chased away the sun. [Children holding blue balloons group together to form a cloud; they move in front of sun while the sun children run to a corner of room.]

The thunder roared. [Children make their balloons thunder by snapping the surface, hitting them together, etc.]

Conversations

Who's going over my bridge?
It's only me—Billy goat gruff.

"I'm going to get you," said the Troll.

Somebody's been eating my porridge and ate it all
up.

Somebody slept in my bed and there she is.

Don't eat me bears. Don't eat me. Let me go home.

The rainbow went all over the world, all over the
world, all over the world.

Hello, folks. Now is the show. We're gonna sing for
you. Be still.

. . . An then the big dragon came and chased
everyone away. But the Owl said, "I'll save you."
"Help, help. Here I am. Everything is fine."

What's your name.
My name is Puppet. I want you to be my friend.
O.K.

I'm Bobo the talking dog. I can say bow-wow. But I
can talk to.
What do you want.
I want to find the elephant. Did you see the
elephant?
We don't have elephants here. We can't.
Then just give me my dinner.

Dramatizations of this kind can be created for almost any occasion. As long as the story plan is kept very simple, the children will enjoy pantomiming the actions as they come along. They like stories involving animals, vehicles of all kinds, and happy family occasions.

One favorite plot is about a little pig that talks only to children but not to adults. When some children want to bring the pig home to live, their mother objects. The children insist that the pig can talk, but as long as the mother is present the pig only says, "Oink, oink." The children become very dramatic in trying to coax the pig to talk. The audience becomes involved, too, saying, "Talk, pig, talk. Please talk." Finally, when the tension has built up to great dramatic heights, the pig finally talks to the mother and the story has a happy ending.

I originally presented this story to the children as a marionette show, purely for their entertainment. But the plot was so child-oriented, they quickly picked it up as their own property, and are frequently seen dramatizing it, with or without an audience.

Sometimes the dramatizations that develop are enactments of experiences the children may have had on a field trip to a bakery, zoo, pet store, or dairy, for example. Or they may reenact the ride on the bus. With guidance, the children will introduce and portray many more characters than is usually observed in their spontaneous day-to-day dramatic play scripts.

Many times the dramatizations that take place at school are simply brief moments of interplay between adult and children. For example, a teacher might say very dramatically, "Oh, I'm so glad you came to school today. I've been waiting and waiting, all night long." Children will respond to this kind of game quickly and may answer, in perhaps a falsetto voice, "Oh, yes! You've waited long enough!" This will go on for a few moments with everyone using false voices and exaggerated movements. Soon the teacher will bring it all back to normal by a casual comment such as, "Okay, you had better go to your rooms and see what's there today."

LANGUAGE AND STORYTELLING

Children under the age of five have very small vocabularies and must therefore rely heavily on their imaginations in order to communicate with others. Adults who are involved with young children must also rely heavily on imagination to bridge the gap between a child's vocabulary and his or her own. Some "television-nurtured" children may actually be able to *say* more words than their pre-television counterparts, but that does not mean they are able to understand what those words mean. Understanding comes with use—and this is where creative play comes into the picture. The creative play program, with its emphasis on movement skills and self-determination and its deemphasis on periods of enforced silence, which is so much a part of many traditional classrooms, provides a setting in which children have an opportunity to develop their language abilities to the fullest at their individual rates of growth and development.

A child's cultural and family background has an effect on how he develops his capacity to communicate. Children in bilingual families may be confused by the necessity of processing two different grammatical structures at the same time. This does not indicate a language deficiency, but does indicate a need for more time to assimilate the rules that apply to each separate language. Teachers commonly make the mistake of failing to give such children sufficient time to absorb what has been said to them, translate it into their native language, think of the words for a response, and then translate those words back into the second language for verbalization. Impatience in this kind of situation makes the child feel stupid and appear that way to others. By showing patience and displaying an expression of confidence while waiting for the child to process his response, the teacher can help him feel good about communicating in the second language.

In many areas of language development, children learn a great deal from their peers. Adults who are involved with the activities of the children in the creative play program can provide a focal point for language development on the part of individual children. Because there is always a place for meaningful conversation, language experiences do not have to be "created." They are part and parcel of the program, with casual communication, both verbal and nonverbal, something that everyone is aware of.

Teachers frequently say, "Come and talk with me. I want to hear about what's been going on." She might say that to an individual or to a group. If it's to a two-year-old, the teacher might add, "You played with the toys and then you put the big truck on the bottom shelf." The child may nod his head. Or he may answer, "I played with toys. Put truck away." Either way, he is having a meaningful conversation with another person. Many three- and four-year-olds are so used to being told to be quiet that it always seems to surprise them when an adult indicates that he would really like to have a conversation.

The subject of the conversation at this age is not nearly so important as the opportunity to communicate with an interested party, someone who is really trying to find out what the child is "feeling" or "experiencing" than in worrying about grammatical constructions. These will come in time.

Some of the principles of language encouragement that guide the adults involved in the creative play program are:

1. Helping children be aware of and to recognize sounds.
2. Helping children attach meanings to words.
3. Helping children *listen* to what others are saying.
4. Helping children recall past events.
5. Helping children project future events.
6. Helping children describe present events (their own actions).
7. Helping children verbalize their feelings.
8. Helping children realize that other people appreciate, understand, and enjoy the words they use.
9. Helping children describe things they see.
10. Helping children describe things they hear.

Before children can learn to read, they have to be aware of, and then know the meaning of, words. In order to do so, they need unlimited opportunities to hear and use those words. As in all areas of learning, it is easier for a child to acquire an understanding of what words mean by using them. When children are given the trust, the freedom, and the help they need in order to do things for themselves—at their own levels of ability and experience—they acquire language skills as a result of the natural course of verbal interaction that stems from the need to ask questions, exchange information, make observations, answer questions, and express feelings and ideas. Adults respond to the children and encourage them to respond to each other. The children feel free to respond to the adults.

Sensory-motor and perceptual-motor skills are important to the acquisition of language skills. Therefore, it is important to provide activities that promote the development of these skills in all phases of the play program.

Dramatic play encourages verbal communication between children. Observant adults can use these experiences to introduce new vocabulary, just as they do in *all* areas of the program. Inasmuch as dramatic play goes on wherever the children are, it is a good idea for the adults to take note of all the children's conversations and verbalizations, and then suggest new words whenever the opportunity arises. Adults should make every effort to show recognition and appreciation for the children's language abilities as much as for their other areas of growth.

One way to encourage creative expression through language and story telling is for the adults to set a pattern and then provide ample opportunities for the children to respond to it. One effective technique is to write down the children's conversations and read them back to the children later —with as much seriousness as reading stories from a book. The children involved in the "story" are delighted to hear their conversations read back to them, and their peers who recognize the characters in the story are just as interested. When children see an adult writing near their play area, they sometimes ask, "Are you writing *me*?"

In addition to recording what the children say in play situations, it is a good idea to set aside time for individual children to dictate stories for an adult to write down. The adult should point out that particular words are represented by various written letters and that they can be read again at any time just like stories in books. A good way to encourage a child to tell a story is to say, "If you tell me the story about your picture, I'll write it down and then we can read it later." (Conversely, it is not a good idea to ask three- or four-year-olds to "illustrate" a story they have already dictated. There is no point in confusing the creativity of making up a story with the noncreativity of making a specific illustration. Five-year-olds, however, begin to show signs of wanting to tell stories through their paintings and drawings. When these children show evidence of having reached that stage of development, they are encouraged to illustrate their dictated stories—if they want to.

When you ask a child to tell you a story, it is sometimes helpful to offer him a topic. One interesting technique is to show the child a picture that he will find something in to react to. If the child has a limited vocabulary for his or her age, this is an opportunity for you to help extend that vocabulary by asking questions about the picture and helping to articulate the answers or reactions by suggesting appropriate words.

The following stories were dictated by three children in response to a picture of a burning house. The children were 3, 4, and 5 years old.

Three-year-old boy

The house is on fire. A hook and ladder will come. The man will put water on it. It will be all gone. Then mommy can cook dinner. That's all.

Four-year-old boy

A little boy was playing with matches. So the house burned. So his daddy got mad at the boy. So the fireman came and fixed it. He put it all out. There was no more fire. So the dad didn't get mad anymore. So they lived happily after.

Five-year-old girl

There was a house and it was on fire. It was flaming all over. The people in the house were getting burned. Some of them were getting killed. The fire engine came. No one could go in because it was too hot. They said, "How did it start?" The mother said there was a red thing in the fireplace. She said it blew out of the room. She said her children were in the house. She said her baby was playing on the floor. The children didn't hear the fire so they stayed inside. No one could get them. The mother wished she had another baby, so she got a new baby. And she got a new house. And they lived happily ever after. And the fireman said not to make a fire again.

The child's ability to reason, to use imagination, and to complicate the plot seems to increase as he grows older. From the earliest age, children tell stories that are as interesting to themselves as they can make them.

Here is an example of a story dictated by three children—3, 4, and 5 years old in response to the question, "If you could be any animal you wanted to be in the whole world, what would you be?"

Three-year-old girl

I would like to be an owl. I would like to be a monkey. I would eat things. I would like to be a bee. It stings you. I want to be a bird. I would fly with wings. I would like to be a flower. A green flower.

Four-year-old boy

I would like to be a dragon. I would have fire inside of me. Fire is all different colors. If someone tried to hurt me I would spit fire at them. I would be a big dragon. I would be purple. I would have big teeth.

Five-year-old boy

If I could be an animal I would be a giraffe. I would get leaves with my long neck. I would like to go through the crawlbox. I would just bang through the wall. I would bite trees down because I have very sharp teeth, very very very sharp teeth. I could carry things in my mouth.

Here are the responses to the question, "What if you could be anything you wanted to be?"

Three-year-old girl

I would like to be a daddy. I would work. I would clean house. I would lock gates. I would go to the store to get candy. I would answer the door if somebody is at the door. I would get the toys and put them under the tables. I would draw things.

Four-year-old girl
I would like to be a baby. I would cry. I would like to be a mommy. I would work. I would pick babies up. I would call somebody. I would eat food. I would feed babies. I would go in my room. I would put pictures up on the wall. I would put records on the record player.

Five-year-old boy
I want to be a motorcycle. I'd do skids and mow everyone's yard up. I'd go "rrrrrrrrr." I'd lay skids in everyone's face. Smoke comes out of the back of the motorcycle. I'd lay skids on the street.

Here are some responses to the request, "Tell me a story all your own."

Four-year-old girl
Mommie picks the babies up. She puts the babies down. After that the babies cry because they want to be picked up. She goes outside and puts the flowers down. She comes inside because the babies are still crying. She comes inside to get her shorts and then she goes back outside. Then she stays inside. Then Daddy takes sister to the donut shop.

Five-year-old boy
Bambi was a little Bambi who was lost in the woods. He bumped into an old bear and asked the bear if he can live with him. The bear said, "O. K. you can live with me."

Five-year-old girl
These people are on a boat. It is going to China. The people have to move the paddles to make the boat go. There is a mother and a father and all of the children, too. They are getting ready to have a party. The party will be later. Everyone has to wait. There is a nurse to take care of the people. Everyone is laughing at the party. The boat is going now. The party is on the boat. They are in the water. When they got to China the party was all over.

Four-year-old girl
Once upon a time there was a Mother Goose. She went to the market. She buys her groceries. She buys her milk. She buys some sodas. She went back home. She takes care of her children. She went to bed and the children went to bed, too. Then she read some books and she cooked and she ate some food. She made words out of paper. That's all.

Five-year-old boy
Once upon a time there was a wolf and a cat. They were friends. They played together a lot. This great big lion came up to them and said, "I'm going to kill you." The wolf and the cat ran away. They got lost in the forest. A little

talking butterfly came around to lead them back to their house. The wolf and the cat didn't remember their mother. But they remembered their daddy. They went out for a walk around the block. They couldn't go into the forest anymore. They lived happily ever after.

Overweight five-year-old boy

This is a story about three chickens. One chicken went for a walk and found a rooster and ate the rooster. The third chicken found a leaf and ate it for supper. Then the second one took a shortcut to the forest and found a bear, and ate the bear. He just pecked at it and then ate it. Then the three chickens went home. The end.

Four-and-a-half-year-old girl

Do you know the story of a little girl that broke her leg? Well, this little girl was walking down a street and a car passed her and ran over her leg. Because she was walking in the street. She got hit. So she had to go to the hospital. So her Mom took her to the hospital. So she had to go into a cast all the way up to her neck. The doctor said she might stay away from home three or four days. The mother wasn't so upset because that wasn't that long. The father was working at the hospital. The father worked with the kid so she wouldn't cry because she was only four years old. They went back home and after a few days they took the cast off. And they lived happily ever after.

Four-year-old girl

I have a new puppie. His name is Mr. Sam. He poopies outside. He sleeps at night. In the morning he wakes up. He eats doggie food. I fix it with hot boiling water. He's half Brittany Spaniel. We don't know the other half. He's this large. An inch big. He has little white boots on his feet. He's all black. He has a black nose. Part of his nose is black. The other part is white. He has some toys. He likes to play with us. He cries when we're gone. He bites. But just when he has problems. He likes me.

Sometimes several children in a group contribute to the development of the plot of a story. They usually include each other's names as well as the name of their teacher or other adults who are of interest to them. The following story was created by a group of four-year-olds who were inspired by a dignified older gentleman who occasionally volunteered to do odd jobs at their school.

One day Mr. Sam came to the school and sawed some wood outside. He broke his leg. He said, "Oooooouch." Michael and Alicia took him to the doctor. Liana and Jennifer went, too. Mr. Sam said to the doctor, "You're a Dodo." The doctor said a bad word. Jennifer stood on a chair and fixed Mr. Sam's leg. He could walk on his leg and could still come to the nursery school. The end.

Here is another created by the same group of children.

> One day there was a mommy who washed the dishes. A monster came and snuck some food. The mommy locked the food in the oven and the monster couldn't get it. He broke the oven and ate the food. The little boy named Marc fell on his head. Maureen helped Marc up. The monster got punched in the nose by the mommy. The monster got his hat and ran away. He had a yo-yo in his hand. It was the little boy's yo-yo. The monster put the yo-yo in the dungeon. Mary unlocked the door and somebody got the yo-yo. The end.

Asking each child to add an original sentence to the story encourages creativity. Four-year-olds are beginning to understand the sequencing of events. They also show evidence of the need to establish a hero—a need that becomes more obvious as they grow older.

> There was a dinosaur called Willie. He went to the store and bought some ice cream and bubblegum and mushrooms. He bought candy, too. He broke the store because he was a giant. He went back where his cave was. Somebody locked him in the cave. He broke his cave open and broke the door and got out. All the dinosaurs came and ate lunch with him. Then Willie locked the children in the cave. Some alligators came and let the children out.

> A mommy and a dog went to the store. Their car didn't work. The mommy told the dog to stay at the store and she got the car started. They bought some milk, a candy bar, a bubble gum for the daddy. A monster came and a snake came. The snake went around the monster's leg. The monster flew away and got untangled with the snake. The mommy and the dog were scared. The mommy and doggie hid in the box. Then they went home. The daddy said, "Where did you go?" The mommy said, "We went to the store and were buying some food. We were buying bubble gum for you." The daddy said, "I bought my own bubble gum." So the bubble gum was for the mommy."

Now here is a third story by the same group of children. Notice how they incorporated parts of the previous stories into their new ideas.

> A dog went to the market. He played with the toys in the market. He fell and broke his leg. He broke his knee. Jennifer helped him. She took him to the doctor. The doctor gave him a brand new leg. Jennifer took the dog home. She named him Bridget. The dog had spots and he was ticklish. Diana came and took Bridget for a walk to the woods. There was a snake there. He was a good snake and his name was Sammy. The dog and the snake became friends.

POEMS

Nursery rhymes are frequently children's first exposure to the rhythm and drama of words. Unfortunately for too many children, no further opportu-

Conversations

That's the United States of America.
It is not, it's a house. Oh, I see a shotgun.
Don't touch it. It'll hurtcha.
That weapon doesn't hurt. Only in war.
I think they're killing him. Touch him. Ohhh! Blood.

Some boys grow up to be captains. Some don't. My
daddy did.
My dad's a kid, because he grew up out of a kid.

I know what that is. I seen that. It makes cars go.
Whrrrrrrr! That's how they go.

This is your house, little horsie. Sleep in your house.
Now it's fire.

All the trucks are going on the freeway. They'll crash.
No, see? They didn't crash.

I have a house like that. I has big stairs and you go up,
and up and up. Bobby cries. It's dark in the stairs.

Turn the pages. Turn the pages. Turn the pages.
Ohhhhh. Look. O.K. Next page.

I know that word. M-o-t-h-e-r. I know that spells my
Mom.

This is easy. The cat said, "Meow." The dog said,
"bow-wow." The cow said "moo."

I don't like boys. But I like daddys because they give
you things.

nities to become familiar with poetry are forthcoming. Children should be exposed to many kinds of poetry and helped to memorize short poems, which they can repeat over and over again. Even if they do not understand all the words, children come to appreciate the power and beauty of words.

Playing word-rhyming games will encourage children to be aware of words. For instance, the teacher can mention a word and ask the children to suggest other words that rhyme with it. Then teacher and children together can make up a poem using the rhyming words. For example,

> Aunt Mary
>
> Sat on a berry
>
> It was scary
>
> Said Aunt Mary

Children can also be encouraged to make up poems with words that are "opposites." This idea is fairly easy for children to comprehend once they are able to make simple comparisons, such as the opposite of *hot* is *cold.* Once they become familiar with such word pairs as *big/little, hard/soft, under/over, tall/short,* and so on, they will eventually become aware that such words as *yesterday, winter, comfortable,* and *asleep* also have "opposite" meanings. Here is a poem based on this concept by a five-year-old:

> Big is tall
>
> But little is small.

A four-year-old made this one up:

> That is hot.
>
> This is not.
>
> But it's cold
>
> Because it's old.

When these games are played, it is important that every child involved be encouraged to contribute, even if he has missed the point. For example, once when a very eager, but not very skillful four-year-old was asked to make up a rhymed poem, she contributed this:

> Afraid, afraid, afraid. Cry.

When she noticed that the teacher was writing down her poem and that the other children were not interrupting her, she went on. Her finished poem read:

Afraid, afraid, afraid.

Cry.

Afraid. Run, run.

No! No! No!

Big.

While the child was dictating her extraordinarily sophisticated poem, her face expressed fear during the first three lines. Then she looked very stern as she said, "No! No! No!" Then she produced a big smile when she said, "Big."

OBSERVATIONS AND CONCLUSIONS

Creative expression through dramatizating and storytelling and general opportunities for conversation and other language experiences guides children's physical development and the things that they learn in the same directions. First, and most readily evident, is the increased ability at overall *language skills,* including *pronounciation* of words, *differentiation between sounds,* sentence and *grammatical construction,* and, most importantly, increased *vocabulary* and knowledge of the *meanings of words.* They develop the ability to *recall* and *describe* past events, tell things in proper sequence, and project what they are going to say. They learn to use *descriptive words* to explain what they have seen or heard, and also to express their *feelings.* As the child uses language in coordination with various movements involved in play and other experiences, he develops *auditory-motor perception,* which enables him to distinguish sounds as he moves. Children learn to identify words that *rhyme* or that are the opposite of each other. These dramatizations and language experiences help children clarify ideas derived from other experiences, and to unify many separate learnings into a more coherent whole.

I also observe that the advancing ability to use language improves children's *self-esteem, cooperativeness,* and *social skills.* They also learn to *mimic, portray others, echo, satirize,* and display other dramatic skills.

Children who have these opportunities develop their *conversational* skills and grow in their ability to *listen* and respond to what others are saying.

13 Dramatic Play and Other Forms of Make-believe

Children interweave several different types of play into their make-believe experiences in order to accommodate their own needs and the immediate needs of the other individuals or groups involved. The simplest of these is *imitative play*, or *role playing*, in which the child is pretending to be someone else. When more than one child participates, it is called *dramatic play*. A more complex form of dramatic play is *sociodramatic* play, which involves a sustained plot. All of these activities can also be called *symbolic* play inasmuch as most of the objects and situations used are symbolic rather than real. A newer approach is to call much of this kind of play *mastery play* since it is being pursued by the child for the purpose of helping him to understand, and thus master, his world. Recognizing these variations, we will primarily use the term *dramatic play*.

Infants first learn about play by imitating their own sounds and movements. They accidentally make a sound and then they try to repeat it. Once they are able to do so, they play with it. In other words, they repeat it again and again, just for the pleasure or satisfaction that doing so gives them. They also imitate what their caregivers do. Games like the universal "peek-a-boo" and "pat-a-cake" give small children further opportunities to imitate. These activities and others performed with adults and peers enable young children to learn about social interaction. It is interesting to note that the most popular games are those that have some type of interactive rhythmic component. For instance, the child makes a noise, then the adult makes a noise. You blink your eyes; the child blinks his. The child throws down a spoon; the adult picks it up—over and over again.

Beginning attempts at verbalization and the first words children master are learned by imitation. They make their first sounds by chance, but usually

214

by the time they are a year old they are repeating certain common sounds. Because adults repeat these sounds back to them, they learn the meaning the adults have given these sounds. Soon they imitate such words as *ma-ma, da-da,* and *bye-bye.* They even learn to imitate the motion of waving the hand for *bye-bye,* and also discover that the wave can be used to symbolize the word.

By the time infants have become toddlers, they have learned to do many other things through imitation—feeding themselves with a spoon, drinking from a cup, shutting a door, opening a cupboard, turning the pages of a book, hugging, and kissing. Much of their play is imitative. For example, I was watching seventeen-month-old Debra playing with some of her toys in the living room. Suddenly she picked up her doll, walked into the bedroom where there was a doll bed. She flung the doll into the bed in a rather haphazard manner, then threw a doll blanket on top of it. She repeated the action several times. She was obviously trying to imitate the way her mother did this. Finally, she dragged the doll out of the bed again by one leg, put it down on the floor, and "fed" it from a play baby bottle.

Then she picked up a purse that had been given her, emptied its contents, put everything back, then emptied it again. Then she looked in my purse and said, "Keys." Taking the keys from my purse, she walked to the front door of the house and held them up to the surface of the door. She showed no interest in looking for the keyhole. She then took the keys back to my purse. Until now, her actions were purely imitative of actions she had observed in her home. But now a new element entered. She liked the jingle and feel of my large yellow plastic key ring with all the little rings and other attachments on it. She decided to keep it. She walked to the place in the living room where she had orginally been playing with her toys when I had arrived. She sat down on the floor, keys in one hand, and began to manipulate some of the toys with her other hand. She allowed me to play with her, once in a while mentioning "keys" to let me know she knew they were mine. But her attitude indicated that she knew that I would eventually take the keys away from her. This had probably been done by others in the past on numerous occasions. When she realized I wasn't making any such attempt, she seemed to become more relaxed and trusting. She held on to the keyring for approximately two hours. Eventually, as she was absorbed in being carried by her daddy, eating dinner, and other stimulations, she let go of the keyring and I quietly slipped it into my purse. A little later, saying good-bye, I was rather taken with the very sweet smile she gave me. I smiled back. Her response was an immediate, "Want keys."

The entire episode, which was part exploratory play, part testing, part social interaction, part imitation, and part routine, enabled me to recognize how this seventeen-month-old child could show anticipation, trust, and persistence within a three-hour time span. Her use of "persuasion through a smile" to attempt to obtain the keys again made me more aware of how even toddlers can use personality, intrigue, persistence, and other means to try to get what they want. She also demonstrated how much personal likes and dislikes influence their activities. These by-plays of interpersonal relationships are going on at all times, but we are usually so involved in the activity itself or the interaction that we don't realize that they are made up of separate parts. Careful observation of a child at play, paying particular attention to his conversations and interactions with others can provide valuable insights into the child's personality.

In the following instance, three-year-old Christa was playing with a doll. She put it in the doll bed, covered it with a blanket, and then fed it. Then she took it out of the bed, put it on the floor, rearranged the bedding, and put it back in the bed. She covered it again and fed it once more—more imitative play. However, being three years old, she was probably also role playing. She was not just imitating her mother, but was trying out how it feels to act like a mother. One interesting thing about this episode was the object Christa used for the baby bottle. It was the cone-shaped base on which colored stacking discs are supposed to be placed in descending sizes. Needing a baby bottle and not finding one, she improvised. The cone became *symbolic* of the bottle. By listening to Christa's conversation, it was evident that the doll was symbolic of a real baby, and that all the equipment she was using was real, as far as she was concerned.

In some cases, it is the child, rather than the doll, that is symbolic of the baby. The child may sometimes have played being mother or father or some other family member, even the dog, but sometimes he needs to play baby. A child might volunteer to play baby simply because, in the make-believe play that is going on, someone needs to perform that role. Sometimes a child is "ordered" to by another child. Sometimes a child who has suffered rejection will find comfort in the doll bed.

The solace that can be derived from pretending to be a baby can be described in the experience of Morgan, aged three. Morgan was new in school and was finding it difficult to adjust to the new situation. He was receiving nothing but negative reactions from the people around him. Not only was the school experience new, but he was in a strange town, having come with his mother and twin brother to visit his grandparents while his father was away on a three-month trip. On his second day at school, Morgan suddenly looked around the room, retreated to the doll bed, covered himself with a blanket, and sucked his thumb. From this secure vantage point he listened to the story the teacher was telling the other children.

Morgan was role playing being a baby, but he was not engaging in dramatic play. He repeated the experience several times during the next few days. By Morgan's second week in school, he was able to function in a more socially acceptable manner and was getting acquainted with the other children. His opportunity to play at being a baby had given him a chance to study the situation in the new environment and relieved him of the acute discomfort of not knowing anyone, not understanding what was expected of him, and not being able to control his own impulses.

A few weeks later I observed Morgan playing in a housekeeping situation with two other children. He was the mother, busy cooking "supper for daddy." More at ease in the group situation, he could now utilize his play time to explore some of his inner feelings about his father being away for so long. It was reassuring for him to play the mother role. When his mother prepared dinner at home, his father usually arrived shortly afterwards to eat it. He was still role playing, but now his activities were in the context of dramatic play.

As children grow in experience and maturity, the sequencing of their play experiences becomes more complex and more specific. They may devise elaborate rules for the various types of make-believe experiences, adding to the rules each time they play. The rule making itself becomes a kind of game. As the children become more adept at using their imaginations, their expanding abilities at fantasy require the balancing influence of their simultaneously emerging sense of logic.

EVALUATING CHILDREN'S NEEDS

Careful evaluation of the children's dramatic play activities may provide some insights into the personalities of their parents and the atmosphere of their homes, as well as vital clues to their individual needs. In making such observations it is important to be aware of several things:

1. What the children are doing may not necessarily reflect traumatic or anxiety-producing situations. Children recreate their everyday world in order to acquire a better understanding of it and the roles or people in it.

2. Dramatic play offers children safe ways to explore their awareness of their own growing abilities and changing roles and their relationships to others.

3. Sometimes their play activities are being used as a means of expressing antisocial ideas and impulses.

4. The words and actions the child uses in imitation of his parents are usually grossly exaggerated and may not necessarily reflect the exact language used in the home.

5. Some activities may stem from the need to work out anxieties or misunderstanding about impending events of which the children have been informed, or have heard about, but do not understand. An expected baby, moving to another house, a single parent's remarriage could all fall under this category.

6. Children who repeat one kind of dramatization over and over to the exclusion of other types may be doing so because of an ongoing burden in the home. There may be a new baby, an invalid or dying relative, bickering parents, pressing economic problem, alcoholism, impending hospitalization of a family member, or similar problems. Some children also replay a single traumatic episode that may have lasted only a moment, but made such an impression that it is difficult to handle, even though it is replayed over and over again.

7. The children may merely be responding to their ongoing need for creative expression.

EXPRESSING FEELINGS AND EMOTIONS

In all of these situations, dramatic play experiences are important in that they provide for children to examine their feelings. In their nonplay experiences, children are constantly reminded to control their natural feelings and impulses. Adults have usually had their own feelings suppressed in exactly the same way, making it sometimes difficult for us to remember that children's emotional reactions are legitimate—whether they are pleasant or unpleasant. Feelings affect children as strongly as they affect adults. Understanding this one important point is the key to empathic relationships. You will hear them struggling to differentiate between love, helpfulness, and permissive actions on the one hand, and rules, punishment, and negative attitudes on the other. The same parent who loves and cares for a child and tucks him into bed at night with a hug and kiss may also be the one who spanks him and tells him to go play somewhere else.

In most kinds of minor problems, children will manage to handle them in a *natural* manner through a series of dramatized episodes, and they will move on to other types of explorations and make-believe. The play itself is self-resolving. Having reenacted parts of real life situations symbolically, children are better able to cope with similar situations either in their imagination or in real life.

By listening to the children, however, you can begin to recognize when some situation seems to be an obsession in a particular child's play. This might indicate a need to try to find out more about the situation the child is acting out, talking with a parent, if necessary, to try to discover the real reasons for the feelings he is demonstrating.

Frequently there is a physical reason for persistent negative-type dramatic play. This can usually be determined by watching children in their other play activities. They may be hungry, overtired, overstimulated, or hyperkinetic. They may be coming down with an illness or just recovering from one. They may feel physically unable to control their world. These children may behave in the same ways that children with a troublesome emotional problem do—for example, incessant crying, whining, yelling, kicking, hitting, running away, or other antisocial actions. Often these children are told not to cry, when instead they could be told, "I know you are not happy," or, "You are feeling really unhappy." Actually, whatever means they use to express negative feelings, whether the reason is physical or emotional, they are actually using these behaviors as a means of communication. It is your responsibility to respond to that communication in positive ways that will help alleviate the negative feelings without making the child feel that it is wrong to have such feelings. When children are saying, "I can't handle it," it is important to try to find out why.

In evaluating the feelings children are expressing through play, never jump to conclusions. The following example is one in which I jumped to conclusions: One morning when Billy arrived at school, he said, "Mommy cried." I said, "Mommy cried and that made you unhappy." He said, "Daddy went away." I said, "Daddy will come home pretty soon." Billy said, crying, "No. No. Daddy took his suitcase and went far away. Mommy cried." I tried to reassure him further but he continued to cry, interspersing the sobs with an occasional, "Daddy's not coming home."

After a few minutes, Billy stopped crying and went to his classroom. I alerted his teacher to his behavior. She, I, and the other staff members concluded that his parents had separated. We showed Billy an unusual amount of love, tenderness, and compassion that morning.

An hour later, I saw Billy in the playground arranging some empty boxes and saying, "This is a train. Toot! Toot!" Then he picked up a coffee pot from the sandpile and said, "This is my suitcase. I got to go." He got into the "train" and several children joined him. At first Billy kept saying, "We got to go. We got to go." Suddenly he was quiet. And then, as though trying to convince himself, he started singing, "Daddy's coming. Daddy's coming." Soon he jumped out of the train, leaving it to the other children. Billy became absorbed in other play activities. First on the jungle gym, then a turn on the tire swing. Then over to the bike yard to ride his favorite Big Wheel. Then indoors for other kinds of play.

When Billy's mother came to pick him up, I intercepted her. I told her that her son had a happy morning. She said, "Oh, that's good. We took his father to the train station last night, because he's going on a business trip. I started crying when we said good-bye. Billy was sure upset, but I just couldn't explain it to him."

Fortunately for Billy, his family was intact, but the anxiety he felt was real. The play through which he was able to try out his father's role and measure his belief that he would come back relieved him of the inner conflict caused by his mother's assurance that he would return versus his mother's tears.

Not all problems are worked out so easily, nor is the reason for them always easy to determine. No generalized rules can be applied to evaluating them because each child and situation is unique. However, some generalized types of play-scripts are observed more frequently than others. Here are some examples:

A three-year-old is busily spanking the teddy bear. She spanks with exaggerated vigor, shouting, "I don't like you," over and over again. She throws the teddy bear down with force, saying, "You're bad." She puts her hands on her hips, feet apart, and surveys the room, turning from side to side. What she saw was not a hostile world, but people she knew and played with and who helped her when she needed help. She saw her teacher smiling reassurance rather than condemning her actions. She looked down at the bear and her expression softened a little. Suddenly she relaxed. She picked up the stuffed animal and hugged it tightly. Then she dropped it in a corner and ran off to other play activities.

Very possibly, the teddy bear represented the child's parents—or perhaps herself. After the scene was over, the child played rather joyfully for the remainder of the morning.

Another frequently enacted sequence is that of the doctor or nurse performing examinations and offering cures. Broken legs are commonly the problem. Seldom do the "patients" have such illnesses as flu, tonsilitis, colds, or stomachaches. It may be too difficult for the children to role play the real illnesses with which they are familiar, so we see broken legs.

The important characters in this kind of play are always the doctor and the nurse. They are usually trying to alleviate anxiety, which may take several repetitive sessions to accomplish. When the children really become involved in pretending to be the one giving care, they discover that they genuinely want to be kind and helpful. Even though they may approach the "patient" with great force as they give their "shots," they are not trying to hurt him or her. They seem to develop an understanding of the kinds of feelings one has when trying to help a sick person, and will begin to look at the doctor and nurse as friends.

JEALOUSY

Jealousy is a normal human emotion. Everyone experiences it at one time or another. As with other emotions, its only harmful when it produces guilt feelings and is constantly being repressed. Much of this guilt can be relieved through dramatic play experiences and role playing. Children who are jealous of the attention a new baby is receiving, may want to play being that baby and getting the same kind of attention. Or they may play very aggressive roles and display much hostility in their behavior and language toward others. Or they may become withdrawn. Many children manage the first year of a new sibling's life fairly well. By time the baby starts to walk and talk, however, the threat becomes more real. Many children undergo dramatic personality changes about the time their baby brothers and sisters are from twelve to sixteen months old. These personality changes are seldom permanent. They are the children's way of saying, "Hey! Remember me. I'm important too." It is hard for two- and three-year-olds to share toys. Imagine, then, the idea of sharing their parents, their home, and their time. The following example describes the reactions at nursery school of a child who was jealous of a younger brother. She had been building up to the extremes revealed in this dramatization for several weeks.

Jennifer was obviously upset about something when she entered school Monday morning. She stomped, rather than walked, into the building. When I greeted her she looked back at me with angry, tear-stained eyes. Her mother seemed tense and nervous, and also rather helpless. She said, "Good-bye, Jennifer." But Jennifer did not respond. In the classroom a few minutes later, Jennifer was sitting on the floor next to the wall in an isolated corner wanting nothing to do with anyone. About ten minutes passed. She got up and walked over to the painting area and looked expectantly at the teacher. "You may put on an apron and paint," the teacher said. Jennifer started to do so, but she suddenly dropped the apron and ran to the housekeeping area, where she started to busy herself with setting the table. She arranged two dolls on chairs on opposite sides of the table. She placed some "food" on the table. Then she said, "No. I have to feed the baby." She then picked up a doll, started to feed it with a spoon, and then sat down on a chair and started spanking the doll. Just then, Sandy entered the play area. Jennifer looked at him and said, "Well, Dad, I'm glad you came home. I have a headache." Then she picked up a second doll by one leg, thrust it into Sandy's hand, and said "He's bad. I don't want him here." Sandy, loving the spirit of the game, threw the doll out of the area. "I locked the door," he said. Jennifer, dropping the first doll on the doll bed, then told Sandy to sit down and said, "We're having a party. We're having a party." She pretended to eat. In a few minutes she turned around and ran out of the housekeeping area over to where some boys were playing with blocks. She brushed by their structure rather casually, knocking two or three blocks down as though by accident. She picked the blocks up and said she was sorry. Then she went to the painting area and put on the apron she had previously thrown down.

Ten minutes later Jennifer was playing on the rug with two of her special friends. She seemed relaxed. Her rapport with her friends was positive. Through the remainder of the morning, she continued to be the helpful, cooperative, and friendly child she normally was. The ensuing weeks, brought out two or three similar emotional episodes. Always the older "child" was shut out of the house leaving the baby alone with the "mother." Finally, the episodes ceased. Jennifer's home behavior improved dramatically. Her emotions, having been tried out, examined, and released, were now under better control. Her feelings of jealousy were a normal reacton that was alleviated, in her case, by her ability to transfer her own role to that of an imaginary brother. He became the one who was jealous of the baby and who was punished by the mother. With this transference, her own anger disappeared. At school we encouraged conversation about babies, and about how helpless they are. We talked about how they need someone to do everything for them. Jennifer wholeheartedly agreed, and told us about some of the ways babies needed help. She was even able to express the thought, "Sometimes, they're sure a lot of trouble."

Aggression

In evaluating the aggression that we see in children's dramatic play experiences, we need to consider the child's home and community environment. Some inner-city children, for example, may be so familiar with law-enforcement officers, weapons, street fights, and similar events that any acting out of these events may be more imitative than symbolic. Since intimidated children from deprived environments have not usually had the opportunity to develop their imaginations and have not had many opportunities for role playing, these imitative episodes can be used as a starting point to helping them learn to symbolize and play out their feelings. For example, the child who is acting the part of the officer and is intimidating another, might be asked to reverse roles. Or the child who is constantly bullying and starting fights, might be asked to play the role of the law-enforcement officer and help the others do what is right. Gradually, you can ask the children's help in creating the playscript, which will begin to reflect their fears and anxieties that may have been causing them to be aggressive.

All children need opportunities to enact certain threatening situations, and to role-play dominant and aggressive characters. But they also need to be shown that there are alternative ways of expressing these feelings that are also a natural part of human nature. Rather than glorifying killing and hate, offer such activities as mountain climbing, fire department play, ditch digging, exploring and camping, road building, and other activities that involve considerable gross motor activity. These will allow for wholesome physical contact, and at the same time, allow the children to develop play-scripts involving aggression and dominance.

One of the favorite play-scripts of aggressive children, most usually boys, is one in which they play tigers, lions, or other wild animals, chasing people. A typical episode may start out with the initiator suggesting "Let's be tigers," or "Let's be wild animals and chase the girls." As a result of the influence of television, these wild animals are sometimes various kinds of monsters.

Whether the "chasers" are wild animals or monsters, they all include common elements of having the power to instill fear, male-female interaction, and submission. Occasionally a girl will become the aggressor. But rather than playing the role of wild animal or monster, she will usually be a witch. The rules seem to be that monsters can't conquer witches, but witches can, on occasion, conquer monsters.

Children also like to play the roles of nonthreatening animals. For example:

Andy, Jill, Matt, Jeff and Deana are in the housekeeping area. Their average age is four and a half.

Matt:	[reading a book at the table] Dogs should have dog food everyday.
Jeff:	Get the dog food.
Jill:	I'm the dog.
Matt:	[getting up and going to Jill] Here, Doggie, eat.
Jill:	Now I'm the mother.
Matt:	Get up! Get up!
Jill:	No. I'm sleeping.
Matt:	Get up!
Jill:	No. I said I'm sleeping.
Matt:	O.K.! I'm leaving! I'm going to work! [He goes to the telephone and says, "Ding-a-ling-a-ling."]
Matt:	Hello, mother. What's wrong. Something wrong? O.K. I'm coming home in an hour.
Jill:	[now the mother] Come at 10 o'clock.
Matt:	No, I'll come at one.
Deana:	[to Andy] I know what you can be. You can be the dog.
Jeff:	I want to be the dog.
Deana:	I know. You can be the kitty. And Andy can be a kitty, too.
Andy:	O.K.

Deana: [giving plates to each of the "kitties"] Here, kitty, kitty.
[The two boys got down on the floor and "lapped" up the make-believe food.]

Jill: I'm the dog again.

Jill, who started out to be the dog, apparently decided it might be more prestigious or that she'd have more control by playing the mother instead. However, the ease with which she slipped from one role to the other may indicate that both the dog and the mother represented her role playing of her mother. Jill seemed to want to be catered to throughout the episode. She may have felt that switching back to being "dog" would get more of a reaction than being "mother" did. As "mother," her not wanting to get up only meant that "father" left the house. Then when he said he was coming back, she was unable to get him to return at the time she wanted him to. He set the time. Deana apparently needed to get the situation into her own control. She did so by appointing two kitties, whom she fed equally and to whom she was very tender. This was typical of her true personality.

These kinds of dramatic play experiences allow children to make necessary adjustments to their perceptions by what they learn through their play in addition to giving them an outlet for their feelings and emotions.

Paul (3½): I'll take my fire engine.

Chris (3½): No, wait a minute. [Pushing Paul's engine] Whooooh!

Paul: I'll take my fire truck. [Pushing engine] Whooooh! [Pushes the toy to the hallway door and looks around.] I'll have to stop here. [Looks at teacher for approval. Turns around and goes the other way.] Get the hoses everybody. Fire's over.

Chris: Now the firemen have to go back to their house.

At this point, Paul went to play elsewhere. He was new at school and did not know if he was allowed to go out into the hall. Therefore, he set his own limits by the boundaries of the room. Chris, not having control of the engine, used simple logic to stop the game. If, as Paul said, the fire was over, the firemen could now leave. They both did.

Julie (5): Jed's Daddy cutted off my navel when I was a baby.

Dan (4): What?

Julie: Jed's Daddy cutted off my navel.

Dan: Why?

Julie: Because it wasn't cutted off yet. It has to be cutted off.

Dan: Oh. There's a real storm. Get the wheelbarrow away quick. I want to get away fast cause there's a storm.

Apparently the idea of severing the umbilical cord was too much for Dan.

Dominance

In almost all play involving more than one person, especially in dramatic play, there is an ongoing struggle for dominance. This is an authentic means for children to find out what their roles are within various social groups. Well-adjusted children are more apt to take turns playing the dominant role. Some children, however, have an urgent need to keep the upper hand at all times and will be very ingenious in finding ways to do so.

The following episode involved four- and five-year-olds.

Michael: I'm the truck driver. Michele, David, Tina, Joey, Corey, and Jennifer, you're the wood logs. I have to bring you to another town. [All agreed. Michael not only established control of the entire group, but he appointed the others to roles that would prevent them from taking any kind of interfering action.] Here we start. We're in Riverside, let's go to Los Angeles. Brrrrrrrr. We're still going. O.K. Here we are. Everybody out. [To the other children] You're the wood we're unloading [meaning he's unloading]. I put you in the river and you go riding down the river. [Now he even succeeded in eliminating everyone else from the immediate play action.]

Michael: [starting all over again]: Let's go ride the train. [There is a play train in the school yard.] I'll be the engineer. All aboard. You're the coal car, you're the milk car, you're the oil car, you're the wood car, and you're the corn flakes car. I'm the engineer. Chug, chug, chug, chug, chug. Toot-toot. Here we go to the bakery shop. [Again Michael saw to it that he was the only "alive" actor in the episode, thus eliminating all competition.]

All of Michael's play falls into similar categories. He is always appointing roles to others and they are usually roles that are nonthreatening to him. His ideas are often quite innovative, so children like to join his games. But he is never able to follow anyone else's suggestions, and is unable to relate to more than one peer at a time on a friend-to-friend basis. Even then, he must assume control, or else he simply goes off to play by himself. Since this type of behavior has followed the same pattern for several months, the staff attempts to redirect some of Michael's activities. They sometimes step in and become the ones who appoint the role, thus giving other children opportunities to have the dominant position. At first, Michael was confused and resentful. He simply walked away from the situation. But gradually he began to allow the teacher to assign a minor role to him, and he played it very dramatically, with

225

all of the imaginative skills he showed in the leadership roles. The number of his friendships increased and he is apparently achieving a more wholesome balance to his personality.

The dramatic play experiences are all experiences of self-discovery. They cannot be programmed. You can't insure that even when you plan an episode, such as in the case with Michael, that the reactions will be what you anticipated. The value of symbolism and role playing through dramatization and make-believe is that the results, whatever they may be, spring from the inner needs of the individual children.

An observant teacher can help extend the *direction* the play is taking by a casual comment such as, "Sometimes a family packs suitcases to go to live in another house." Or she can add to the play activity by an action such as, "Here are two more boxes that can be pretend suitcases. Now your whole family (the play family) can have their own suitcase." Or perhaps she'll provide a large carton and say, "This can be the bus that takes you on the trip," or "This can be the truck that moves you to your new house," or even, "This can be the motel that you stay in until your new house is finished."

Adding materials and props, or even ideas, to an already existing play-script takes great sensitivity on the teacher's part. Be absolutely certain that your momentary involvement will not be interpreted as an intrusion. Choose only those moments when involvement is really called for to prevent a situation from disintegrating, to provide positive reinforcement of needed props, or to reinforce certain concepts that seem to be developing, or to help some children develop dramatic play skills. Be equally aware of those times when it is best to let what is happening go on without adult intervention of any kind.

There are times when the children are really playing constructively, but too many children are attempting to use a limited space. Or perhaps one particular child is really disturbing the others and not allowing the playing to continue. Or it may be that entire group is excluding one child. Each case is unique and must be handled on its own merits in a way that is most helpful to all participants. When I see simple quarrels going on that are on the verge of getting out of hand, I pass on a simple, "Play nicely." The reminder helps everyone to regain control of his particular role in the play that is unfolding. The only basic rules to cover all situations are those of fairness, consistency, and a kind, but firm attitude, which tells the children in a nice way that you mean business. The term "firm attitude" does not mean inflexibility. If you want children to be flexible, they must be able to see that you are able to be flexible. All facets of each situation must be carefully weighed against one another to determine the best direction to take.

The vast majority of dramatic play incidents center around themes of the home, the family, other people who frequent the home, and pets. This is logical since the home is where young children spend most of their time and where most of their emotional ties are. As the child's world expands, so do the themes for dramatic play and the roles to be played. First they will extend into the community—to the various shops and professional offices they are taken. Their play will also include various community workers that they observe in and around the home, the school, and the community. Soon their play will include places they visit on vacations or family excursions. Kinds of transportation are especially interesting to young children and are frequently the theme for their play activities. The programs they see on television also play a part in setting themes and defining roles to be tried out.

Much is lacking yet in making television an always positive influence in the life of the preschool child. Many people are pleased with the advanced vocabulary that children who watch television acquire. However, much of this vocabulary means little because the child has not yet had the real experiences that will enable him to understand the real meanings of many words.

As children grow in the ability to separate reality from fantasy, they become more and more involved in basing some of their play activities on literary fantasies. These will usually be related to stories, fairytales, and folklore told to them by adults. Many of those chosen for acting out are likely to be those which, due to the way the adult has presented them, have a connotation of satisfaction and accomplishment such as "The Three Bears," "The Billy Goats Gruff," "Little Red Riding Hood," and "The Three Little Pigs." There has been some concern during recent years that these stories and others like them may foster unwholesome attitudes in the children toward killing, male dominance, and other present-day concerns.

Actually, these stories have developed through the ages, though in ever-changing forms, because they *are* important to both storyteller and listener. Those stories have survived while thousands of others have gotten lost along the way. Those which have survived parallel, in their sequence of events, symbolic sequences of events that are universal in the lives of all people. They are all concerned with overcoming threatening situations and they generally have happy endings. The symbolism finds its universalism in the fact that children's thought processes, and thus human thought processes, all develop in the same way.

The acting out of favorite stories gives children opportunities to act out problem-solving situations in which they already know how the problem is going to be solved. Unlike their dreams, which often follow similar sequences but which just as often leave the story of symbolism hanging in midair, the happy endings of these stories are of great importance to children. They help children develop optimism, hope, endurance, industriousness, close family relationships, and other qualities that will lead to wholesome life attitudes.

227

Conversations

You're the grandmother. Grandmothers sit in rockers.

Quick. Get it before they get back. Let's cook it all up.

There's a deal I have. How old are you? Get five turns if you're five. Get four turns if you're four.

I want those.

Get out of our place.

Here's some more. That's broken.

You've got these things, too. Put them there.

Why don't you get away from here.
He doesn't have to.

I'm a rabbit.
Can I pet you, rabbit?
I like you, rabbit.
I love you. (kiss, kiss, kiss)
I'll give you a toy, rabbit.
And I'll give you a toy.

Come in. Here's a hat for you.
I don't want it. I don't wear a hat. 'Bye. I can't stay.
I'm getting the tea ready. Two cups pouring. Three cups pouring. Who wants to have some.
Can't I have some?
Noooooo!

When I bring my doll I'll let you hold it. I just have one black doll and lots of white dolls.
I want to feed your doll.
I don't want anybody to feed her. I'll let you hold it.
I'll let you put her clothes on.

229

The suspense-building sequences of these plots develop an emotional climate that enables the listener to take great satisfaction in the ultimate "victory."

SPACE AND MATERIALS FOR DRAMATIC PLAY

Basic materials for dramatic play activities can easily be provided for specific kinds of play. Large numbers of things are not necessary. To allow children to give their imaginations full reign, it is better to have "less" rather than "more." Children are perfectly capable of creating an imaginary environment out of thin air with no props whatsoever. The reason for providing any props is to give impetus to the imagination they will probably use anyway.

The Home

Play areas for homemaking activities should include housekeeping materials and equipment. Child-sized sinks, stoves, tables, chairs, and beds are the basic equipment. The furniture can be commercially manufactured, with functioning doors, windows, and shelves. However, children will play just as enthusiastically with the simplest of home-made, improvised equipment. The kitchen can be a box with "burners" painted on the top of it. Or the burners can be plastic coffee can tops fastened to a box or a table. With pots, pans, and stirring spoons, children will prepare just as elaborate a "meal" on this stove as they would on an expensive replica of a real stove. Sinks, too, can be improvised. One easy way is to stand two boxes on end 15 inches apart. Place a plastic dishpan in between with the lip of the dishpan clinging to the boxes on each side. Empty cable spools can serve as tables, as can a large board set on some kind of support, such as a coffee table or old end table. End tables can be purchased cheaply in second-hand stores. "Beds" can be made from empty boxes. Even cardboard boxes will do, if wooden ones are not available. A cardboard "bed" can be made by fitting one box inside another to double the strength. The beds should be strong enough to hold children as well as dolls. Chairs can be taken from the regular classroom supply or they can be improvised from boxes, hollow blocks, or stools.

Whether you buy the furniture, make it, or improvise it, it should be painted in colors that harmonize with the rest of the room. Its best to paint these types of playthings in light, neutral shades. Furniture painted neutral colors will need repainting less frequently than that painted with bright colors.

Play furniture should be the right size for the children. Doll furniture is usually too small. Beds should be big enough for a child to get into. Tables should be big enough for a party of four. Pots and pans should include some of the smaller pieces that adults use. Children like play dishes and play utensils, but they also like to have a few bigger pieces in which to do their "real" cooking. Be sure to include an eggbeater and other food preparation tools.

In the play centering around housekeeping areas, you can add various props if the children seem to need them. It doesn't matter whether the item you give them is real or not. Offer something else to the children as a substitute, saying, "Here, you can use this for the adding machine."

Props for such use can be kept in a place where the children have access to them. Be sure they are familiar with what is in the collection. Sometimes you might set out some of the props before the children have arrived in order to stimulate their imaginations. These types of things could include party decorations, doll bathing supplies, suitcases, tea party materials, wedding accessories, spring housecleaning supplies, pretend "foods," and dry breakfast cereal to really serve and eat.

Along with the make-believe furniture and accessories, you should have on hand an ample supply of costuming materials. These should include dresses, skirts, blouses, petticoats, jackets, vests, hats, purses, gloves, ladies' and men's shoes, jewelry, belts, canes, uniforms, and whatever else you can collect. Be sure to have some large safety pins available to help in "fitting" if requested—but only give help when a child asks for it. As a rule, the children get a great deal of enjoyment out of dressing themselves up in their own way. Adults must be careful not to impose their suggestions on the originality children show.

The Store

As the children realize the satisfactions of dramatic play, they will engage in it more and more. The home and family playing will eventually be enlarged to include "going to the store." This activity sometimes involves simply telephoning the father to stop at the store on his way home from work.

A toy cash register is all the equipment needed to motivate store-play activities. However, these are experiences that most children have participated in with their families. Providing many props and supplies enables them to expand on these experiences more fully. We usually start out by sending notes home to the parents and requesting that they send to school empty food containers that have clear illustrations on them. We prefer small containers to large ones, and do not use any empty cans that have sharp edges.

With the 2½-year olds and 3½-year olds, we give them a small number of containers. They take turns piling them into a plastic grocery cart. As long as they can play with the cash register, they don't care if they are "buying" food

Conversations

Sean won't play with me.
I won't play because she messed up the store. When she cleans it up, I'll play.

What's that?
Cereal.
But what's that on it? Oh, I know. That makes a juggling thing.

We have cheese, corn, anything.
No that's not corn. It's butter. O.K.?

I need two dozen eggs. I have to have company.

WAIT!!!!! The store's not open. I have to fix the cash register. It won't open.

Hey, you can't buy everything.

I'll put it in this sack so you can carry it. Then bring it back, O.K.?

How 'bout special season stuff you put on spaghetti? Its really good food. Well, don't you want my coffee?
It does look more like coffee. But I love candy.
O.K. Have some of this dessert.

Fish, fish, fish, stuff, o.k. I'm making fish. I need a lot.
I forgot to add water to fish. Five dollars. Has anybody seen the money?

We don't need too much people—only two at a time.

containers or blocks. The fun for them is in piling things in the cart. After some experience in this type of play, one teacher selects cans and boxes that are predominately either red, blue or yellow. She lines one shelf with yellow paper, one with blue, and one with red. The containers are then placed on the appropriate colors of paper. She then might say to a child, "Please buy me a red can of soup." Soon the children catch on to the color categorizing and, after they have removed all the containers from the shelves, they put them back according to color, if given a little guidance.

Children of four and five develop quite complex store-play situations. They will spend a lot of time arranging and rearranging the shelves before they even start to play. The older they get, the more time they spend in preparing the setting in advance. They are beginning to understand the principles of communication and want to be sure that everyone involved is able to realize what is going on. As with the younger children, the supplies are arranged rather haphazardly at first, in whatever space is available. We gradually introduce the idea of categorizing by placing soaps and other cleaning items in one area, dry foods in another, canned foods in another, and refrigerated foods in the "cold" area. Along with the cash register, we usually supply paper sacks and shopping bags. A small grocery cart is a favorite shopping aid, but the children have to be constantly reminded that it is used only for collecting what they want to buy, and that they have to take their items away in a sack. Children occasionally quarrel over who gets to play the roles of storekeeper, cashier, and shopper, but, for the most part, they interchange them rather freely. It seems to be just as much fun to play one type role as the other.

The children spend a large part of their store-play time getting dressed. This involves all the fineries of the costume closet—especially purses.

Grocery store play can lead to other types of shopping play. With a supply of discarded adult shoes and the intrigue of an authentic shoe-store foot "measurer," you can play shoe-store. Baked goods are frequently put on sale by the sandbox bakers. Children also like to use a supply of broken toys and bits of lost puzzles and other games as sale items. Two or three times yearly, we lend the children real pennies, which they use to "purchase" these "variety" items. Their selections have to be made from items marked 1¢, 2¢ or 3¢. Children spend a lot of time studying the situation and figuring out whether to buy three items for 1¢ each or one "big" item for the entire 3¢.

Finally, late in the school year, one teacher sets up a "Giggly Grape Store." This functions similar to the other play store activities except that the items being "sold" are real midmorning snacks. The children are given pennies with which they can purchase such delicacies as: five carrot sticks and one juice; one carrot stick, one juice, and one cracker; two crackers and one juice; or no crackers or carrot sticks, but three juices. The decision making is real, but the choices are entirely the child's. Exchanges are freely allowed. It is sometimes quite a shock to a child to see someone with six things (five carrot sicks and one juice) while he only got three things (one juice, one cracker, and one carrot stick). The children's primary motivation seems to be how to get the most items—not what the items are. Whatever the items for this activity, it is set up with the cash register and two or three storekeepers to take charge.

A similar experience involving real money takes place around Valentine's Day. The children are each given an opportunity to count out ten pennies for themselves in their classroom. They take their pennies to the office where they count them out to the "banker" who gives them each a dime in exchange. Then the children walk to a nearby post office where they use the dime to buy a postage stamp. Each child brings his stamp back to school and sticks it on an envelope in which he mails a Valentine home to himself. Although these situations are organized by adults, the children draw on them for their ongoing everyday play experiences.

Other props can be introduced to the children in various ways. As you listen to the children's conversation while they are playing, you may realize that you have just the thing they need for what they are doing. Or you put out the prop before the children arrive in a prearranged play center, where it waits to be "discovered." The children may not use it the way you had thought they would, but the joy of play is the right of participants to choose how they will do it. Also, the children should know where the dramatic play props are stored and they should feel free to use them whenever they need them.

Prop Boxes

The best way to store props is in boxes or "kits" that keep together the items that may be needed for a particular type of activity. For example:

> *Post Office* Stamp pads, rubber stamps, gummed labels (to use as stamps), envelopes, rubber bands, writing pad, pencil, small postal scale.

> *Vehicles* Sets of cars, airplanes, boats, trucks, and other miniature vehicles to use, as needed, with blocks, in sandbox, or wherever else dramatic play is going on. These should be kept on open shelves because they will probably be used almost daily by children alone or in groups.

Human Figures Collections of various types of "people to use as needed for dramatic play activities. These should include a variety of sizes, materials, expressions, and roles. Some can be miniature plastic figures that you can buy by the hundreds. Some can be wooden cutouts that stand up. Some can be miniature dolls. Some should represent various ethnic groups. Some should be children, others adults.

Plasterer Plastering tools and painters caps to be used with water, sand, and a surface to "plaster."

Painter Painter's brushes, buckets, and painter's caps to be used with water, on a variety of surfaces.

Doll Beauty Shop Hair curlers, combs, barrettes, hair brush, mirror, hair nets, scarves, and bobby pins to be used with doll heads mounted on stands.

Real Beauty Shop Clean, wide-toothed combs; small, sparsely bristled, easy-to-wash, brushes, large plastic hair curlers small hand mirrors; bobby pins to be used with real heads.

Barber Shop Old-fashioned shaving soap in a jar, shaving brush, toy plastic razor, stand-up mirror, paper towels, plastic "barber cloths" to place around shoulders while "shaving."

Doctor's Office A real stethoscope, play thermometer, stop watch, cloth for bandages, doctor's smock, doctor's headpiece (a paper crown with extension in front to represent light), and toy hypodermic needle.

Telephone Repair Pliers, wires, two toy telephones, assorted parts from broken toy telephones, plastic electrical tape, small scissors to cut tape, miscellaneous tools.

Furniture Repair Assorted screwdrivers, screws, nuts, bolts, and a few pieces of wood with holes to put the screws or nuts and bolts into.

Radio and Phonograph Repair Assorted screwdrivers and pliers, and other tools to use with discarded radios and phonographs.

OBSERVATIONS AND CONCLUSIONS

Dramatic play experiences occur continually during play time. Practically everything that children learn from all of their other experiences is intertwined with what they learn from role playing, imitation, and dramatic play activities. However, these dramatic play experiences give children the opportunities to *evaluate* the other things they have been learning, such as their own *understandings* about their lives and their environments, ways to *integrate* what they are learning, doing, and feeling, as well as what they have previously experienced, want to experience, and think they are expected to experience.

Through *imitation*, children first learn to make *sounds* and deliberate *movements*. As they develop physically, they elaborate on their imitations in order to try to find meaning in the actions of people in their environment. From imitative play, they soon learn to *pretend* they are the person they want to imitate, and they spend a great deal of time at this new activity. *Role playing* encourages them to use *symbolic* objects in place of the real thing. They learn that they can use this means of play as a legitimate outlet for feelings, especially negative ones, but also for other *emotions* as well.

As they become more experienced at role playing, they learn to separate what is *make-believe* from what is *real*. They learn that there are many different ways of expressing *emotional feelings*, and with this knowledge comes an increased ability to *control* those emotions.

They usually begin with episodes concerning their *homes,* immediate *family*, and very closest *friends, neighbors,* and *relatives* with whom they have frequent contact. They gradually expand this world to take in other people, such as delivery men, community workers, and people who work in the various business establishments they may be taken to by their parents. As children expand their knowledge of the world they live in, they enlarge their techniques, and simple imitation and role playing gives way to increasingly more complex *dramatic play* situations. Children involved with one another in dramatic play discover their own and other people's feelings about the environment and the people in it, and they develop skills in *interpersonal relationships*.

They continuously struggle for the *dominant* role, and very soon establish set patterns within various play groups that dictate the hierarchy of control within that group. Those who become relegated to a *secondary role* may carry on an ongoing struggle for a more

important role. This struggle enables them to learn many *techniques* that will help them work into the role that they want.

They also begin to develop *rules* and procedures for various dramatic plays, adding to them as they go along. Those playing the dominant roles frequently keep changing or adding to the rules to keep things going to their own advantage.

As children enlarge on their dramatic play games, they learn to use *fantasy* to help them cope with the problems and intrigues of their ever-expanding world. They renew their efforts at learning to identify *reality*, which is easier to do when they can contrast it with fantasy. While they are developing their *imaginations* and *creative abilities*, they are also learning how to handle their own *anxieties*. They practice their growing abilities in a wide variety of *make-believe* situations. Some of these accomplishments will be useful when they grow older. They learn about the many different ways they can resolve their feelings about things that have happened, are happening, or are expected to happen. They learn to *cope* with traumatic experiences by dramatizing the event in various forms over and over until it becomes diluted with time and familiarity, which makes it more understandable or at least more tolerable.

They spend a great deal of time trying to balance out the contradictory forms of treatment, as they perceive it, that they receive from adults, such as *love and hate, acceptance and rejection, permission and refusal, helpfulness and punishment, attention and lack of attention, presence and absence,* and what they consider to be other forms of *inconsistency*. In games, that a particular child controls to the extent that he can make the ending come out to his advantage, the child develops understandings of such positive feelings as *hope, optimism,* and *empathy,* and of qualities such as *industriousness* and *endurance.*

As a result of play activities based on homemaking experiences, children develop a better understanding of their environment and learn to *accept* their own role in it. They also come to understand differences between the various roles that other family members play. They develop an embryonic awareness of some of the intracacies of *housekeeping.*

During their play-store experiences, they learn to *classify, categorize, count,* and do simple *addition* involving three or four numbers. They practice the *use and division of space* as they arrange their goods on the available shelves and as they try to pack as many things as possible into their shopping bags, carts, or other containers. This activity increases their knowledge of *volume* as well.

From play in doctor-nurse situations, children acquire a better understanding that people in the medical profession are helpful and that it is not necessary to be afraid of them. In each of the different types of play situations that children enjoy *dramatizing*, they acquire knowledge that will help them develop increasingly more realistic perceptions and *conceptualizations* of their own early lifehood experiences and the people with whom they share them.

Appendix

A BRIEF HISTORY OF YOUNG CHILDREN'S PLAY

Play has always been an integral part of human life. It has taken many forms, including dance, poetry, storytelling, music, mime, drama, art, crafts, games, sports, and other forms of cultural communication. Historically, what we know about play largely pertains to youth and adults rather than young children. However, since the play of youth and adults has always been similar to the types of play they engage in today, it can be assumed that the play of young children has likewise always been similar to the play of young children today.

Prehistoric man most likely directed some of his early efforts toward the satisfaction of his basic physiological needs. As societal groups increased in number, they probably began to develop games and "plays" to help them understand the actions of the world and the unknown forces by which they seemed to be controlled. They utilized movement experiences to recreate by mimicry the high points of their day-to-day lives, such as the hunt and other life-sustaining experiences. Simple mimicry evolved into complex dance forms and dramas. Themes were enlarged upon to include all aspects of life, such as birth, sexual rituals, marriage, and death. Complex symbolic rituals developed by which success could be assured, even in the face of the mysterious powers that seemed to control the world.

At the same time these dance games were evolving, people also began to devise simple tools, thus enabling them to develop new skills in eye-hand coordination, which in turn provided new abilities to integrate body and mind. This advance led to new perceptions and subsequently new concepts and increasingly logical thought processes. These new skills enabled early

241

man to record the high points of his life and beliefs through cave drawings.

Cultural achievements in the form of art and dance, all of which helped early man cope with the unknown, were passed on from generation to generation and from community to community, thus marking the beginning of the ongoing development of our own cultures, including such components as religion, mythology, customs, and *play.*

All human infants develop in much the same way. Their first strivings are directed toward the satisfaction of their basic physiological needs. As their world begins to expand, they gradually learn to "play" little games, that provoke reactions from both people and things in their environments. They begin to mimic those about them. This behavior gives way to imitative play in which they pretend to be someone else in order to help them to understand that person's actions. They begin to symbolize. At this point in their development, their playthings become environmental objects, the use of which they desperately want to understand. Through this type of play, they learn that they can manipulate parts of their environment, thus giving them the power to control that environment. They learn to use simple tools and they begin to develop coordination between eye and hand, and integration between body and mind. Perceptual processes are enhanced, concepts take form, and logical thought evolves.

Until very recent times, families for the most part were much less concerned about the play of their children than they were about their mere survival. Before the twentieth century, the mortality rate was so high that keeping infants and toddlers alive was of far greater importance than play. Children who lived supplied manpower for labor and soldiers for warfare. They also ensured, in a sense, the parents' immortality and future remembrance, and, of course, their welfare in their old age. In societies that incorporate ancestor worship, parents take great care of their offspring to insure their own later care and veneration. Apart from religious practice and economic concern, mankind in general shares universal feelings of the need to produce offspring, knowing that the continuation of life depends on this process.

Historical evidence suggests age-old concern for the welfare of the young and an interest in their need to play. Excavations in Egypt have uncovered miniature dishes and other toy utensils, marbles, tenpins, tops, and toy wagons, bouncing balls and balls made of porcelain and other objects believed to have been playthings. Near the Step Pyramid at Saqqara is the tomb of a Vizier of Egypt who lived about 2400 B.C. Friezes in this tomb depict scenes of his life selected by him while he was still alive. One of these scenes shows the Vizier watching children at play. Excavations in Asian countries have unearthed playthings used thousands of years ago.

Plato, in his *Laws,* listed the types of playthings every household should have for its children. For infants, there were to be rattles. For older children, there were to be balls, hoops, tops, swings, and stilts, as well as dolls for girls and toy carts for boys. These were to be in addition to toys that children made for themselves or other things they found to play with. Jewish writers of the Talmudic Period (A.D. 100–400) referred to children's toys. A rabbi wrote that he bought earthenware dishes for his children to play with "in order to satisfy their impulses for breaking things." Childrens' playthings have also been found in American Indian sites.

Ancient games, as well as toys, were similar to those we know today. The number and variety of games seemed to be in direct proportion to the complexity of the culture in which they were invented and played. The importance of play and games was in proportion to the prosperity of a society and the resultant time for leisure. Even slaves and laborers with little time for leisure found time for play and games during holidays and holy days. Some religious practices included revelry in celebration of religious holidays, which provided the same kind of relief.

Many of the games that have come down through the ages are out-growths of the tribal dances and dance dramas of prehistoric times. Games such as Eeny-Meeny-Miny-Mo, Blindman's Buff, Hide and Seek, Drop the Handkerchief, and other kinds of tag games have their origins in legendary behavior related to pursuit, escape, sacrifice, bondage, and other traumatic experiences. Even though the symbolic behaviors and ritual words have changed, the actions performed in many games have remained remarkably similar. Athletic skills required for ball games, jumping ropes, wrestling, boxing, archery, swimming, tennis, hockey, and many other of the games and sports we participate in today were practiced as far back as 2,500 years ago. Chess, checkers, and card games have been played for centuries. Kite flying too is an ancient past time.

The similarities in the way children play are modified in particular societies according to cultural attitudes and socioeconomic status. Consider two contrasting paintings of children at play.[1] The first of the late Sung dynasty in China, probably painted around A.D. 1200. Titled *One Hundred Children at Play*, it depicts obviously pampered, privileged children, in a luxurious courtyard setting, playing the roles of the adults in their aristocratic world. They appear decorous, well mannered, automatic, and very formal. They reflect a society in which children are separated from its mainstream and shielded from reality. Other Sung paintings show children from middle-class society playing games and pursuing activities that are closely allied to those seen in Pieter Brueghel's 1560 painting, *Children's Games*. This Flemish

---

[1] *Horizon*, Winter 1971. See Bibliography, Opie, Peter.

painting gives a bird's-eye view of two hundred and fifty children engaged in seventy-five separate play activities. If the buildings and clothing were modernized, the painting could easily be a portrayal of children playing in an American city today. They are completely absorbed in their interaction with one another, free of artificially imposed adult restrictions. At first glance it seems to be bedlam. But just as we find in playgrounds of today, when large numbers of children are engaged in play their play spaces are organized into harmonious, rhythmic, fluid areas. The games include such activities as bubble blowing, tree climbing, tug of war, making mud pies, walking on stilts, and playing out make-believe weddings and other adult events. They include games of skill, rivalry, and fantasy. The children seem to have their own rules, and they are self-disciplining. There is a strong spirit of comradary, vigor, pleasure, individuality, and above all, playfulness.

Through other paintings, as well as writings of that period, we know that Brueghal's children did not play only children's games. The lives of European children during the Middle Ages and until fairly recent times were so closely interwoven with adults that they were exposed to all of the more sophisticated adult pleasures from earliest childhood. Although we may show dismay at some of these adult activities in which children participated, at least what they saw wasn't distorted as are the unrealities of the adult world to which they are exposed on American television. They were not shut off from the mainstream of their families' world like the children in the Sung painting or as in much of our society today.

By 1700, attitudes toward children began to change. A strong religious influence began to spread and many adult pastimes were forbidden to children. Gradually Western culture began to take a new view of the period between ages six or seven up to adolescence and developed an attitude of protecting these children from the influence of adult "sins." By the early nineteenth century, great changes were evident. Children's reading was censored. Casual sports and free activities began to give way to highly organized team games, foreshadowing the Little Leagues of today. Children had always been dressed similar to adults, but special styles of clothing began to develop. School children wore uniforms. Children were isolated from adults, even in their own homes, as much as space and supervision permitted. Finally, childhood as we know it today—a separate world, with its own clothing, food, literature, social structure—had developed.

In lower socioeconomic groups, the changes did not spread very rapidly. Children who are forced to live in close quarters with adults, even today, cannot have their lives separated from the adults, and it is difficult for adults to conceal their activities from children. In societies where survival of the family depends on long hours of hard work, such as in the United States before World War II, children have been expected to share in that work from the earliest possible age. The natural imitative play of children was thus put to use for utilitarian purposes. They have performed a wide variety of jobs—from simple household chores to heavy work in fields and factories —according to their ability and the community.

During the nineteenth and early twentieth centuries, many European immigrants in this country had to work hard, frequently to the detriment of their health, to pay for their children's educations. They expected their children to work hard, too, and play was not a great concern. But though these children did not have the opportunity to learn some things that can be learned through play, they acquired other valuable learning through close family relationships and their positive roles within the family. They became adults who had a strong sense of responsibility. They learned to accept themselves as competent human beings. Many creative people had their imaginations stimulated during childhood, not by creative teachers and play, but as a result of a vigorous involvement with life. Not all of these children were required to work. Their play, however, reflected their need to imitate the work of the people around them, as do many of the children today.

In recent years, a new class of poor has developed, people whose horizons have been limited by successive generations of a family knowing only welfare as its source of income. Children in such families don't have models of workers to imitate. Many such children have only limited ability to fantasize in their play, a reflection of the limited viewpoints of the adults with whom they are in close daily contact. Many of these children are now having opportunities through the growing field of early lifehood education to be involved in play activities in which imagination, self-esteem, and sense of responsibility may hopefully be developed to the point where they can break through their family limitations and expand the possibilities of their own lives.

PLAY-LEARNING THEORIES

The groundwork for play theories of today was laid by thinkers of the past. New theories do not completely obliterate old ones—rather they add new dimensions to fit the understandings and knowledge, as well as the needs, of new periods of time. Each new theory builds on previous knowledge, research, understandings, and experience. The following list acknowledges the contributions of thinkers of the past and present.

427–347 B.C. PLATO. Greek philosopher. Plato showed an almost modern concern for children, writing, " . . . a child must be happy, free from sorrow and pain as far as its childish desires permit . . . From three to six years of age children should be absorbed in play, in games of their own devising . . . "

384–322 B.C. ARISTOTLE. Greek philosopher. He agreed with Plato on the need for children to play, anticipating the surplus-energy theory, saying, " . . . a young thing cannot be quiet."

106–43 B.C. CICERO, MARCUS TULLIUS. Roman statesman. He promoted the principles of early childhood education. He related the importance of children's activities during their first six years of life to their total development throughout life.

A.D. 35–95. QUNITILIANUS (QUINTILIAN) MARCUS FABIUS. Spanish born rhetorician and teacher of oratory in Rome. He combined Plato's and Aristotle's ideas on play with Cicero's ideas on early childhood education. The result was the promotion of the use of play as a means of promoting learning.

1495–1553. RABELAIS, FRANÇOIS. French writer. He proposed an educational system related to the realities of life, rather than to books alone. He stressed the importance of the individual, the educational value of freedom as opposed to restraint, and of gentleness as opposed to harshness. His writing was important to the future of learning-play theories because of his tremendous influence on Rousseau and Pestalozzi.

1533–1592. MONTAIGNE, MICHAEL DE. French essayist. He considered play to be the means by which children develop the kinds of qualities they would display in maturity. Thus, if a child played with vigor, he would pursue his adult activities with vigor. He protested learning by rote, promoted learning by doing, especially by interaction with others. He felt that the educational process should be geared toward creating a desire to learn by making learning pleasurable.

1592–1671. COMENIUS (or KOMENSKY), JOHANN AMOS. Moravian bishop and educator. He published the earliest known picture book for children, *Orbis sensualium pictus*, in 1658. He promoted puzzles and three-dimensional toys as aids to learning and encouraged mothers of young children to give them many opportunities to play.

1604–1676. SCHALLER, JACOB. German philosopher. He influenced later theorists by promoting the idea that play was needed in order to recharge one's exhausted energies.

1712–1778. ROUSSEAU, JEAN JACQUES. Swiss-born French philosopher and author. Influenced by Rabelais and Montaigne, he promoted the importance of handling each stage of growth of the young child differently. He believed that experience was necessary to perceptual formations, including play experiences. He felt that pleasurable attitudes, curiosity, play, and similar means should be used to create in the child a desire to learn.

1746–1827. PESTALOZZI, JOHANN HEINRICH. Swiss educational reformer. Greatly influenced by Rousseau, he promoted the principles of step-by-step learning, from the elementary through to the complex, based on the child's individual needs. He promoted learning through self-initiated activities, such as play. He believed sensory impressions to be the foundation of all human knowledge, and thus, education.

1748–1803. TIEDEMANN, DIETRICH. German philosopher and psychologist. In 1783 he published the earliest known study of infant development, and the early development of human intelligence, based probably on the study of his own child, who was then three years of age. Study, by observation, of one's own child was a popular practice of educated men of that period.

1759–1805. SCHILLER, JOHANNE CHRISTOPH FRIEDRICH VON. German dramatist and poet. He defined art as the "expression of a human play-drive . . . " He believed that play is necessary to use up muscular energy and exuberance that is not used in other activities. He paved the way for the development of the *surplus-energy theory* of play promoted by Herbert Spencer.

1771–1858. OWEN, ROBERT. Welsh-born English manufacturer and pioneer in British socialism, philanthropist, and educational reformer. In 1816 he established the first infant school in Great Britain, and abolished the practice of employing very young children in the cotton mills of New Lanark, Scotland. He established the first infant school in the United States in New Harmony, Indiana, in 1826. He promoted the importance of outdoor play and of learning that occurs through the natural curiosity of a child.

1775–1854. SCHELLING, FRIEDRICH WILHELM JOSEPH VON. German philosopher and aesthetician. He influenced the evolving philosophies and theories of play by promoting the importance of self-expression for people of all ages, including very young children. He believed self-determination to be the primary condition of all consciousness.

1782–1852. FROEBEL, FRIEDRICH WILHELM AUGUST. German philosopher, philanthropist, and educational reformer. He opened the first Kindergarten in Germany in 1837, in which he promoted the principles of learning through play and games, and the importance of developing health and skills through physical activity. Like Plato and Pestalozzi, he stressed the importance of giving mothers instruction in how to care for and promote the play of their children. He felt that in addition, specially trained people should have some part in children's early upbringing. His ideas spread throughout Europe and the United States.

1824–1903. LAZARUS, MORITZ. German philosopher and Hebrew scholar. He promoted the theory that play is a *restorative* force. He defined recreation as the opposite of work but different from idleness.

1805–1879. ROSENKRANZ, JOHANN KARL FRIEDRICH. German philosopher and educator. He promoted the *recreation* theory of play, encouraging play as a means of both exercising creative ingenuity and refreshing the ability to work. He believed children needed space, time, and opportunity for play as a respite from nonplay activities. He distinguished work from play by stating, "Work is laid out for the pupil by his teacher authoritatively, but in his play he is left to himself."

1812–1880. SEQUIN, EDOUARD. French physician and educator. His pioneer work with retarded children promoted the principles of sensory-motor training and the integration of body and mind. He believed that the education of young children should be conducted in an atmosphere of happiness and laughter. Maria Montessori based her methods on the work of Dr. Sequin.

1820–1903. SPENCER, HERBERT. English philosopher and social scientist. Greatly influenced by Schiller, he promoted the idea of play as a means of utilizing unused energy, known as the *surplus-energy* theory of play, but sometimes referred to as the Schiller-Spencer theory. He looks upon play as (1) compensatory: a substitute for other satisfactions that have not been met; (2) rivalry: through play, victories can be achieved; (3) instinctive: play is often imitative, and imitation is instinctual. He also considered art to be a form of play. Although he had many valid ideas, he considered play to be unnecessary to life.

1841–1897. PREYER, WILHELM THEIRRY. German physiologist. His book, *Mind of the Child*, published in 1882, was the first book written on child psychology. He recorded the progress of the development of his own son from the first automatic movements of infancy to the increasingly complex movements of each succeeding stage of growth.

1842–1919. JAMES, WILLIAM. American philosopher, educator, psychologist and physiologist. He promoted the idea that play was the result of *instinct*. He advanced the principle that children learn best when they are motivated by their own interests, and when their own ideas and their emotions were given consideration.

1844–1924. HALL, GRANVILLE STANLEY. American psychologist and educator and founder of the *American Journal of Psychology*. His *recapitulation theory* of play promoted the idea that children developed phylogenetically, or in accordance with the evolutionary development of man. He viewed play as a way to provide children with an outlet for primitive instincts, as a necessary process for learning control of them in order to achieve maturity. His theory, although very controversial, led to an intensified interest in child study and the study of children's play.

1856–1939. FREUD, SIGMUND. Austrian-born physician, originator of psychoanalysis. He felt that the repetition of stress situations in children's play activities, allowing for them to use trial-and-error methods, would encourage children to resolve many of their own problems. He believed that efforts to master the environment through the repetition of activities (such as play) were one of the fundamental drives of children. He theorized that surplus energy was expressed through sexuality rather than play.

1857–1949. PATRICK, G.T.W. Influenced by Moritz Lazarus, Patrick developed the *relaxation* theory of play, in which he views play as a restorative process. However, where Lazarus looked upon all play as a response to an escape from fatigue, Patrick considered it applicable only to play activities related to the "pursuits of primitive man."

1859–1952. DEWEY, JOHN. American educator and philosopher. He advocated changes in school curriculae in order to promote the principle of learning by doing. As a result of his efforts, the development of education and schooling in the United States made great advances, promoting increased concern for the value of practical experience as an adjunct to formal lessons. He also influenced educational systems to add programs for physical, emotional, and social growth to those for intellectual growth.

1860–1931. McMILLAN, MARGARET. British educational reformer. She organized nursery schools for children of working mothers in London, promoting the belief that children should be allowed to play and develop naturally to assure maximum physiological and intellectual growth.

248

1861–1946. GROOS, KARL. Swiss professor of philosophy. He refuted the then-prevalent idea of play as an expression of surplus energy, promoting instead the *instinct-practice* theory of play, which was also referred to as the *rehearsal* or *pre-exercise* theory. He insisted that play was practice and preparation for life, a belief that is strongly held by many to this day. He recognized the basic instinct to imitate, then related all play to this instinct.

1867–1934. JOHNSON, HARRIET M. American nursery school educator. With Lucy Sprague Mitchell, she founded what is known today as the Bank Street College of Education in New York City, a school that pioneered in early childhood education. She contributed much to the development and understanding of play theories by her voluminous records of her observations of the play behavior of children.

1867–1954. PRATT, CAROLINE. American educator. She believed in learning through play and developed both schools and materials to promote her beliefs. She originated the unit blocks and the hollow blocks, two types of playthings prevalent in nursery schools and kindergartens today.

1870–1952. MONTESSORI, MARIA. Italian physician and educator. She promoted the principles of structuring the play environment for maximum learning by promoting sensory-motor growth and manipulative skills through didactic self-correcting play materials, which she developed. She promoted the self-selection of activities within a structured environment, but discouraged spontaneous play and non-structured performance of tasks.

1872–1945. HUIZINGA, JOHAN. Dutch historian. He related play to all elements of culture and promoted the *cultural* theory of play. He considered play to have a *genetic* base. He felt that play should not be considered separately from the main activity of life, but rather should be integrated with it wholly.

1885–1948. ISAACS, SUSAN. British educator, psychoanalyst, and child psychiatrist. She considered play to be related to all aspects of child development, including physical growth, social understandings, reasoning and competition, and the ability to handle one's emotions. She strongly advocated allowing children to use their playthings in their own way for maximum value of the activity and as vehicles for learning and understanding.

1891–1964. ALEXANDER, FRANZ. Psychoanalyst. He was the first exponent of the *psychoanalytic* theory of play, promoting the principle of deriving pleasure from the repetition of situations presenting problems and causing stress, through play. He believed: (1) Play rejuvenates the body both physically and mentally; (2) play allows for trial and error at achieving understanding of procedures needed for nonplay activities; and that (3) surplus energy is energy that is not needed for survival, but may be applied to utilitarian activities.

1893– • BUEHLER, CHARLOTTE B. German-born American professor of psychology; clinical developmental and humanistic psychologist. She considered play to be a way that a child could derive pleasure from his actions. She classified play as being of four types: construction activities; play geared toward the development of sensory-motor skills; make believe and illusion; and passive play, such as reading books.

1895– • FREUD, ANNA. British psychiatrist and psychoanalyst. Her work has centered on her belief that play is as important for the child as work is for adults. She suggests that clues to a child's normalcy or disturbance can be deduced from his ability to play. For example, repetitive, monotonous, overimaginative play, as opposed to constructive play, may be a sign that a child is neurotically halted at a particular stage of development.

1896– • PIAGET, JEAN. Swiss psychologist, biologist, and *developmental* theorist. He looks upon play as a means by which the child can transform reality by assimilation to the needs of the self. He looks upon imitation as an accommodation to external models and intelligence as an "equilibration between assimilation and accommodation." He defines four categories of play: (1) Exercise play, which is the only type of play that takes place during the sensory-motor period, from birth to age two. This is a primitive form of play consisting primarily of repeating for pleasure activities picked up through imitation and exploration. (2) Symbolic play, which reaches its peak between the ages of two to three and five to six. This type of play provides the child with a means for self-expression through the use of symbols developed by the self and modified or reconstructed according to self-needs and wishes. (3) Games with rules, which are social games like marbles or hopscotch, that are passed on from child to child. (4) Games of construction, which develop from symbolic play and are first geared toward play symbolism but then develop into mechanical constructions and other creations.

1914– • AXLINE, V.M. She pioneered in the field of play therapy, a process by which the child is helped to understand his feelings through spontaneous play activities.

1928– • SMILANSKY, SARA. Israeli professor of psychology. She developed the theory of *sociodramatic play*, which is dramatic play involving two or more children and containing some verbal interaction. She found that some children from socioeconomically deprived backgrounds do not participate easily in sociodramatic play, but rather persist in operating on a sensory-motor level beyond the usual developmental age of most children. She promotes the importance of adult intervention in helping children acquire play techniques by helping them learn to role play, make-believe, persist in the play experience, interact with two or more others, and communicate verbally with them while doing so.

1899–1964. CARR, HARRIET HELEN. She wrote on the theory that play was a *catharsis*, a sort of safety valve. The theory was first suggested by Aristotle and later promoted by Groos and others. Closely related to the surplus-energy theory, this theory advocates the need for play to be emotional, rather than physical, and considers play to be necessary as a means of releasing tensions and to help the survival of man.

1902– • ERIKSON, ERIK HOMBURGER. American psychiatrist, psychoanalyst, and specialist in the field of human development. He agreed with the psychoanalytic theory of play and thought of play as an attempt to master the problems of reality. He also considered it as a means by which the child organizes his life and integrates his varied experiences. He saw in spontaneous play valuable self-curative effects, as in play therapy.

1903– • BETTELHEIM, BRUNO. Austrian-born psychiatrist and child psychoanalyst, and professor of educational psychology. He promoted the theory that play is important because it gives children the security they need by allowing them opportunities to be in control of situations. Their need to be able to manipulate their physical world is seen as crucial to their mental and emotional health.

1906– • GESSELL, ARNOLD L. Psychologist, child specialist, and physician. He has had a tremendous infiuence on the contemporary development of play theories because of the wide acceptance by the public of his research on the play of infants and preschool children in relation to their ages and stages of development. Aside from the validity of his studies, this acceptance was possible because of the popularity of his many books for parents.

1911–1973. KEPHART, NEWELL C. Educator, psychologist, and author. Kephart's pioneering work in the field of special education has had a positive influence on bringing motor activities into the classroom, and promoting the importance of pre-academic skills. His contributions in the field of muscular responses as a basis for behavior and achievement have not only been promulgated by others in the fields of remediation and special education, but have influenced many educators to develop preventative approaches in preschool education.

1916– • ELLIS, MICHAEL J. He looks upon play as *arousal-seeking*, caused "by the need to generate interactions with the environment or self that elevate arousal (level of interest or stimulation) towards the optimal for the individual." He also sees play as *competence effectance*: "Play is caused by a need to produce effects in the environment. Such effects demonstrate competence and result in feelings of effectance."

1924– • SUTTON-SMITH, BRIAN. Research theorist. He distinguishes between various types of activities that lead to play and are usually called play activities. He urges educators to make the same distinctions—and then cautions against defining these activities too strictly because children tend to switch constantly from preplay activities to play and back again. The distinctions to which he refers are: (1) investigation (exploratory learning); (2) repetition of adequate response to make things happen, thus achieving mastery; (3) combination of responses; and finally, (4) play. He defines play as *voluntary behavior*, (as opposed to compulsory) a *reversal of power* (as opposed to being under the control of others), and a condensation or *vivication of experience*—allowing people to live vividly.

Selected Bibliography

ALMY, MILDRED (ed.), *Early Childhood Play* (New York: Selected Academic Readings, 1968).

AXLINE, VIRGINIA M., *Play Therapy* (Boston: Houghton Mifflin, 1947).

BUHLER, CHARLOTTE B., *From Birth to Maturity* (London: Routlege & Kegan, Paul, 1935).

CAPLAN, FRANK, and THERESA CAPLAN, *The Power of Play* (Garden City, N.Y.: Anchor Books, 1974).

CASTLE, E.B., *Ancient Education and Today* (Baltimore, Md.: Penguin Books, 1961).

CHARLES, C.M., *Teacher's Petit Piaget* (Belmont, Ca.: Fearon, 1974).

CHERRY, CLARE, *Creative Art for the Developing Child* (Belmont, Ca.: Fearon, 1972).

———, *Creative Movement for the Developing Child* (rev. ed.) (Belmont, Ca.: Fearon, 1971).

———, *Learning Centers for Early Childhood* (chart) (San Bernardino, Ca.: CATEC, 1972). Available from Fearon Publishers.

———, *Motivational Curriculum Chart for Early Childhood* (chart) (San Bernardino, Ca.: CATEC, 1969). Available from Fearon Publishers.

CHERRY, CLARE, BARBARA HARKNESS, and KAY KUZMA, *Nursery School Management Guide* (Belmont, Ca.: Fearon, 1974).

COHEN, DOROTHY H., *The Learning Child (New York: Random House, 1972).*

ELLIS MICHAEL J., *Why People Play* (Englewood Cliffs, N.J.: Prentice-Hall, 1973).

ERIKSON, ERIK H., *Childhood and Society* (New York: Norton, 1950).

FRANKFORT, H.A. *et al., Before Philosophy* (Baltimore, Md.: Penguin Books, 1961).

FROEBEL, FRIEDRICH, *Education of Man*, translated by W.N. Hailman and reprinted in *Classics in Education* (New York: Philosophical Library, 1966).

FREUD, ANNA, *The Psychonalytical Treatment of Children* (New York: Schocken, 1964).

FREUD, SIGMUND, *Beyond the Pleasure Principle* (London: Hogarth, 1948).

GERHARDT, LYDIA A., *Moving and Knowing: The Young Child Orients Himself to Space* (Englewood Cliffs, N.J.: Prentice-Hall, 1973).

GROOS, KARL, *The Play of Man* (New York: Appleton, 1901).

GESELL, ARNOLD, *The First Five Years of Life* (New York: Harper & Row, 1940).

HARTLEY, RUTH E. and ROBERT M. GOLDENSON, *The Complete Book of Children's Play* (New York: Crowell, rev. ed. 1963).

HERRON, R., and BRIAN SUTTON-SMITH, *Child's Play* (New York: Wiley, 1971).

HOLT, JOHN, *How Children Learn* (New York: Dell, 1974).

HOOKE, S.H., *Middle Eastern Mythology* (Baltimore, Md.: Penguin Books, 1963).

HUIZINGA, JOHAN, *Homo Ludens, A Study of the Play Element in Culture* (Boston: Beacon, 1950).

ISAACS, SUSAN, *Intellectual Growth in Young Children* (New York: Shocken, 1966).

JAMES, WILLIAM, *Talks to Teachers on Psychology* (New York: Dover, 1899).

KEPHART, NEWELL C., *The Slow Learner in the Classroom* (Columbus, Ohio: Charles E. Merrill, 1960).

KRISHNAMURTI, J., *Education and the Significance of Life* (New York: Harper & Row, 1953).

MATTERSON, E.M., *Play and Playthings for the Preschool Child* (rev. ed.) (Baltimore, Md.: Penguin Books, 1967).

MILLAR, SUSANNA, *The Psychology of Play* (Baltimore, Md.: Pelican Books, 1968).

MOFFITT, MARY, and EVELINE OMWAKE, *The Intellectual Content of Play* (New York: New York State Association for the Education of Young Children, 1966).

MONTAIGNE, MICHEL DE, *Essays* ("On the Education of Children"), translated by Charles Cotton and reprinted in *Classics of Education* (New York: Philosophical Library, 1966).

OPIE, PETER AND IONA, "Games (Young) People Play", Plumb, J.H., "The Great Change in Children," and Schafer, Edward H., "Playing Grownup", *Horizon*, Vol. XIII, No. 1., pp. 4–23 (New York: American Heritage, 1971).

PATRICK, GEORGE T.W., *The Psychology of Relaxation* (Boston: Houghton Mifflin, 1916).

PESTALOZZI, JOHANN HEINRICH, *The Method, A Report by Pestalozzi* reprinted in *Readings in Public Education in the United States* edited by Ellwood P. Cubberly (Boston: Houghton Mifflin, 1934).

PIAGET, JEAN, *Play, Dreams and Imitation in Childhood* (New York: W. W. Norton, 1962).

_____, and BARBEL INHELDER, *The Psychology of the Child* (New York: Basic Books, 1969).

253

PLATO, *Laws* (New York: Dutton, 1961).

PREYER, WILHELM T., *Mind of the Child* (New York: Appleton, 1882).

RABELAIS, FRANÇOIS, *Gargantua and Pantagruel* (New York: Penguin, 1962).

RICHARDS, MARTIN P.M., *The Integration of a Child into a Social World* (New York: Cambridge University Press, 1974).

ROBISON, HELEN F., and BERNARD SPODEK, *New Directions in the Kindergarten* (New York: Teachers College Press, 1965).

ROSENKRANZ, JOHANN, *Philosophy of Education* (excerpt from "Pedagogy as a System") reprinted in *Modern Philosophy of Education* by John Strain (New York: Random House, 1971).

ROUSSEAU, JEAN JACQUES, *Emil, or Education*, reprinted in *Three Thousand Years of Educational Wisdom*, edited by Robert Ulich (Cambridge, Mass.: Harvard University Press, 1961).

SAPORA, A.V., and E.D. MITCHELL, *The Theory of Play and Recreation*, 3rd ed. (New York: Ronald Press, 1961).

SCHELLING, FRIEDRICH, *Ages of the World*, translated by F. de Wolfe Polman (New York: AMS Press, 1942).

SCHILLER, JOHANNE, *Letters on the Aesthetic Education of Man*, translated by Reginald Snell (New Haven, Conn.: Ungar, 1954).

SPENCER, HERBERT, *The Principles of Psychology* (London: 1855).

SPODEK, BERNARD, "The Problem of Play: Educational or Recreational?" in *Play as a Learning Medium* edited by Doris Sponseller (Washington, D.C.: National Association for the Education of Young Children, 1974).

SPONSELLER, DORIS, "Why Is Play a Learning Medium?" in *Play as a Learning Medium* (Washington, D.C.: National Association for the Education of Young Children, 1974).

SUTTON-SMITH, BRIAN, "The Playful Modes of Knowing" in *Play: The Child Strives Toward Self-realization* edited by Georgia Engstrom (Washington, D.C.: National Association for the Education of Young Children, 1971).

———, "Play as Novelty Training" speech reprinted in *One Child Indivisible* edited by J.D. Andrews (Washington, D.C.: National Association for the Education of the Young Child, 1975).

——— and SHIRLEY SUTTON-SMITH, *How to Play with Your Children (and When Not to)* (New York: Hawthorn Books, 1974).

VALLET, ROBERT, *The Remediation of Learning Disabilities*, 2nd ed. (Belmont, Ca.: Fearon, 1973).

WAELDER, ROBERT, "The Psychonalytic Theory of Play" (in *Psychonalytic Quarterly* 2, 1933, 208–224.

WINNICOTT, D.W., *The Child, the Family, and the Outside World* (Baltimore, Md.: Penguin Books, 1964).

Index